AMBASSADOR IN BLACK
AND WHITE

3

DAVID SCOTT

Ambassador in Black and White

Thirty Years of Changing Africa

WEIDENFELD AND NICOLSON

LONDON

First published in Great Britain by
George Weidenfeld & Nicolson Limited
91 Clapham High Street, London SW4 7TA
1981

Book design by Joyce Chester

ISBN 0 297 77865 X

Printed and bound in Great Britain by
Butler & Tanner Ltd, Frome and London

CONTENTS

CONTENTS

ILLUSTRATIONS

With James Morgan in Northern Rhodesia, 1959.

The Monckton Commission, Victoria Falls, February 1960.

At the Bulawayo Trade Fair, 1961.

Lord and Lady Alport leaving Salisbury at the end of their tour of duty, 1963 (*photo: John McGeorge*).

Robert, Andrew and Diana in Salisbury, 1962.

Three generations of Scotts, Salisbury, 1962 (*photo: John McGeorge*).

Lord Alport meeting Mr Butler at Salisbury airport, 1962 (*photo: John McGeorge*).

Greeting members of the advisory team on the future structure of the Federation of Rhodesia and Nyasaland, 16 July 1962.

The end of the Federation, Victoria Falls Conference, July 1963.

With the Ugandan Minister of Foreign Affairs, Sam Odaka, and the Canadian High Commissioner, Miss Meagher, 1969.

In conversation with Jayant Madhvani, Jinja, 1969.

Brian and Diana Unwin.

Dr Milton Obote, President of Uganda, says farewell to members of the diplomatic corps at Entebbe before leaving for the Commonwealth Presidents, and Prime Ministers, Conference, 4 January 1969.

Michael Fairlie.

Presenting credentials to the South African State President, 17 March 1976.

With Mr Pik Botha at the Queen's Birthday party, Cape Town, 23 April 1978 (*The Cape Times*).

Dr David Owen and Mr Don Jamieson being greeted by Mr Pik Botha on their arrival at Waterloof Airbase, Pretoria, after visiting Windhoek, 1978 (*South African Argus Newspapers*).

Vera with Ann and Nicholas Monsarrat, Gozo, January 1978.

CARTOONS

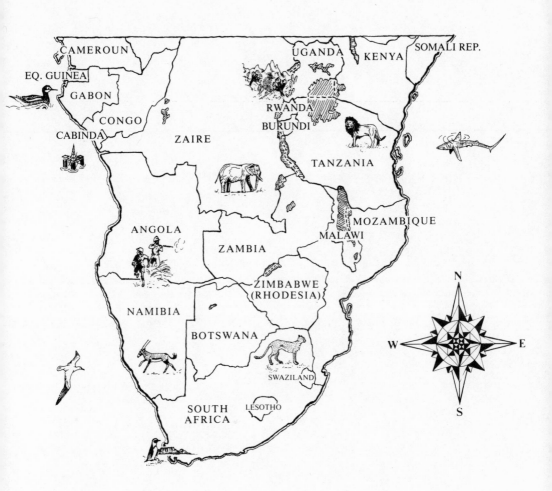

CAMEROUN

EQ. GUINEA

GABON

CONGO

CABINDA

ZAIRE

UGANDA   KENYA   SOMALI REP.

RWANDA
BURUNDI

TANZANIA

ANGOLA

ZAMBIA

MOZAMBIQUE

MALAWI

NAMIBIA

ZIMBABWE
(RHODESIA)

BOTSWANA

SWAZILAND

SOUTH
AFRICA   LESOTHO

N

W   E

S

INTRODUCTION

The conception of this book, in common with other human conceptions, can be traced to an identifiable and pleasurable evening. The date was September 1978, the occasion a small dinner party at our horrendous embassy residence in Pretoria at which my wife and I had arranged to introduce Lord Weidenfeld to a cross-section of the South African establishment.

In its primary role, the party was a disaster. The South African Government was in the grip of simultaneous crises relating to Namibia and the Information Department – of which more hereafter – and a minister and a leading academic had already politely refused our invitation on the unassailable ground that they had previous engagements. A second minister, together with a pair of senior civil servants and their wives, who had accepted, were called away at the last moment for engagements outside South Africa. We were left with what I can only describe as the hard core: George Weidenfeld himself; Group Captain Leslie Swart, my Defence Attaché, and his charming wife Mary-Anne, and Vera and myself.

Perhaps for this very reason the occasion turned into a riot. George Weidenfeld was in characteristically expansive form, and struck sparks off the rest of us. In the course of the evening, probably in response to some notable indiscretion on my part, he said, 'I assume you'll be writing a book about all this?' I cautiously admitted that I had considered such a possibility, adding firmly that I was neither competent, nor prepared, to embark on a serious history, nor did my own significance justify a formal autobiography. Nevertheless, I had a number of things to say about the past thirty years: the only problem was that, as a member of the Diplomatic Service, some of the more interesting things I wanted to record would probably fail to get past the beady eye of the official censor. Lord Weidenfeld muttered something about the Crossman diaries and indicated that the surmounting of that particular hurdle was something we could take in due time: if I wrote a book he would like to publish it. So here we are.

Unfortunately, the gestation period of a book relates more to that of the elephant than of the human embryo. In the two years since my retirement in mid-1979, things have not stood still. Nevertheless, I hope that much of what I have to say is still relevant, if not strictly current, in the continuing uncertainties of Africa.

It must be repeated that this is a personal story, dealing with family incidents and developments as well as with international events. As a book of recollections by one who, in the main, did *not* keep a diary, it has no pretension to historical completeness; its aim can only be to entertain, and possibly to open a few windows which might otherwise remain closed to the historian of the future. I hope, nevertheless, that the reader will find, in the words of Jack Point, a grain or two of truth among the chaff.

It is a truism that the test which the diplomat has to apply to his work is the enlightened interest of his own country. In this connection, it needs to be underlined that he is primarily concerned with governmental contacts and affairs; however assiduously he keeps in touch with Opposition thinking, both at home and in the country in which he serves, most of the real action is with ministers and officials. If I appear, therefore, to devote less attention than might be expected to opposition (with a small, as well as a large, 'O') personalities, it is not because I did not know or often sympathize with them but because the bulk of my day-to-day work simply did not lie with them.

A diplomat is expected to preserve a certain detachment: to observe coolly, to avoid excessive commitment, and, while preserving his own standards, to suppress a natural instinct to pass moral judgments. If I add that this detachment has to be combined with an understanding and sympathetic approach to those one meets, a willingness to listen and learn, and an ability to report accurately and dispassionately, I shall be accused of preaching the impossible. I am.

Although this book does not pretend to be a history, some research has inevitably been involved. I am particularly indebted to Sir Roy Welensky, who generously gave me access to his unrivalled collection of personal and official papers covering the period when he was Prime Minister of the Federation of Rhodesia and Nyasaland. Since that country, and his Government, no longer exist, these papers are not bound by the same restrictions on publication as those of the British Government. I do not know of any other diplomat who on his retirement has been fortunate enough to be given similar access to the State papers of a country in which he has served. I have, however, drawn on them only to the extent to which they have a direct bearing on my own first-hand experience.

I am also most grateful to Vera, my wife, who not only took part in most of the events recorded, but remembered many details, particularly dates, which eluded me. Amongst the many others to whom I am indebted for information, comments or corrections are the late Sir Roger Stevens, who allowed me access to certain private papers and who gave me invaluable advice and encouragement in the last few days of his life; Lord Alport, Lord Blake, Lieutenant-Colonel H.N. Crawford, Michael Fairlie, Mrs Cicely Morgan, who allowed me to see the diaries of her husband, the late James Morgan, my sons, Robert and Andrew Scott, Sir Robert Taylor, Sir Mark Tennant, Lord Trend, Brian and Diana Unwin and Dr Rex Wilson. I am also delighted to thank my eldest grandson, Michael Unwin, for the map and for the line drawings on the title page and at the beginning of each part.

Since as a former public servant my manuscript had to be submitted for departmental scrutiny, I should like also to express appreciation for the patience and tolerance with which Miss Blayney and her colleagues at the Foreign and Commonwealth Library discussed with me such changes as were suggested to enable the book to comply with the rules governing the publication of memoirs by former members of HM Diplomatic Service. I need hardly add that she bears no responsibility whatever for any of the views expressed. Last, but not least, I am grateful to Liza Gane, who not only took part in some of the events in Uganda, but also typed the manuscript, much of it more than once.

PART ONE

UNION OF SOUTH AFRICA
1950–53

CHAPTER 1

AHOY, *CAPE TOWN CASTLE*

ALTHOUGH THIS STORY begins in 1950, we were even at that stage not total strangers to Africa. At the end of the war, while still in the Army, I had been seconded to a semi-diplomatic appointment in Cairo where Vera, my wife, and the two elder children joined me early in 1946. My appointment was as Chief Radar Adviser in the British Military Mission to the Egyptian Army. If this sounds impressive, it can appropriately be put in perspective by recalling that it was almost entirely due to her radar deficiencies that Egypt lost the Six Day War to Israel in 1967. In self-defence I could perhaps add that it was by then a different generation of radar; no one could have expected to win a war on the meagre supplies of obsolescent equipment on which I was instructing the Egyptians in 1945.

Shortly after she and the children joined me in January 1946, Vera became the first diplomat in the family by taking up a job in the publicity section of the British Embassy in Cairo under the direction of the late Lord Kinross.

My earlier background can be disposed of quickly. I was born in 1919. My father was a housemaster at Wellington College, an English Public School with a reputation for toughness, though he himself, as I have every reason to know, was both understanding and enlightened. My mother, after a long career as his wife, and effectively as full-time manager and public relations officer of a Public School boarding house, took to local politics after my father's retirement. She became successively a member and then chairman of a rural district council, Justice of the Peace, county councillor and, finally, Chairman of the Berkshire County Council Education Committee, where she disposed of a far larger budget than I have ever had to handle.

Launched into a classical education at a rival educational establishment, Charterhouse, I subsequently switched to science and in 1938 went to Birmingham University with an engineering scholarship from Trepca Mines, a subsidiary of Selection Trust Limited, intending to enter the mining industry as one of the late Sir Chester Beatty's young men. At Birmingham I met my

3

future wife, Vera Ibbitson, who was then reading commerce and economics at the feet of Professor Sargent Florence.

At this point the war intervened. Reaching a firm and immediate personal conclusion that hostilities were *not* going to be over quickly, I joined the Army in November 1939 on the realistic but somewhat mercenary assumption that it might be easier to get promotion in the Army by getting in on the ground floor than to persevere with the more hazardous task of completing my degree. Vera, on the other hand, completed hers against all the odds in May 1940. She caught German measles about a fortnight before her finals and, on the day they started, learned that her brother Eric, an officer in The Queens West Surrey Regiment, was missing at Dunkirk. However, all ended well: she got her B.Comm. and Eric not only turned up but achieved an MC in the process.

We spent the autumn of 1940 listening to each other's bombs down the telephone – she in Birmingham and I in Chester – and decided that we might as well hear the same ones by getting married. This we did in January 1941. My war was mainly a technical one, much of it spent as an instructor in anti-aircraft radar; most of hers was as a civil servant.

Having deferred my release from the Army for eighteen months to take up the job in Egypt, I eventually returned to the private sector in April 1947 with aspirations for a career in journalism. As a freelance I earned precisely £23. 4s. 5d. in the four months after my demobilization; even in those days an inadequate sum on which to support a wife and two children. In September I secured a somewhat improbable engagement from *Time and Tide* to represent them at the Radlett air show. This should have earned me at least £10, but shortly before the opening day *Time and Tide* reconsidered their requirement for an aeronautical correspondent. By that time, however, I had a press card and went anyway. At the show I met an old army friend who had just joined the Decca Navigator Company; thanks to his interest I found myself within a few days as personal assistant to Group Captain Ned (later Sir Edward) Fennessy, the Managing Director, and, under his guidance, responsible for technical publications. By that time I had already put in my application to take the civil service reconstruction exams, so my stay with Decca was regrettably short. I entered the Commonwealth Relations Office as a rather elderly Assistant Principal on 1 January 1948. I was not to rejoin the private sector until my retirement thirty-two years later.

After a year learning the ropes in a political department, I did a further nine months as Assistant Private Secretary to that most delightful and undemanding Secretary of State, Mr Philip Noel-Baker. Francis Cumming-Bruce (later Lord Thurlow, and Governor of the Bahamas) was his Principal Private Secretary, but the political side of the Private Office was dominated by the attractive and dynamic Patricia Llewelyn Davies. She and her husband Richard, the architect, were later to make history as the first husband and wife pair of life peers.

During this time, Vera and I were extremely impoverished. Even by the standards of 1948, the £500 a year earned by an Assistant Principal was a fairly minimal salary on which to cover mortgage repayments (on a semi-detached house in Chislehurst), food and rail fares, not to mention day-school fees for the two small children. The additional £100 allowance given to a Private Secretary added a welcome 20 per cent in 1949, and towards the end of that year my promotion to the rank of Principal on £1,200 a year took me nearly back to what I had been earning two years earlier as a major in the Egyptian Army. The lure which kept us – and our bank manager – going was the prospect that sooner or later we should be offered an overseas posting with its accompanying allowances.

In July 1950 we received the long-awaited news. I heard that I was being sent as First Secretary (Political) to the office of the British High Commissioner in South Africa. A few days later we spent a short holiday near Hythe in the New Forest. We all remember rowing out on Southampton Water in a small boat and passing the Union Castle mailship *Cape Town Castle* at anchor in the stream. It was tremendously exciting to realize that in four or five months' time we should ourselves be sailing for Cape Town in her or one of her sister ships. We wanted somehow to make ourselves known to the solitary crew member leaning idly over the stern rail. 'Ahoy, *Cape Town Castle*, what's the time?' was the best we could think of. We didn't really want the answer. But we had made our point.

At this distance in time one has to make a conscious effort to recall the conditions of austerity in which we in England were still living more than five years after the end of the war. Not only was rationing still in force for a wide range of foods, but domestic items such as china and glass were either unobtainable or available to the home market only in utility versions at controlled prices. But for export everything was different. Vera still vividly remembers the almost immoral *frisson* of being taken behind a curtain in the china department at Heal's to see the dazzling range of decorated china incredibly available for us to choose from. We had even been advanced some money to buy it with.

My first contact with South Africa came sooner than I expected. In October, Field Marshal Smuts, by then leader of the Opposition in the

South African Parliament, died. In Britain, more perhaps than in his own country, he was recognized as a world figure. A lifelong friend of Mr Churchill, he was a principal partner in victory and an architect and founder of the United Nations. A full-scale memorial service was held in Westminster Abbey, attended by members of the Royal Family, by virtually the whole of Mr Attlee's Cabinet and by Mr Churchill himself. I was an usher in the North Transept.

CHAPTER 2

THE LAST PRO-CONSUL

UNTIL A FEW sad years ago the traditional – one could almost say the only – way of travelling from Britain to South Africa was by the Union Castle Company's weekly mailship, widely advertised as leaving Southampton for Cape Town every Thursday at 4 o'clock. On the morning of Thursday 4 January 1951, a small party of Scotts, consisting of Vera and myself and two wildly excited children, Diana, aged eight-and-a-half, and Robert, aged nearly seven, caught the boat train at Waterloo station to join RMS *Pretoria Castle* at Southampton.

Only a fortnight earlier it had seemed highly unlikely that we should be on the train at all. Shortly before Christmas, Vera and I had been sent on the customary industrial tour arranged by the Central Office of Information to brief officers and their wives departing for overseas postings. Being the proud possessors of our first new car ever – a Morris Oxford – we had started our tour with a visit to the British Motor Corporation's factory at Cowley. As we left the factory, driving sleet was beginning to turn into snow. The public relations officer who had organized the visit came to the entrance to see us off. His parting words, delivered with every sign of sincerity, were, 'Well, Mr Scott, if there is anything we can do for you at any time don't hesitate to let me know. Here's my telephone number.'

Poor man. He little knew what he had let himself in for. Half an hour later, the road beginning to cover with snow, we came over the brow of Deddington Hill on our way north to Birmingham. A hundred yards ahead of us down the slope a confused mass of vehicles were tangled in a multiple crash. I put on the brakes – with no perceptible effect whatever. At about twenty-five mph we slid inexorably under the tail of a lorry. We were the thirteenth vehicle in the pile-up. My immediate reaction was to remember that a mile back we had passed a huge articulated lorry and trailer carrying more BMC vehicles. I got out of my car, and immediately fell flat on my back on the ice. But I picked myself up, and got back to the crest of the hill just in time to flag the lorry down before it completed our destruction.

7

An hour later, having abandoned the car where it lay, we were in a hotel in Banbury. It was too late to do anything that night, but first thing in the morning I was on the telephone to our friend the Cowley public relations officer.

'You remember what you said last night,' I began, I hope not too sadistically. 'Well, here's your big chance, I'm afraid.' I explained that we had a wrecked radiator and fan, a stove-in bonnet cover and grille and damaged off-side wing and lights. 'The garage here in Banbury tell me that it will take them seven months to get the parts; they say they are all going for export. We are supposed to be sailing in just under three weeks. Can you possibly help?'

There was a deep hush at the other end of the line. 'Three weeks, you said?' 'Yes. And I'm afraid that several days can be taken out of that for Christmas.'

The stiffening of the upper lip was almost audible, but the answer was brave. 'What did you say the name of the garage is?' I told him. 'Well, Mr Scott, I'll see what I can do. I'll ring you back in about an hour after I've talked to our spares division and the garage.'

He was as good as his word. Miraculously, the car was ready three days after Christmas. When I picked it up the garage was grudging, but clearly impressed. 'I don't know how you managed to get the spares,' they said. 'I suppose you realize that a lot of our regular customers have been waiting for months.' I expressed polite sympathy and departed.

After the accident we left Banbury by train on our way to Birmingham to salvage as much as we could of the remains of our tour. That day we visited the Dunlop factory at Castle Bromwich. In the evening I rang my parents, who were looking after Robert, to tell them of the disaster. My mother listened with what I thought at the time was a certain lack of sympathy. When I had finished, she said, 'I'm afraid I've got some bad news for you, too. Robert wasn't feeling very well last night. This morning the doctor came in to see him. The dear boy's got mumps. Not badly – but thoroughly. I can't remember if you've had them yourself.' I hadn't.

I'm afraid Christmas was something of a nightmare for my parents. Poor Robert was firmly in bed and allowed to be visited only by those members of the household who had had the disease, which fortunately included Vera. I was not allowed nearer than the door. On 1 January we set off to spend our last two nights in Worthing with Vera's parents, who had been looking after Diana, before we came up to London to catch the boat train.

As we steamed down the Solent and past the Isle of Wight, the 6 o'clock news greeted us with gale warnings. The first two days were rough, but by the time we reached Madeira the weather was perfect. Robert was over his mumps, and the sea voyage was just what the doctor might have ordered for all of us.

Two weeks later, on Thursday 18 January, we woke before sunrise. Out on deck the stars were still in the sky, the Southern Cross hanging inverted on the starboard bow. Ahead of us, its outline just visible against the faint glow in the south-eastern sky, was the unmistakable outline of Table Mountain. As the sky brightened the mountain itself began to pick up light and colour until every detail could be seen. I do not know of any port in the world which makes a more startlingly beautiful first impression.

Once we had been through customs and completed the other formalities we were taken to Conzella, the comfortable, if slightly down-at-heel, house in Woolsack Road, Rosebank (now, alas, destroyed to make way for one of Cape Town's countless motorways), which was to be our home for the next five months. Just above us was a row of modern prefabricated houses belonging to the University of Cape Town, which, as we soon discovered, catered for married undergraduates, many of whom had served in the defence forces during the war and who were rather older than the general run of students. The houses were officially called *Protem*, but were more usually known by their inhabitants, unfairly, as Belsen. We had already noticed a slightly battered Morris Minor in one of our two garages, and later that day one of our neighbours from Belsen called on us to ask if we had a second car of our own, and if not whether we would mind their continuing to keep their car in our garage. So started a lifelong friendship with two families – Rex and Mardee Wilson and their two boys, Patrick and Rory, and Chuckie and Mary Knutzen and their sons, Victor and Robert. Both the men were medical students and nearing the end of their course.

The next two days were mainly spent in settling in, though on Friday I was taken round the office and introduced to all the staff, both home-based and locally recruited. On Saturday we went for a long exploratory drive round False Bay with a family we had got to know on the ship who were emigrating to Rhodesia. When we came back in the late afternoon, Diana was fretful and clearly far from well. I also had developed a slight headache, which I attributed to the unaccustomed sun. Neither of us felt any better on Sunday morning, however, and during the course of the day it became only too apparent that we both had mumps – Diana mildly, but I both thoroughly and painfully.

We had, of course, by then had no time to contact a local doctor. Since there was no possible doubt about the diagnosis, Vera was reluctant first to find and then to call in a strange doctor on Sunday evening. She did, however, remember the medical students next door. With some trepidation she walked up the garden, knocked on Rex Wilson's door and explained the situation. What should she do for a husband suffering from a sharpish attack of mumps? Very properly, Rex started with a disclaimer. 'Well, ma'am,' he began, 'I'm afraid I'm not qualified. So I'm not allowed to give you medical advice. But we did mumps in our third year. You must get a doctor in the morning, but in the meantime my advice is to keep his balls warm.' Mardee even lent us a hot-water bottle for the purpose. The treatment was effective, as was positively demonstrated later.

So much for our long-awaited introduction to the glamour of diplomatic life. Our new Secretary of State, Mr Patrick Gordon-Walker, was due to make his first official visit to South Africa in three weeks' time and, in Sir Evelyn Baring's absence on a home visit, the Acting High Commissioner was deeply worried that my initial hand-shaking tour round the office might already have set in train a mumps epidemic to coincide with the Secretary of State's arrival. A solemn edict was therefore issued forbidding anyone connected with the staff, husbands or wives, whether or not they had already had mumps, from visiting us. As a result, Vera had to unpack and settle into an entirely strange house – and country – without any of the moral or physical support one can normally rely on from one's colleagues. It was only some ten days later, when Sir Evelyn and Lady Mary Baring got back from London, that we had contact with anyone other than doctors or tradesmen. Fortunately, Lady Mary sized up the situation at a glance, and from that moment on we were never short of visitors or books. I almost regretted that not a single soul caught mumps from either of us.

This is perhaps the moment to say something about the Barings. Evelyn Baring's own career has been fully and sympathetically reported in Charles Douglas-Home's biography, under the appropriate sub-title 'The Last Pro-Consul'. For both Vera and myself the Barings provided our first working experience of the aristocracy in the traditional sense of the word, and we were deeply – and in retrospect justifiably – impressed. Although totally professional in his dual career as a diplomat and a Colonial Governor, both aspects of which were applicable to his appointment in South Africa, Baring also exuded a sense of detached self-confidence which stood him in good stead in the many difficult situations and negotiations in which he was involved throughout his career. He was, perhaps, interested more in things than people, though he was a man whom people followed confidently. He was an enthusiastic walker and climber, and a first-class amateur naturalist. When I displayed an interest in wild flowers in the course of an early walk with him on Table Mountain, he made the illuminating comment that it was a great pity that Linnaeus had been compelled to base his classification of species mainly on specimens available from the northern hemisphere. If he had been able to acquire a wider knowledge of the fauna and flora of southern Africa and Australasia, his great work might have come out rather differently. There were, for example, several hundred species of the family *Erica* in the Cape alone, compared with the six or eight heaths listed in northern Europe; and many of the specialized southern hemisphere families, including the Proteas and the gums, had no northern equivalents at all.

The British High Commission in South Africa in the early 1950s consisted of two separate offices under a single High Commissioner. One office fulfilled the orthodox diplomatic role of representing the Government of the United Kingdom in South Africa. Thus, wearing his diplomatic hat, the High Commissioner carried out virtually all the normal functions of an ambassador accredited to the Union Government. Wearing his other hat, however, he was Governor of the so-called High Commission Territories: Basutoland (now Lesotho), the Bechuanaland Protectorate (Botswana) and Swaziland.

The diplomatic side of the office came under the supervision of a counsellor, the Deputy High Commissioner, who at the time of our arrival was Algy (later Sir Algernon) Rumbold, a former member of the India Office. Two First Secretaries, John Wakely (later HM Ambassador to Burma) and myself, supported by a Second Secretary, formed what would now be called the Chancery. In parallel with us was a Defence Liaison Staff, headed by the Commander-in-Chief, South Atlantic, at that time a Vice-Admiral. The economic and commercial side of the office was run by a Senior Trade Commissioner, Sir William Peters, with subordinate offices in Johannesburg, Cape Town and Durban. Last, but not least, the British Information Office in Johannesburg was run by Nicholas Monsarrat, who quickly became a friend and was shortly to become famous as author of *The Cruel Sea*.

The Territories side of the office was an entirely separate operation under a Chief Secretary, Roland Turnbull, who as Sir Roland later became Governor of British North Borneo. He and his staff were responsible for the administration of the High Commission Territories, each of which was run by a Resident Commissioner living in the territory itself. Although the Territories were staffed by members of the Colonial Service, they, together with the self-governing Colony of Southern Rhodesia, were in Whitehall the responsibility of the Commonwealth Relations Office (CRO) rather than the Colonial Office

(CO). Within the CRO the department concerned, of which some years later I became head, was known as the Central African and Territories Department and was also responsible for relations with Southern Rhodesia.

As if this structural complication were not enough, there was also the problem of the annual migration. This dated back to the settlement enshrined in the South Africa Act of 1909. Under this it was agreed that Pretoria, the capital of the Transvaal Republic, should become the administrative capital of the Union of South Africa; Cape Town became the parliamentary capital, and Bloemfontein (Orange Free State) the seat of the judiciary. Durban, the capital of Natal, was left out, but was more than compensated, so tradition has it, by being allocated the principal meeting in the South African racing calendar, the July Handicap.

The annual parliamentary session in Cape Town normally lasted – and indeed still lasts today – about five months, from the second half of January to late June. During the session, all the people involved, including South African ministers and civil servants as well as a majority of the diplomatic corps, had to have accommodation there instead of in Pretoria. Although most of the South Africans were provided with flats or houses in a specially built suburb known as Acacia Park, in those days we had to find our own houses in both Cape Town and Pretoria. Twice a year, therefore, househunting became a major, and very time-consuming, occupation.

It was through Sir Evelyn Baring, wearing his Territories hat, that I gained my first insight into the Southern Rhodesia scene. One of his responsibilities was membership of the Higher Authority for the Rhodesia Railways. This appointment derived from the fact that the railway line running through the Bechuanaland Protectorate from Mafeking to Bulawayo, which provided Rhodesia's vital rail outlet to the Atlantic at Cape Town, was operated on behalf of the Bechuanaland Government by Rhodesia Railways, who were also responsible for providing much of the rolling stock. The High Commissioner was thus *ex officio* a member of the Authority; the fact that Baring's previous appointment had been as Governor of Southern Rhodesia was not strictly relevant, though it inevitably made him specially conscious of the atmosphere in Salisbury.

On his return to Cape Town after one of the periodic meetings of the Authority, Baring commented at his weekly staff meeting on the enormous post-war influx of immigrants, almost all from the United Kingdom, into Southern Rhodesia. The whole character of the country seemed to have changed since he had left Salisbury in 1947.

'I could hardly believe what the Secretary of the Salisbury Club told me yesterday,' he said. 'Four out of five present members of the club only arrived in the territory after the war. That means that most of the top leadership of the country is entirely new: the old settlers are only a small minority.'

That was in 1951, less than six years after the end of the war. I often thought of his words afterwards, when people talked of the sterling pioneering attributes of white Rhodesians. Of course, the real pioneers were immensely tough; they achieved miracles in converting 'miles and miles of bloody Africa' into prosperous farms, often in the face of an unreliable water supply and some human hostility. In the process they built up a wealthy and beautiful country and brought prosperity to the blacks as well as to themselves. But many of the newcomers were in a different mould. The main aim for most of them was the achievement of a standard of living no longer obtainable at home. Lest I be accused of personal bias, the following quotation from Frank Clements,[1] himself a Rhodesian immigrant, puts the matter in a nutshell:

They were the misfits of British society; that is, of course, not the same thing as the failures and the rejects, though indeed they themselves had decided that they were not equipped to succeed at home. In no field of activity, from accountancy to welding, from journalism to selling, did Rhodesia offer inducements to the successful or the conspicuously talented.

CHAPTER 3

APARTHEID IN ACTION

POLITICALLY, THE UNION of South Africa in 1951 was in a state of transition. Most South Africans still prided themselves on the fact that the Union was a founder member of the 'old' Commonwealth, consciously and characteristically regarding India, Pakistan and Ceylon, the 'new' members, with an element of contempt. It was because of the Commonwealth relationship that our office was a High Commission rather than an embassy. King George VI, who, with the Queen and the two Princesses, had paid a State Visit to South Africa in 1947, remained King of South Africa, though he was, as elsewhere in the Commonwealth, normally represented there by a Governor-General.

But this relationship was already beginning to weaken. In 1948 the National Party, under Dr Daniel Malan, had defeated General Smuts's United Party at the General Election. During the two-and-a-half years the Nationalists had been in power, the policy of *apartheid*, or separateness between the races, had begun to emerge as the official legislative policy of the new South African Government. In saying this, it is only fair to add that the fact of *apartheid* was not a new development. The new element was rather that for the first time it was codified as an ideological objective in its own right. The Smuts Government had traditionally acted on the assumption that the blacks were not yet ready to assume power; they were, however, prepared to leave the political doors ajar for the ultimate enfranchisement of those who, through education or the accumulation of wealth, in their view became qualified to take on the responsibilities of the vote. In other words, they were following broadly the pattern in nineteenth-century Britain, where the franchise was gradually, but in practice inexorably, extended to additional classes of voters. This was not as the result of a belief in the absolute validity of the concept of one man, one vote; but rather on the pragmatic basis that those who could be expected to exercise the vote responsibly should have it.

The National Party, on the other hand, believing passionately in the God of the Old Testament, convinced themselves that the differences between black and white were differences of kind, not of degree. Moreover, they were brought up in a legislative system based on the Roman-Dutch law, under which it was considered necessary to crystallize policy in legislation rather than to allow the law to be gradually modified by precedents based on judgments in the courts. If in the South African context it seemed right, therefore, that blacks and whites should lead separate lives, living in separate areas, using different transport and not mingling in sport, sex, or church, it was axiomatic that this should be laid down in legislation and not left to the good sense of individuals, who were necessarily weak and fallible.

The prolonged legislative process under which, over the next fifteen years, this belief was to be relentlessly translated into the statute book, was just beginning. Nevertheless, in 1951 the United Party still remained an alternative government, and many people shared their alarm at the rapid erosion of civil liberties that was becoming evident. In March 1952, the Torch Commando movement came into being. Forty thousand people, led by an Afrikaner war hero, Group Captain 'Sailor' Malan, marched through the streets of Cape Town to lay a petition before Parliament protesting against the bill proposing the removal of the Coloured (mixed race) voters from the common roll.

Many of our local friends were members of the Torch Commando, and I vividly remember standing at the top of Adderley Street one evening watching the seemingly endless column of marchers, many carrying flaming torches, pass on the last lap of their procession to Parliament. Among the crowds lining the streets the large number of silent Coloured spectators alone may have realized that they were the victims of a lost cause.

To newcomers to South Africa from Europe, especially to those arriving in Cape Town, the impact of *apartheid* took a little time to be felt. Indeed, for many new immigrants in the immediate post-war period it was probably hardly felt at all, except in the sense that it continued to ensure a plentiful supply of cheap labour to undertake the more menial household chores. But for those who were employed in a British Government office, as we were, it posed problems in both a personal and a political context. These problems were of special sensitivity in the light of the High Commissioner's dual role in relation to the South African Government on the one hand and as Governor of the High Commission Territories on the other.

In our official capacity we were encouraged to meet and entertain blacks, even though to do so was discouraged by the South African Government. In practical terms, however, our social contacts with educated black people were infrequent and mostly limited to clergymen and school teachers, though in the Cape it was also possible to get to know some of the leading Coloured politicians. Even in those days, however, when the Coloureds were still on the voters' roll, they could not themselves stand for Parliament, but had to be represented by white MPs. This did not make the life of a Coloured politician a particularly rewarding or responsible one.

As for most new arrivals – and indeed for almost all white South Africans – our first, and most lasting, personal contacts with individual blacks were with our servants. We had been particularly lucky in inheriting as our cook from our predecessors, Jim and Barbara Bottomley, a delightful and intelligent lady called Lydia Modishane. It would have come as a shock to most South Africans to learn that on two occasions in our first few weeks in Cape Town I found her reading my office copy of the *Economist*; thereafter I lent it to her every week before passing it on to the next office recipient. We discovered that she had the equivalent of five matriculation passes at what would now be called 'O' level: the fact that she had to be content with employment as a cook was a reflection of the extent to which racial job reservation limited the openings available to educated blacks.

Lydia's husband, Johnnie Modishane, whom by virtue of her job she was able to accompany on the move between Pretoria and Cape Town (unlike most blacks, who were compelled to leave their families behind in a Pretoria 'location', or African township), was employed as personal valet by the then Governor-General. We heard later that this arrangement continued throughout our successor's tour of duty. However, a subsequent Governor-General decided that it was inappropriate for his clothes to be handled by a black man and Johnnie was replaced by a Dutchman. Even in our time, however, the Modishanes had to leave their two daughters at school in the Transvaal because the children were not eligible for permits to travel to Cape Town for the session, even though their parents were.

At a political level the effects of *apartheid* had two years previously erupted in acute form in the Bechuanaland Protectorate as a result of the decision by Seretse Khama, the heir presumptive to the chieftainship of the Bamangwato tribe, to marry a white girl, Ruth Williams. It goes without saying that, from a purely United Kingdom point of view, this marriage would have presented no problems. But the South Africans made it only too clear that they would look with disfavour on the idea of a black leader in a neighbouring state contracting a mixed marriage which would be illegal in South Africa itself. It was felt by many in Britain, on the other hand, that the matrimonial arrangements of a Chief under British protection should be a personal matter for him, or at most for the tribe, and should not be influenced by the racial prejudices of the South African Government.

It was this political problem that Sir Evelyn Baring had been in London to discuss when we landed in Cape Town. It was one which greatly preoccupied the Territories side of the office, and successive High Commissioners personally, throughout our time in South Africa. It also worried the Commonwealth Relations Office, where it tended to fall into the 'too difficult' category. It was widely, though perhaps apocryphally, alleged in the service that the then head of the Central African and Territories Department spent an entire morning locked in the lavatory in order to avoid being forced to discuss the question, and perhaps to take decisions on it, during one of Evelyn Baring's periodic visits to London. Nicholas Monsarrat was at that time, *inter alia*, Baring's press attaché, and some of the public relations aspects – though not the facts – of the case are set out with feeling in *The Tribe that Lost its Head*.[1]

There was another problem which also greatly exercised the territories Administration. This was the recrudescence in Basutoland of a spate of ritual murders, usually involving children or young people, carried out at the instigation of certain chiefs and headmen. The victims were mutilated, sometimes while still alive, in order to provide medicine to enhance the perpetrator's standing or to give him supernatural powers against his enemies. Inevitably, it was difficult to persuade witnesses to come forward to give evidence in cases of this kind, especially when the evidence could be expected to implicate the witness's own chief.

Underlying these symptoms of tribal stress was the wider and politically more delicate problem of the line which HMG should adopt in their role as protecting power of the High Commission Territories towards a possible South African claim for the incorporation of the territories in the Union. This claim, which behind the scenes the National Party Government were beginning to press, derived from a provision in the South Africa Act under which the government of the High Commission Territories might, by Order in Council, be transferred to the Union Government following a request by both Houses of the South African Parliament. In the event, the request was never formally made, for the good reason that the moment never arrived that the inhabitants of the territories would have accepted the transfer, and it went without saying that British ministers could only have approved it with the territories' agreement. But the possibility of such a request being made could not be wholly disregarded and was a potential source of anxiety to successive British Governments.

CHAPTER 4

SETTLING DOWN TO LIFE
IN SOUTH AFRICA

NOT LONG AFTER our arrival in Cape Town we decided to buy a dog. We had lengthy family conclaves on the important question of breed. The only dog we had possessed up to then had been a Labrador, but we found that two of the most popular breeds in South Africa at that time were Rhodesian ridgebacks and boxers. After a long debate we settled on a boxer. So one Saturday afternoon we drove down to a recommended kennel not far from the naval base at Simonstown. We came back with an enchanting little tan bitch puppy aged about ten weeks, which we called Sarie after the heroine of the South African Huguenot song, *Sarie Marais*. Sarie immediately became a firm family favourite, and with her we explored the various beaches of the Cape Peninsula, the walks around the fringes of Table Mountain and, nearer home, Rondebosch Common, where Diana and Robert were learning to ride bicycles for the first time.

Living as we did almost within the campus of the University of Cape Town, we naturally began to build up contacts with the staff as well as with undergraduates. One in particular became a lifelong friend: Rupert Shephard, the Michaelis Professor of Fine Art who, under the influence of his attractive South African wife Lorna, had come to Cape Town only a year or two previously. Rupert was – and is – a distinguished painter and engraver, and our own interest in collecting pictures can be said to have begun when we bought our first two paintings from him later that year. Those pictures, one the portrait of a beautiful African girl employed as a cleaner at the Michaelis School of Art, still provide two of our most evocative reminders of South Africa.

One of the problems of the half-yearly move between Cape Town and Pretoria was the question of schools. Robert was safely fixed at a local kindergarten in Cape Town. But we had some difficulty finding a primary school that would take Diana for only five months. Eventually she was accepted for two terms by a Seventh-Day Adventist school just round the corner from where we lived. The interview with the headmaster had slightly shaken Vera, since his desk featured a small display, representing works of the Devil. This consisted of a bottle of beer, a pack of cards and a packet of cigarettes, which, presumably, parents as well as pupils were expected to eschew. I am not sure that he had ever encountered a diplomatic mother before, but Vera made it clear that, while we neither smoked nor, at least seriously, gambled, a modest consumption of alcohol reflected an almost unavoidable representational element in our lives. She denies admitting that we also liked it.

We soon realized that, if the children were to get a measure of continuity in their education, it might be necessary for them to go to boarding school for half the year, either in Cape Town or Pretoria. We had, I think, assumed that, because the Cape had been a British colony for a couple of centuries before Union, schools oriented towards the English system of education would be easier to find in Cape Town than in the Transvaal. Curiously enough the converse turned out to be the case. Perhaps because the Cape had been English-speaking for so long, the Province had developed an excellent curriculum of its own which was no longer closely related to the examination syllabus in the United Kingdom; the Transvaal, on the other hand, because the majority of its white population spoke Afrikaans, continued in its English-medium schools to use many of the English exams. Unexpectedly, therefore, the Transvaal syllabus was nearer to an English one than that of the Cape. Although the children moved back to Cape Town for two terms in the following year, though not to the same schools, in their final year we left them as boarders in Pretoria. It was satisfactory to find, when they eventually returned to England in late 1953, that they had lost little ground in relation to their English contemporaries; in terms of breadth of experience they had, of course, gained enormously.

Although the migration between Cape Town and Pretoria was a considerable administrative headache, at the same time it provided an unrivalled opportunity to see something of the country. To drive by car the nine-hundred-odd miles from the extreme south-western tip of the country to Pretoria in the north was to get an impression of its size and variety which could never be gained from an aeroplane at 30,000 feet. Moreover, there was a wide choice of route. At different times we travelled via Kimberley and the north-western Cape, via the Orange Free State and Basutoland, and via the Garden Route to Port Elizabeth, the Transkei and southern Natal. Within these routes there could be an almost infinite range of variations, so that after three years we had probably seen more of the country than most South Africans.

On our first journey north we decided to take the central and most direct route across the Karroo through Beaufort West and Bloemfontein. We did, however, allow ourselves a detour from Bloemfontein to enable us to see something of Basutoland. Setting out in the late afternoon we only travelled eighty miles to Worcester the first night. Even that relatively short journey took us out of the predominantly European atmosphere of the Cape peninsula and over the first great range of the Drakenstein Mountains. In the long descent to Worcester on the new road over Du Toit's Kloof we saw our first wild baboons, and felt that we had at last truly arrived in Africa.

The next morning we set off at first light and climbed the spectacular Hex River valley through the vineyards and orchards of De Doorns to the plateau of the Great Karroo. It had been snowing on the high ground during the night, and it was bitterly cold. Although we had explained to the children that we should be driving a hundred miles before breakfast, the journey strained their endurance almost to breaking point. However, breakfast at the Lord Milner Hotel at Matjiesfontein, when we reached it, made up for a lot.

The Karroo has to be seen to be believed. It is a semi-desert area of rolling scrub-covered land stretching for some four hundred miles north of the Drakensberg and capable of supporting only a limited number of sheep. In calculating the sheep-carrying capacity of the land it used to be said that a farmer needed up to a thousand acres a head. But since there are around a hundred million acres of Karroo, that still provides for quite a lot of sheep.

This was our first long journey in South Africa in our new car, and later in the day, through ignorance, we found ourselves running out of petrol when we were still about fifty miles short of Beaufort West. With petrol pumps on the main road anything up to a hundred miles apart, we guessed that a dirt track disappearing across the veld to our right must with any luck lead to a farm. We just hoped that it would not be further than a few miles.

We were in luck; only about three miles off the main road we came to an attractive farm set in an oasis of gum trees. Even more important, we saw a primitive hand-operated petrol pump beside a large barn.

The only trouble was that there seemed to be nobody about. Eventually, after banging loudly on a number of doors, an elderly and somewhat deaf lady appeared to whom we made our needs known. In halting English she said that her husband was busy at the moment, but that he should be free in twenty minutes or half an hour and that if we were prepared to wait he would probably be able to let us have some petrol. Although we still had an uncomfortably long way to go to our planned overnight stop at Colesberg, we clearly had no alternative but to accept what she said, and settled down with as good a grace as we could for what we thought might be a long wait. In fact, after only about ten minutes the farmer emerged, a rugged elderly man with an unexpectedly friendly smile. When we introduced ourselves he displayed great interest that we came from the British High Commission. 'If I had known you were here, man, I would have asked you in,' he said. 'I have just been listening to the Test Match from Old Trafford, and my wife knows not to disturb me during the cricket. The Springboks don't seem to be doing so good. But they've stopped for lunch, and I can get on with some work now.'

He insisted on showing us round the farm before filling us up with petrol, and in the process explained that he was half Afrikaner, a quarter Scottish and a quarter German. Apart from his farm, cricket was clearly his main interest. Our encounter with him underlined the fact that international sport, particularly rugby football and cricket, provided the most important contacts with the outside world for most South Africans, no matter how far out in the back blocks they might live. This goes a long way to explain why sporting boycotts in the international field have been taken so seriously by successive South African Governments and why policy has latterly been considerably modified to avoid them.

In 1951, the decision had already been taken in principle to tar the whole of the north–south trunk road from Cape Town to the Rhodesian border at Beit Bridge. But there were still long stretches of gravel road, mainly in the Northern Cape and the Orange Free State, which had not yet been tarred. A car in the distance could often be detected first by its accompanying cloud of dust; the task of overtaking a fast-moving lorry through an impenetrable trail of dust could be extremely hazardous. When we left Bloemfontein *en route* for the Basutoland border, the road deteriorated even further. If there was a single other vehicle in sight, perhaps two or three miles away, the children claimed that there was a traffic jam.

At the bridge over the Caledon River at Maseru, the sight of the Union Jack flying over the Basutoland immigration post came as an unexpected reminder that Basutoland was still a British colony. The only problem was that, in true British style, there seemed to be more difficulty about getting an animal through the border than there was for a human being, and it looked for a time as if we were going to have to abandon Sarie at the customs post for the night. Fortunately for her, we carried an introduction to a member of the Secretariat in Maseru, and after a lot of telephoning the dog was eventually allowed in.

When we checked in at the hotel we found roaring fires in our hotel bedrooms, and were alarmed to be told that there could be up to 25° of frost at night. We had filled up with anti-freeze after our accident at Deddington Hill six months (could it be only six months?) earlier; but the point was confirmed the next morning when we found that the shallow drifts (fords) in the road northwards to Teyateyaneng were still frozen solid at 10 o'clock.

Later in the morning we stopped for a picnic lunch. In order to get at the food we had had to take a number of things out of the boot, some of which I put temporarily on the roof rack while we were eating. After lunch we passed through several small villages, consisting mostly of traditional Basuto ronda-vels, and were somewhat surprised at the warmth of the welcome we received. It was normal for the children to wave, but this time whole villages seemed to rush out of their huts to laugh and cheer. It was only when we stopped to fill up with petrol that we realized the cause of the enthusiasm: on top of the pile of luggage on the roof rack, its rim neatly tucked under the securing ropes, was my top hat. Seldom can a status symbol so shamelessly displayed have been so generously applauded.

CHAPTER 5

THE TRANSVAAL

IN AUGUST 1951 the Barings left South Africa at the end of their tour of duty and were succeeded by Sir John and Lady Le Rougetel. Before they finally departed the Barings took Vera and myself to a farewell dinner in Johannesburg in aid of Father Trevor Huddleston's mission in the African township of Sophiatown, one of the forerunners of the vast conurbation of Johannesburg townships known today as Soweto. Father Huddleston made a deep impression on us; his calm and all-embracing Christianity was, however, too much for most of the South African establishment, whose God was of an altogether more selective nature. Lady Mary devoted much time and effort to supporting inter-racial Christian contacts, and it was clear that the Barings' departure came as a personal blow to many of those working in this field.

In contrast with the Barings, the Le Rougetels were entirely new to Africa. Sir John had been posted, somewhat to his surprise, from Brussels, where he had expected to finish his career. It was customary in those days for the High Commissioner to be provided with a Private Secretary from the staff of one of the High Commission Territories. The officer who was appointed as Private Secretary to Sir John was a young Scottish District Commissioner from the Bechuanaland Protectorate, Michael Fairlie, who quickly became one of our closest friends and has remained so to the present day.

Pretoria could scarcely have been more different from Cape Town. Arriving there in late June, in the sunshine of the Transvaal winter, the contrast with the rain and wind we had left behind in Cape Town was delightful. But other comparisons were less favourable. Apart from a couple of fairly undistinguished hotels, Pretoria at that time possessed only one restaurant with any pretensions at all. Theatres and concerts were available in Johannesburg, thirty-five miles away, but the capital itself was something of a cultural desert. Happily things have changed considerably since then.

Nevertheless, it was fascinating to be introduced to the high veld and to find ourselves within reach of the first, and still one of the finest, game reserves in the world, the Kruger National Park. Although for many years

23

after the Boer War President Kruger tended to be regarded as a great reactionary, especially by the British, he was in some ways surprisingly ahead of his time. Already at the end of the nineteenth century he realized, long before most of his contemporaries, that unless a significant area of land could be put aside to enable wild animals to live undisturbed by man, there would soon be no animals left in the wild at all. He accordingly put in hand a very substantial programme of purchasing land which was permitted to be used for neither farming nor hunting. The final result – possibly his most lasting memorial – was the establishment in 1898 of the Kruger National Park.

We paid our first visit to the park with John and Peggy Wakely, and their two sons Charles and Richard, in September 1951. In those days the road to the eastern Transvaal was a good deal rougher than it is today, and the journey took us longer than we expected. It has always been a rule of the park that visitors should be in camp by dark, but we missed the closing of the gate by half an hour and had to pay a token fine for arriving late. As it turned out, the fine was well worth it: the impala grazing along the roadside in the dusk were fascinated by our headlights and competed with each other to see how high they could jump across the beams. This complicated the driving, since we were determined not to compound the error of our late arrival with the crime of running over a buck, but it gave us some very unusual and attractive game-watching.

It took some time after its inception for the Kruger Park to be effectively managed and policed, and in the meantime the wild life had already been depleted by uncontrolled hunting, particularly of the larger game. During that first visit we failed to see a single elephant; they existed in any numbers only in the extreme north of the park. Today, at least partly as a result of the remarkable conservation work carried out by the South African National Parks Board since the war, elephants are re-established almost to Komatipoort, where the main road from Johannesburg to Maputo runs close to the southern border of the park. Even if we did not see elephants on that first occasion, however, we were lucky enough to see a pair of cheetah, the rarest of the big cats, on a kill. We also began to see something of the birds for which South Africa is famous: saddlebill and marabou storks, lilac-breasted rollers, sacred ibises, kori bustards and a wide selection of vultures and birds of prey. It was on that trip, largely as a result of John Wakely's tuition, that bird-watching first got a real grip on me: today when I go to a nature reserve it is the birds that I tend to concentrate on rather than the animals.

Shortly after our visit to the Kruger Park, the Shephards joined us for a fortnight's holiday to see something of the Transvaal. It was their first visit, and Rupert was captivated by the vivid colours both of the country itself and of its people. He was particularly fascinated – and indeed for a time influenced – by the art of the Mapogga tribe, a South African branch of the Ndebele (Matabele) people, who had built a model village, decorated with their remarkable and characteristic murals, only a short distance north of Pretoria. It was an interesting demonstration of Cape Town's isolation from the African population of South Africa that he had seen virtually no African art in its home setting before coming north on this visit.

A few weeks later we paid our first visit to the Bechuanaland Protectorate. At that time, and indeed right up to independence, the British Resident Commissioner for the Protectorate had his headquarters at Mafeking in the Northern Cape Province. It was highly anomalous that the capital of a British dependent territory should in effect be on foreign soil – particularly the soil of South Africa. Mafeking was some fifteen miles south of the border and forty miles from Lobatse, the nearest town in the protectorate, but the administration operated within a self-contained British enclave known as the Imperial Reserve – an arrangement which dated back to 1910.

During our time in Pretoria a minor tragedy hit us. Sarie, the boxer, who was by now nearly fully grown, had settled down well in our new house in Colbyn, a Pretoria suburb. One evening, after the children had been playing with her in the garden, she disappeared, apparently into the garden next door. A minute or two later she reappeared in a very weak state and collapsed panting on the path outside the front door. When we looked at her we found that she had a deep cut at the top of her chest. She was not bleeding much, but was obviously sick, and we took her straight to the vet. He confirmed our view that the wound did not look too serious, but said she was suffering from shock and that he would like to put her in his kennels overnight to keep an eye on her. In the morning, to our dismay, he telephoned to say that, in spite of the fact that he had been up to see her several times during the night, she had died in the early morning. An autopsy revealed that she had somehow impaled herself on a bamboo stake which had pierced her lung and broken off inside her chest. He thought that she might have done it while jumping through a hedge onto a staked plant; but there was also the remote possibility that she might have been deliberately attacked. We were all very shaken by her death and, remembering that any dog we took back to England would have to go into quarantine for six months, we decided to leave the purchase of a successor until the end of our tour.

Most of my work in the office was politically oriented, but I was already learning that a diplomat could expect to be called on to deal with a wide range of matters, covering almost every aspect of human activity. During the course of my career I have had to arrange funerals, co-ordinate an aid programme on family planning, and to register births and marriages. I now found myself flogging small boats. But perhaps that requires some explanation.

For the first five or six years after the war the main air service between Europe and South Africa had been provided by the 'c'-class flying boats of Imperial Airways, later BOAC. These splendid aircraft winged their leisurely way down Africa at about 100 mph, taking a week on the journey and putting their passengers ashore in comfortable hotels every night. During our service in Egypt we had watched them landing on the Nile at Cairo and Luxor, but by the time we arrived in South Africa they had, sadly, just been taken off the route. One of my first jobs when we arrived in Pretoria was to arrange for the sale of a number of 'pram' dinghies belonging to the (British) Ministry of Transport, which had been used to handle the mooring cables used by the flying boats when they landed at the terminal on the Vaaldam, not far from Johannesburg.

As a result of this chore I had got to know Ted Bilbrough, the senior BOAC manager in South Africa, and when, towards the end of 1951, the first proving flight of the de Haviland Comet to Johannesburg was announced, Vera and I and the children were invited over to see it. There were great crowds at Palmietfontein airport, most of them doubtless ordinary members of the public, but including senior representatives of South African Airways and the SAAF. The first arrival of a commercial jet aircraft was regarded throughout South Africa as an historic occasion, and it provided a tremendous boost for Britain as well as for BOAC. Unfortunately the triumph was short-lived. The first Comet crash at Elba took place less than two years later, and by the time the fuselage was redesigned and the aircraft brought back into airline service, the Boeing 707 had been ordered by South African Airways.

CHAPTER 6

VAN RIEBEECK TERCENTENARY

As WE OFTEN found in our later postings, the middle year of our three-year tour of duty in South Africa turned out in retrospect to be the most rewarding. There is a certain logic about this. In one's first year there is everything to learn: the fact that one is often faint but pursuing can lead to a sense of frustration and the feeling that one could be doing everything much better if only one knew exactly what to do or whom to contact. In one's last year, on the other hand, there can come a sense of staleness: at a certain stage one inevitably begins to look ahead to the next posting.

For these, and a number of other reasons, 1952 was a good year. We left Pretoria early in the New Year and arrived in Cape Town in time to take a short holiday at Ysterfontein, a small fishing village about sixty miles north of Cape Town up the coast. The Knutzens had been lent a double rondavel very close to the beach, and asked the four of us to join them for a fortnight. For the first week I was on leave myself, and we had a splendid time relaxing on the beach and in the sea.

One particular event of that holiday can appropriately be introduced by the fact that Vera managed to sprain her ankle in bed. She spent most of one sunny Sunday soaking it in a bucket of sea water and numbing the pain with gin and tonic – much to the amusement of Mike Fairlie and another member of the office who had come up from Cape Town to spend the day with us. A month or so later she discovered she was pregnant, so at least she had something to show for her injury.

Shortly after we had settled down in our own house in Cape Town, we became involved in a new official experience, that of a post inspection. The objects of a diplomatic service inspection are to review the staffing of the post in relation to the tasks it has to carry out; to look into the pay and allowances of the officers involved, and to report on the general efficiency of the post. Nowadays, inspections are carried out by a small cadre of regular diplomatic service officers who normally spend about two years in the inspectorate, during the course of which they will inspect a number of overseas posts and perhaps one or two home departments. But in the Commonwealth Relations Office in the immediate post-war period inspections were arranged on an *ad hoc* basis, often by senior retired officers who were re-employed for this specific purpose.

Our inspector turned out to be Sir Harry Batterbee, a former High Commissioner in New Zealand who had retired shortly after the end of the war. One of his tasks was to see how the families lived and, *inter alia*, whether their allowances were adequate for the entertaining they were expected to do. In the process of checking the style and cost of our entertaining against our allowances, it was customary for the inspector to have a meal with each of the home-based officers. We had found our allowances during our first year to be distinctly parsimonious, and we debated whether we should give him a meagre dinner to demonstrate that we could not afford anything better, or whether we should aim to soften him up by giving him the best possible meal within Lydia's capabilities.

Not surprisingly we decided on the second alternative, but it may be that Vera overdid the build-up with Lydia. The first course went well, but it was evident that she was more nervous than usual. When with the second course the moment arrived to hand the vegetables to Sir Harry, she somehow managed to upset an entire dish of peas in his lap. He took it very well. As a footnote I should perhaps add that our allowances were put up by about 20 per cent, which in those pre-inflation days represented a handsome increase in real terms. When I announced this to the family at supper some two months later, Vera and the children rose to their feet and sang 'God bless Sir Harry Batterbee'.

Sir Harry was still in Cape Town when the news of the death of King George VI was received. This event served to illustrate the reality of South Africa's continuing links with the Crown. A period of State mourning was announced, and a special memorial service was held at the Anglican Cathedral. This was attended by Ministers, by the diplomatic corps, among which the Commonwealth High Commissioners took precedence, and by the Mayor and other local civil and military dignitaries. Sir John Le Rougetel read the lesson. Vera, who by then was two-and-a-half-months pregnant, and I sat immediately behind him and his wife. Vera still vividly remembers the agony she went through trying not to pass out during the long service.

In South African history, 1952 marked the tercentenary of the occupation of the Cape by the Netherlands East India Company under its first Governor, Jan van Riebeeck. To celebrate the occasion Cape Town had organized an impressive Festival and Trade Fair in which a large number of governments and firms took part. As South Africa's leading trading partner, the British Government were persuaded to make a major contribution to the fair. The Central Office of Information, working in close collaboration with the Board of Trade, commissioned Sir Hugh Casson, fresh from his success at the Festival of Britain, to design a prestige pavilion to display a wide selection of British goods and activities. Nicholas Monsarrat, as Director of Information Services, was in charge of the project in its early stages, though the design and content were largely settled in London.

As always on these occasions, the construction of the pavilion had to be carried out within a tight timetable. All went well until, almost exactly six weeks before the fair was due to open, the structural steelwork began to go up. When half the steel frame had been erected, but before it had been properly trussed, a tremendous south-easterly gale blew up. By morning the frame was a tangled mass of girders on the ground. It was agreed by the architect, the local contractors and the Central Office of Information that the post-mortem would be left until later. All that mattered was to make sure the pavilion opened on time. This was not easy, as the steel frame had been specially fabricated. To repeat the order, clear the site, re-erect the frame and complete the building in the space of five-and-a-half weeks seemed almost impossible. In order to help with the technicalities the Ministry of Works sent out a clerk of works, and Nicholas, with characteristic naval efficiency, had everyone working round the clock. Hugh Casson himself arrived a few days later and, as a result of tremendous efforts on the part of all concerned and no further interference from the weather, the pavilion opened on time. It was generally regarded as a great success; it featured a major exhibition of aspects of British parliamentary democracy, with special emphasis on the Palace of Westminster. This choice of theme did not pass unnoticed by many South Africans.

The festival as a whole was immensely popular. The Dutch Embassy had sponsored a small-scale replica of the town square at Culemborg, van Rie-beeck's birthplace, complete with a reproduction of the carillon of bells for which its church is famous. Every evening dancing was organized in the square to the music of a traditional steam organ. At night the exhibition, and indeed the whole of Cape Town, was dominated by the illumination with batteries of floodlights of the vast front of Table Mountain; to see the mountain hanging silently, a huge back-cloth to the city, was a sight no one could forget. The lights are in fact still operated today during the autumn months, to the great admiration of overseas tourists, and visitors from other parts of the Republic.

Nicholas had other things on his mind that year, including divorce proceedings and the publication of *The Cruel Sea*. Overnight he became famous. I remember his coming into the office one day and asking if we could put in an application to the South African authorities for permission for him to import a Jaguar XK 120. 'If they're worried about currency,' he said, 'tell them I can pay for it in dollars, or in francs or in marks – or even in drachmas if they like.' I never heard what currency they selected, but the car duly turned up a month or two later. Shortly before the end of the session he gave a tremendous party at the Vineyard Hotel 'to celebrate the first hundred thousand'. I for one assumed that this meant the sale of the first 100,000 copies of the book; only years later we found out that it was to celebrate the first £100,000 derived from sales, royalties, film rights and the rest.

At the party I met for the first time Philippa Crosby, who later became his second wife. She was a high-powered journalist in her own right, with her own weekly column in *Femina*, a glossy magazine published in Johannesburg. She and Nicholas were perhaps both too characterful for the marriage to be a success; sadly it broke up a few years later in Canada.

CHAPTER 7

HOLIDAY IN THE RHODESIAS

THE BABY TO which, in common with our other children, we had for no known reason given the pre-natal name of 'Little Llewellyn', was due in October. We realized, therefore, that if we were to do any serious sightseeing before we left South Africa, it would be wise to do it as soon as possible after the end of the 1952 parliamentary session. Apart from wanting a short change from the South African scene we were particularly anxious to see something of the Rhodesias, which we had no reason to believe we should be able to visit again.

Shortly after our return to Pretoria, therefore, we took three weeks' leave. We worked out a round trip of some twenty-five hundred miles, designed to take us north through Pietersburg and Wyliespoort to the Southern Rhodesian border at Beit Bridge, and thence to Bulawayo and the Victoria Falls. We planned to return to Pretoria through the Bechuanaland Protectorate. This was, of course, all well-trodden tourist ground. But it was new to us and we felt a real sense of adventure as we set out. Although we did not intend to camp, we were advised to take a certain amount of equipment, including a tow-rope, axes and a spade for digging ourselves out of sand or mud. Even in retrospect, this was a fairly demanding trip for an expectant mother of five months' standing.

The first part of the journey was interesting, but relatively unremarkable. The road through the gorge at Wyliespoort was in those days very spectacular: sadly, the most exciting section is now replaced by a tunnel. The 'great grey-green greasy Limpopo River, all set about with fever trees' was, however, a mild disappointment. The fever trees were all right and, even better, our first sight of baobabs, those strange prehistoric-looking giants known locally as *kerimatata* (cream of tartar) trees. But in the middle of the dry season the Limpopo was little more than a string of dirty, disconnected pools crossed by a useful, but entirely unexciting box-girder bridge. Bulawayo was similarly unmemorable, except for the well-advertised width of the streets. The tourist guides did not, however, mention that at every intersection they

31

dipped down into deep flood drains, which were not always easy to see. By taking one of these depressions too fast I caused Vera to hit the roof, literally, and I had some anxious moments when I wondered if she might not be going to have the baby prematurely.

It was after we left Bulawayo, travelling north-west towards Wankie and the Victoria Falls, that we began to feel that for the first time we were really getting into the wilds. The road in those days consisted only of a pair of tar 'strips' with a soft shoulder on each side. The strips took the wheels of a single car or lorry. When another vehicle was seen approaching both had to move over to the left, leaving only their off-side wheels on what had been the near-side strips. Tourists began by moving over as soon as they saw a vehicle in the distance; seasoned Rhodesians, on the other hand, were inclined to play 'chicken' and to leave the move to the last possible moment. To overtake, one had somehow to persuade the vehicle in front to move over. This operation became particularly interesting when, as was usually the case in winter, the shoulders were covered in a thick layer of dust.

In order to save money, the roads were built to a minimum specification. Bridges, for example, were provided only if absolutely necessary, which was hardly ever. Thus, when crossing stream beds, the road was liable to drop down with little warning onto concrete slabs, or 'Irish bridges'. The stream beds, or *dongas*, were normally dry, but in wet weather could turn into raging torrents at short notice; they were matched by equally unpredictable humps in the road which could also prove disconcerting to the unsuspecting traveller. Being the opposite of *dongas*, the children christened these humps 'agnods'. By getting into the habit of using this invented name we greatly puzzled old Rhodesian hands, who sometimes believed that we had got hold of a vernacular word that they should have heard of. I should like to think that 'agnod' now appears in some glossary of Sindebele or Setswana terms.

The only sizeable town between Bulawayo and the Victoria Falls is Wankie, the centre of the Rhodesian coal-mining industry. Miles before the mines could be seen we became aware of a film of grey dust covering everything. The town itself, which I was to get to know better a few years later, was a hive of activity. South and west of Wankie, and covering hundreds of square miles between the railway and the Bechuanaland border, lies the Wankie National Park, which was one of the objectives of our trip. Famous for lion, it also provides a home for some of the largest herds of elephant and buffalo in southern Africa.

But the highlight of the journey was, of course, the Victoria Falls. We could not at that stage afford a family holiday in the famous Victoria Falls

Hotel on the Southern Rhodesian side of the Zambezi, so we booked ourselves, with slight misgivings, into a hutted camp on the Northern Rhodesian
bank. To reach it, we had first to cross the dramatic road-rail bridge over the
gorge just below the Falls. This is unquestionably one of the engineering
wonders of the modern world. The apparently delicate steel arch spans a
canyon more than four hundred feet deep and a thousand feet wide. Vertically
below the bridge, the tremendous flow of water from what was a mile-wide
river upstream of the Falls, boils and seethes as it forces its way into the
narrow gorge downstream. Man's masterpiece provides an elegant and reassuring counterpoint to the untamed energy of nature below.

The Northern Rhodesian camp turned out to be exactly what we wanted.
We were given two twin-bedded thatched rondavels, each having outside it a
barbecue, or *braaivleis*, on which we could cook our own meals. Across the
road from the camp was the vast, and deceptively peaceful, expanse of the
gently flowing Zambezi; the only evidence of the ferocity of the Falls half a
mile downstream was the distant roar, which ebbed and flowed with changes
in the wind.

We spent nearly a week at the Falls. A boat trip on the river showed us our
first hippos, our first goliath heron and, what was for ever afterwards our
favourite African bird, our first fish eagle. The harsh sweetness of the fish
eagle's cry is one of the most evocative sounds to be heard along the rivers of
Africa from the Cape to the Nile. We also visited the excellent Rhodes-
Livingstone Museum in the Northern Rhodesian town of Livingstone, and
spent some time in the nearby Lozi village, which was sponsored by the
museum as a living demonstration of the arts, crafts and customs of Barotseland.

On the river bank not far from our huts was a small bay which, during the
day, was frequented by picnickers and children swimming. When the sun
went down we got into the habit of spending half an hour in this bay
watching the bats come out and the birds winging their way back to their
night-time roosts. One evening, as we were sitting quietly watching the sunset, one of us became aware of a small double projection, looking rather like
a knotted stick, moving silently across the smooth water of the river and into
our bay. It did not take long to realize that there was now a sizeable crocodile
where an hour earlier the children had been swimming. On the following
night the same thing happened. Very few of our fellow tourists ever seemed
to become aware of the crocodile's existence. I assume that he (or she) had
never in fact taken one of the swimmers; otherwise the authorities must
surely have put up warning notices.

Near the camp there was a small airstrip from which we took the children for their first flight – a splendid twenty minutes in which we flew around and over the Falls and a few miles up the river. The view from the air was breathtaking, and showed, as nothing else could, the enormous trench into which the river plunged, and the winding course of the gorge downstream. As the result of millions of years of erosion, the sites of half a dozen previous falls can clearly be seen. As we came back to land, the pilot spotted a crocodile sunning itself on a sandbank well out in the middle of the river. Already quite low above the water, he banked on one wing-tip to give us a better view of the reptile. This slightly alarmed Robert, who has a bad head for heights, but is also alarmed the crocodile, which slid off the bank into the water, where we could still see it swimming slowly beneath the surface. We all speculated whether it was the one we had seen in our bay the night before.

We also spent a morning walking around the Falls on the Southern Rhodesian bank, where the constant fall of spray creates an area of rain forest, quite uncharacteristic of the dry mopani bush through which the river passes for much of its course. This forest presents a self-contained mini-ecology, including trees and birds which do not occur elsewhere in the area for several hundred miles. One of the most conspicuous of the birds is the trumpeter hornbill, whose large casqued beak and undignified call, strongly reminiscent of a toy trumpet, are characteristic.

While we were in the rain forest we were surprised to hear the whistle of a powerful jet aircraft – an unaccustomed sound in the wilds of Africa in those days. It turned out to be a south-bound Comet flight circling the Falls before landing at Livingstone, which was its last stop on the weekly flight from London to Johannesburg. It was surprisingly romantic to see this sophisticated aircraft in that remote outpost of western civilization. A month or two later, back in Pretoria, I was talking to Ted Bilbrough of BOAC, who had just returned from a flying visit to London. 'The Victoria Falls looked wonderful from the Comet,' he said, not without a certain smugness. 'As a matter of fact, the Comet looked rather good from the Falls,' I was able to answer. Score: fifteen all.

After leaving the Falls, we had to retrace our route as far as Bulawayo. From there we visited the grave of Cecil John Rhodes in the Matopo Hills, some forty miles south of the city. The grave consists of a flat stone set in the rounded top of a granitic outcrop two or three hundred feet high, and is surrounded by a group of enormous weathered granite boulders. Even today it remains a place of great atmosphere: before his death it had been the site of Rhodes's historic negotiations with the Ndebele leader, Lobengula. That night we spent at Plumtree on the Bechuanaland border. This small town contains a well-known Rhodesian private boys' school, whose alumni are appetizingly identified as Old Prunitians.

The next day we crossed the border into the Bechuanaland Protectorate and drove the relatively short distance to Francistown. Francistown was then a dusty settlement on the edge of the Kalahari Desert served by two friendly, but fairly basic, hotels, the Grand and the Tati; the latter built at the time of the Tati mining concession. There wasn't much to choose between them, we gathered, but it was said locally that the Grand was rather tartier than the Tati – and that was where we stayed. In the afternoon, we were taken round the town by the District Commissioner. There wasn't a great deal to see, but we were asked in particular to admire the gardens of the offices and official residences. These were in splendid condition, being looked after by the only long-term white prisoner in the local gaol, a man who, we were told afterwards, was serving a life sentence for murdering his wife. Whatever the crime that put him inside, he certainly succeeded in making the desert flower.

The road south from Francistown follows the railway, and most of the European settlements in the protectorate lay along this line of rail. The road surface consisted mainly of sand; routine maintenance was carried out by a small team equipped with two or four donkeys pulling the leafy branch of a tree in order to smooth out the corrugations. Our final stop in the territory was at Palapye Road, from which we spent a day visiting Serowe, the administrative centre of the Bamangwato tribe and Tshekedi Khama's seat of government. Serowe was at that time said to be the biggest entirely black city in Africa. It consisted of an enormous conurbation of *kraals* spreading along a relatively well-watered valley running back into the Kalahari and dominated by the rocky *kopje* on which the ancestral chiefs of the Bamangwato are buried. Seretse Khama was still, with Ruth, in exile in the United Kingdom, and we did not meet them until a year or two later.

At Palapye Road, the front of the hotel formed almost an integral part of the railway station; leading out from it at the back there were two parallel rows of identical bedrooms forming an open-ended square. Shortly after retiring we heard a train approaching, the noise rising to an alarming crescendo as the locomotive came past – so that it felt as if it must be about to burst into our room. The once popular song, 'The railroad runs through the middle of the house', could have been specifically written for the Botswana railway hotels.

Fortunately, as we later discovered, only one or two trains passed through each night. But at about midnight we were woken again, this time by someone pounding on our door. When we asked him to come in, a distinctly querulous and not entirely sober gentleman of Scottish origin poked his head round the door and asked whether we owned a small boy. Honesty, combined with the realization that the question was almost certainly rhetorical, compelled us to admit that we did. 'In that case, will ye kindly remove him from my bed,' he said. Hastily wrapping a dressing gown around me, I looked into the children's room, which was next to our own. Diana was there, sleeping the sleep of the just, but no Robert. One bedroom further down the row, however, just like the gentleman said, there he was, also sleeping peacefully. Evidently he had got up in response to a call of nature and had come back to the wrong room.

The rest of the night was relatively undisturbed, and next day we crossed into the Transvaal at Martin's Drift. By nightfall we were back in our own house in Pretoria.

CHAPTER 8

LAST MONTHS IN SOUTH AFRICA

BACK AT THE office everything seemed very dull. But not for long. Only ten days after we got back from our holiday, in early August, Vera had a violent and unexpected haemorrhage, and was advised by her doctor to take things very easily. A few days later I was on the High Commission tennis court, where I had been made a reluctant conscript to the office doubles tournament. I had warned my partner in advance that in order to underline my amateur status I would be playing in brown 'tackies' (canvas gym shoes), rather than the more orthodox white ones. The game had only just started when Mike Fairlie came onto the court and told me that Lydia had telephoned to say that Vera had been taken ill and was now on her way to the maternity home where the baby was due to be delivered in October. I asked to be excused from the rest of the tennis and shot off.

By a strange coincidence Vera's gynaecologist in Pretoria, Dr Elizabeth MacCallum, was a graduate of St Andrews University, where her professor had been Dr Margaret Fairlie, Michael's aunt. 'Aunt Maggie', as we all knew her, had the distinction of being the first woman appointed to a University Chair in Scotland. She told the story that for ten years the Senate of St Andrews had resolutely and consistently refused to treat her as a full professor, a title which they regarded as a solely male prerogative. She therefore remained in charge of the department in an acting capacity for the whole of that period. It was only when the end of her term of office was in sight that they relented and she became Professor Fairlie. By an even greater coincidence, Aunt Maggie was in Pretoria visiting Mike when Vera was taken ill and, without interfering in any way, she kept a discreet eye on what was going on. She told me in confidence at an early stage that Vera couldn't have been better looked after if she had been in Scotland – the highest compliment she could possibly have paid her former pupil.

Nevertheless, the next few weeks were no fun for Vera. Not only was she under strict instructions to remain flat on her back to avoid the possibility of a miscarriage, but she found the staff of the nursing home not entirely

37

friendly. In particular, the Afrikaner night sister refused to speak English to her, even though she was in fact able to speak it fluently: 'Now you are in my country you should learn to speak Afrikaans.' Vera did her best to argue that English also was an official language in South Africa. But this didn't get her anywhere. To make matters worse, the food was deplorable and I took to sneaking in helpings of Lydia's cooking when the nurses weren't looking.

After five weeks of patient waiting the period of anxiety passed, and Andrew arrived safely. In spite of his pre-natal problems and the fact that he was still a month premature, he was a healthy baby from the start. While Vera was still in hospital, John and Peggy Wakely left South Africa. They were replaced by Roland and Pauline Hunt, with whom we subsequently had much contact, including succeeding them nine years later in Kampala.

When Andrew was only four months old we undertook another trip on our way back to Cape Town in January 1952. Vera was in need of a seaside holiday, so this time we decided to travel by way of Natal and the Transkei, where we spent a happy and relaxing week at a remote but comfortable hotel at Coffee Bay on the Wild Coast. Everything went well until we were leaving Port Elizabeth on the last leg of our journey to Cape Town. It then became obvious that Robert was running a high temperature.

I knew that Rex Wilson had finished his medical course in December, and the first thing I did when we got in was to ring him to find out if he was yet in practice. 'I'm qualified,' he said, 'but I haven't put my plate up yet. Actually, I'm still painting the surgery.'

'In that case you're in business,' I said. 'Robert has developed a high fever and we're very anxious for someone to look at him urgently. Not so long ago we were in Northern and Southern Rhodesia, where he could have picked up sleeping sickness or typhoid, and we have just come from the Transkei, where he might have been in contact with malaria or polio or tick-bite fever. He probably hasn't got any of those things, but we'd like to be sure.'

'Do you really trust me to take him on?' Rex asked. 'If so I'd love to. But I'd better warn you that he will be my very first private patient.'

Rex, who today gives lectures on the problems of the general practitioner to a new generation of medical students at Groote Schuur Hospital, says that he often quotes Robert's case to his classes. Having no other patients, he was determined to leave no stone unturned, and with our approval he firmly refused to put Robert straight onto a wide-spectrum antibiotic. Over the next three days he subjected him to every pathological test in the book. His blood was sampled, his urine, his faeces and his nervous reactions were tested – all inconclusively. In the meantime, however, his temperature began to fall and he was obviously improving rapidly.

'If your first case is a very sick child suffering from a high fever,' Rex says he tells his students, 'and in spite of every test you can't find out what is wrong, don't get too discouraged. Nature is a wonderful thing, and children are on the whole extremely resilient. The chances are at least a hundred to one that the patient will recover. If your only function is to reassure the parents, you will still be doing a useful job.'

Nineteen fifty-three was election year in South Africa and it had been announced that after a short session to dispose of urgent business Parliament would be prorogued so that the election could be held before the onset of winter. With this in mind, most diplomatic missions sent only skeleton staffs to Cape Town that year, leaving the main body in Pretoria. It so happened that I was the sole representative of the political side of the British High Commission in Cape Town, apart from the High Commissioner himself. This meant quite a lot of work preparing political reports for Whitehall, since the United Party were regarded as having a good chance of being re-elected and the election result could by no means be regarded as a foregone conclusion.

Vera and I had once again managed to secure Conzella, the house into which we had moved on our first arrival two years previously. This time, however, the two elder children were booked to return to their Pretoria schools by air at the end of the Christmas holidays. It was the first of many times we were to be parted from the children to attend boarding school, and it was a considerable wrench seeing them off at the airport, even though it was only for one term.

Once Parliament was dissolved in mid-March, the election campaign began in earnest. The United Party built up a great attack on the Government, particularly in relation to the legislation abolishing the parliamentary representatives of the Coloured community. This legislation had been passed during the previous session, but had subsequently been declared *ultra vires* by the Supreme Court. The court's decision seemed likely to have improved the United Party's electoral chances. In the event, however, much to the chagrin of South African liberal opinion, the National Party was returned to power with an increased majority, even though they were supported by only a minority of the electorate as a whole. It was the last occasion on which South Africa could be said to have a credible alternative government.

A contributory reason for the United Party's defeat was the fact that the

1910 Constitution provided for a weighting of votes in the rural areas, which favoured the predominantly Afrikaner, and hence Nationalist, farming community. An average urban constituency at that date consisted of some four thousand voters, whereas most rural constituencies had fewer than three thousand voters on the roll. It had been suggested to General Smuts shortly after the war that this imbalance was wrong in electoral terms, and potentially damaging to the prospects of his own party, since it implanted in the system a permanent bias in favour of conservative rural Afrikanerdom. However, General Smuts rejected out of hand any suggestion that the South Africa Act should be amended to rectify the situation, urging that to tamper with the electoral law would be to upset the delicate balance established in the Constitution between the two communities. It is only in very recent years, with the movement of more Afrikaners to the towns, that some Afrikaners are themselves beginning to wonder if the arrangement is an entirely sensible one.

At the end of February 1953 Mike Fairlie left the High Commissioner's private office on posting to Swaziland as District Commissioner at Mankaiana. One of the first things we did after our return to Pretoria was to spend a long week-end with him in his new surroundings. Diana, who had a mid-term holiday, and Andrew, now seven months old, came with us. Mike's parents were also spending a short holiday with him from Scotland.

Mankaiana, which lies some forty miles south of Mbabane, the capital of Swaziland, is close to the edge of the Usutu Forest, which had recently been established by the Colonial Development Corporation. On our second afternoon there, Mike took Vera, Diana and myself for a short drive up to the top of the escarpment to give us an idea of the scale of the Usutu Forest scheme and to show us something of the country. Andrew was left behind with Mrs Fairlie, who bravely undertook to give him his 6 o'clock feed if we were not back by then. We travelled in our car, which had a distinctly lower clearance than Mike's Chevrolet, and on our way up the very rough track to the viewpoint we bottomed audibly on a large boulder in the middle of the road. When we arrived at the top of the hill we got out of the car to admire the view, which was even more spectacular than we expected. Passing round the back of the car, however, I noticed a fine trail of oil, which all too clearly followed us up the hill. A brief glance under the engine justified my fears: a pool of oil confirmed that the sump was leaking badly. Without waiting for the sunset, which had been one of the promised attractions of the drive, I got everyone back in the car with the idea of driving as far as possible on our way back to Mankaiana before the oil gave out. Even travelling down hill we couldn't go very fast, however, and we had only covered a couple of miles before the tell-tale red light came on to show that the oil was below the danger level.

By that time the daylight was beginning to fade. I parked the car as far off the road as I could manage, and we set off to walk the five miles or so back to the district headquarters. Mike had already told Diana, more to impress her, I suspect, than with any strict regard for accuracy, that there were leopards in them thar hills. He could not easily go back on the story now that we were really facing the wilds, and Diana, summoning all the resources of her training as a Brownie, clearly regarded the whole episode as a tremendous adventure. Although happily no leopards materialized, the journey was not entirely without hazard, since it was a totally moonless night and we had passed through three drifts, or fords, on our way up the escarpment, which we had to wade through on our way back. Apart from the flickering flames of distant village fires, and the occasional firefly, we had no lights at all – none of us was even a smoker. Fortunately we were above the normal altitude for bilharzia, and the streams were too small for crocodiles, but there was no doubt that the journey on foot conveyed an infinitely greater sense of adventure than the same journey in the insulated security of a car.

One additional complication was that we had no means whatever of letting Mrs Fairlie know what had happened; it was clear that we should be home at least two hours later than she expected us. When we eventually got back at about a quarter to nine, the poor woman was seriously considering how she should set about organizing a search party. She told us that she had also been trying to work out for how long, in the event that we had all been killed, she could have gone on looking after a baby on her own.

At Easter we took another few days off, going this time to Rooival, near White River in the eastern Transvaal, to stay with Martli Malherbe and her mother. Martli, who held the post of films officer in Nicholas Monsarrat's Information Office in Johannesburg, had spent most of the war in Britain, where she had initially gone, in company with a number of other South African girls, to make her fortune on the stage. She was not successful in this particular ambition; instead she became a civil servant and ended the war in an important niche in the offices of the War Cabinet. When she returned to South Africa after the war it was natural that she should gravitate to the British High Commission. Her mother was also a woman of great distinction, having become the first woman Mayor of Pretoria, representing the National Party interest, in 1929.

The fifth of June was Coronation Day. In Pretoria the SADF celebrated the occasion by holding a large three-service parade and fly-past at Swartkops airfield. This ceremony was attended by South African ministers, members of the diplomatic corps and a fair crowd of spectators. Unfortunately most of the route of the march past was on grass, a surface on which it is notoriously difficult for the military to keep in step. It was not, I fear, the smartest or best organized parade I have seen, but a good time was had by all.

We were by now nearing the end of our South African tour. Parliament was due to reassemble in Cape Town in early July, and it was agreed that Vera and I should again accompany the High Commissioner to Cape Town and then return directly to England by sea at the end of the session. Shortly before we left Pretoria, I heard that I had been selected to attend the course at the Joint Services Staff College (now the National Defence College) at Latimer, beginning in September. I therefore spent some of my final weeks cultivating the South African Defence Forces in order to get a feel of the military atmosphere I should be immersed in at Latimer. For the first time, a South African naval officer had just been selected to command the Navy; he was Commodore Biermann, known to all his friends as 'Boozy', who had just returned from attending the Royal Navy's Senior Officers' Course at Greenwich in his previous rank of Commander. Shortly after he took up his new appointment we asked him to dinner, in the course of which I congratulated him on his accelerated promotion to Commodore. Looking me firmly in the eye, and with a completely straight face, he said, 'My dear chap, that's nothing. In your Navy there is a contemporary of mine, an officer who has just been promoted from Commander to Admiral of the bloody Fleet. Admittedly he has the advantage of being married to the Queen.'

PART TWO

FEDERATION OF RHODESIA AND NYASALAND
1959–63

CHAPTER 9

CENTRAL AFRICAN AND TERRITORIES DEPARTMENT

THE JOINT SERVICES Staff College provided a welcome break from responsibility; being on a military course means that virtually all decisions are taken by someone else – one merely has to follow the man in front. A week or two before the course ended, I heard that I was to be seconded for a two-year tour of duty to the Cabinet Office. Since we had sold our Chislehurst house before we went to South Africa, we spent a number of week-ends house-hunting, and eventually found a comfortable family house on the outskirts of Guildford, where from April 1954 we lived intermittently for the next sixteen years.

One of the first things we did after settling in our new house was to get another boxer bitch puppy to replace the much-lamented Sarie. We called her Belinda, and for the next twelve years she was very much a member of the family.

My two years in the Cabinet Office are mainly irrelevant to the present story, though during the course of them I spent a fair amount of time on Commonwealth and Colonial affairs. This included a period as one of the Secretaries of the Malta Round Table Conference, and a few hectic weeks in which I was Secretary-General successively (and for a short time concurrently) of the Federation of Malaya Constitutional Conference and of the conference on the proposed Caribbean Federation, both held at Lancaster House. I was also a member of the Secretariat of the 1955 Commonwealth Prime Ministers' Conference at 10 Downing Street, the last to be presided over by Sir Winston Churchill.

It was a great privilege to be able to see the great man, at the end of his working life, in action at first hand. Even though he was past his best, he still managed to dominate the gathering by the power of his presence. At that conference, two other figures were also outstanding: Pandit Jawaharlal Nehru of India, like Churchill an Old Harrovian, and Sir Robert Menzies of Australia. It so happened that my seat, as Assistant Secretary of the conference, was next to that of Lord Malvern, first Prime Minister of the Federation of Rhodesia and Nyasaland. As a humble member of the Secretariat I did not exchange more than a few words with him, but I was able to observe him at close quarters. Since he was virtually stone deaf he was supplied with a hearing aid connected to the amplifier system; it was his practice, when he disagreed with the views being expressed, ostentatiously to unplug his head-set. I was sad to notice that he almost always seemed to switch off when Pandit Nehru was speaking.

It was a pleasant tradition at Commonwealth conferences held in London that the officials involved, both those from the home team and the visitors, together with their wives, were invited to an evening party at Buckingham Palace. I had arranged with Vera that she should pick me up at the Cabinet Office about half an hour before we were due at the Palace, and that we should drive there together. But about ten minutes before she was expected, disaster struck. I was bending down to polish one of my shoes when I heard – and felt – a sinister tearing in the seat of my pants. Only a glance was necessary to confirm that the crucial (in the most literal sense of the word) seam had opened up along almost the whole of its length. My secretary, who just might have had a needle and cotton, had already left.

I locked the door of my room, took off my trousers and inspected the damage. It could hardly have been worse. It was unthinkable that I could risk the prospect of my shirt-tails, or worse, popping out as I bowed to seven members of the Royal Family, even if Vera crowded up behind me. There was not the faintest possibility of getting hold of a new suit; it was a quarter past seven and even Moss Bros would be closed. I thought of using pins, but quickly imagined that what the mumps had spared, the pins might mutilate. But even as I rejected the idea, inspiration struck. I realized that every good civil servant had a remedy to hand for precisely this emergency: HM Stationery Office Stock Item Code Number 57–23, the common stapler. Mine, I discovered, even bore the superb and appropriate inscription, Ofrex Consort. Clearly this was no common stapler – rather a surrogate wife. I turned the trousers inside out, and had begun to apply the Consort to the seam at one-inch intervals, when there was a knock at the door. Vera had arrived. It was all systems go. Months later, when the suit came back from the cleaners, I discovered the staples, still in place and still performing perfectly.

There was one other aspect of my period of service in the Cabinet Office which turned out to be relevant to my continuing connection with southern Africa, though I did not realize it at the time. This was the fact that I became Secretary to a Ministerial Committee on House of Lords reform, the chairman of which was the late Lord Salisbury. For a year or more, therefore, I worked closely with him. I was impressed by, and sympathetic with, the energy which he put into his efforts to breathe new life into the Upper House. For obvious reasons he was particularly concerned to preserve the hereditary principle, and evolved the concept of 'Peers of Parliament', in terms of which members of the House of Lords would have to decide at the start of each Parliament whether they intended to participate in the legislative function of the House. Unless they did so, they would not be entitled to take part in debates. In spite of his efforts, however, he failed to infect his colleagues on the committee with his enthusiasm, and reform of the House of Lords, when it came, took a different form. But I felt then – and I felt still more so later as I caught glimpses of his activities in support of his friends in Rhodesia – that his undoubted gifts were not always employed to the best advantage.

At the end of my two years in the Cabinet Office, I was posted to Singapore on secondment to the Foreign Office as a First Secretary on the staff of the Commissioner-General for South-East Asia, then Sir Robert Scott (no relation). Shortly after our return to London in 1958, I was promoted to take charge of the Central African and Territories Department, dealing now with the Federation of Rhodesia and Nyasaland as well as with Southern Rhodesia and the High Commission Territories. The fact that I had visited, albeit unofficially, all the territories with which my new department dealt, was of great value. In one respect, this department was unique in the CRO, since it was directly responsible for administering the High Commission Territories, and for recommending to the Secretary of State whether or not he should approve certain classes of Southern Rhodesian legislation. Every other department in the Office – at least until the amalgamation with the Colonial Office which took place some ten years later – had strictly diplomatic responsibilities for advising the Secretary of State on the conduct of relations with independent countries.

One of my new responsibilities was to be *ex officio* guardian to Prince Constantine Bereng Seeiso of Basutoland, later King Moshoeshoe II of Lesotho. Until his coming of age the paramount chieftainship was held by a regent, who was, in fact, Prince Constantine's step-mother. It had been decided some years previously that the Prince should have an English education, first at Ampleforth College and later at Oxford. He spent most of his holidays with a family living in the west of England, but we had him to our Guildford house for occasional week-ends.

Prince Bereng was an extremely nice, rather shy young man, whom we got to know well and to like. With the benefit of hindsight, I believe that the decision to give him an exotic education was mistaken, since it isolated him from political thinking in his future kingdom and gave him little opportunity to come to grips with its problems, including, for example, the 'medicine murders' which were still taking place in Basutoland with the connivance of some of the tribal chiefs. Prince Bereng's absence from the scene, while keeping his hands clean of these machinations, unfortunately left him singularly ill-equipped to deal with the local political leadership when he eventually returned as King.

During 1958, a conference was held in London to decide on a new Constitution for Basutoland. This was attended by most of the leading Basutoland politicians including Chief Leabua Jonathan, leader of the Government Party, who was later to become the first Prime Minister of an independent Lesotho. Chief Jonathan had as his constitutional adviser Professor Dennis Cowen, a South African lawyer who was then married to Deborah Duncan, daughter of a former Governor-General of South Africa.

As head of the Department, I was responsible for much of the day-to-day running of the conference, though the British delegation consisted of a large team under Mr C.J.M. Alport, who had just been appointed Minister of State in the CRO. Immediately before the conference assembled, we found that Chief Jonathan had a week-end free, and I was deputed to take him and his party to see Windsor Castle, which he had expressed a wish to visit. Vera and I decided to make this a family affair, and we took Andrew with us. We had a pleasant afternoon looking at the royal treasures with the Basutoland party, several of whom had never before been outside southern Africa.

Over lunch I asked Chief Jonathan about travelling in Basutoland, which in those days was almost entirely by pony. The Chief, who has always been solidly built, has a nice sense of humour, and when I asked him how many miles he normally travelled in a day he said, 'Do you mean me, or an ordinary chap?' I said that I had really meant him, but how many miles could an ordinary chap cover? His answer was perhaps about eighteen, but that if he personally tried to do more than about ten miles the pony was liable to drop dead. All this amid roars of laughter from his companions.

The constitutional talks started next day. The bargaining was tough. Dennis Cowen was a sound constitutional lawyer but was not himself a politician, nor had he any wide experience of inter-governmental negotiations. He therefore tended to see the issues in strictly black and white terms, and encouraged Chief Jonathan to press for a degree of autonomy which did not at that stage seem realistic to the British team. HMG, on the other hand, were only too conscious that any settlement involving constitutional advance for Basutoland would have to be compatible with the territory's continued existence as a British colony situated inside a South Africa deeply committed to a policy of white supremacy. Only if a head-on collision with the Union Government could be avoided would it be sensible or practical even to consider the longer-term possibility of self-government. It is easy at this distance in time to forget that the first African colony to secure independence, Ghana, had achieved it less than two years before, in 1956. Although the British Government was already coming to accept that independence must be the ultimate goal for the larger African colonies, they certainly did not at that stage regard this as attainable in the short term by a country as small and vulnerable as Basutoland.

After several days of negotiation it became clear that there was still a wide gap between the views of the Basutoland delegation and those of the British Government. It was therefore decided to suspend the talks to enable further behind-the-scenes discussions to take place, and the Basutoland delegation returned to Maseru. When the talks were resumed the differences were still very wide, especially in relation to the composition and powers of the proposed Basutoland National Council. At the end of one of the most difficult plenary sessions, therefore, I suggested to Dennis Cowen that perhaps he and I should see if we could privately hammer out some kind of compromise on the outstanding points. He agreed, and invited me to join him at his club, the Athenaeum, to continue the discussion. We retired to the club library and for nearly four hours over beer and sandwiches argued the position backwards and forwards. By the time we had reached broad agreement on a compromise formula for the composition of the Council, I realized that if I did not leave soon I would miss my last train to Guildford. We both took away a draft text in manuscript and agreed to put it to our respective delegations in the morning.

I was very cock-a-hoop at having achieved what I believed to be a considerably better agreement than I had earlier thought possible. As soon as I arrived in the office in the morning, therefore, I had my copy of the text typed and reported to my Under-Secretary what we had managed to agree. In my enthusiasm I probably failed to make it clear that Cowen and I both understood that our text was *ad referendum* to our two delegations. The Under-Secretary, for his part, probably suspected that Cowen was trying to face our delegation, including the CRO legal advisers whom I had obviously not yet had time to consult, with a *fait accompli*. However that might be, instead of the congratulations I had confidently expected, I received a sharp reproof for exceeding my authority in having had any private discussions at all with Cowen, let alone reaching an agreement with him. This led me in turn to blow my top, and with some impropriety I sought an immediate interview with the Minister of State to explain what had happened. I made the obvious point that he was entirely free to reject the text I had secured, but that Cowen was at that moment putting it to the Basutoland delegation and I very much doubted whether, if we turned it down, we could secure a better agreement in a plenary session.

Fortunately for me, Mr Alport accepted my arguments; the legal advisers were squared, and at a plenary meeting after lunch the text was approved by both sides with scarcely any further discussion. This was my first experience of the exhilaration of a successful personal negotiation. Although I learned a lesson in presentation which I never forgot, I also came to realize how important *tête-à-tête* discussions of this kind can be, always assuming that the participants retain the confidence of their own delegations.

About this time I had my first meetings with Seretse Khama of the Bechuanaland Protectorate. His uncle, the former Regent of the Bamangwato tribe, Tshekedi Khama, had just died of a kidney complaint and the question of the appointment of a new chief of the Bamangwato came under active discussion both in Serowe and in London. Somewhat to the surprise of officials in London and Mafeking, Seretse, while he was still in exile in the United Kingdom, had been elected by the elders of the tribe as Tshekedi's heir apparent, notwithstanding his marriage outside tribal custom. On 11 June he called on me, after which I was to take him across Parliament Square to the House of Lords to meet Lord Home, then Commonwealth Secretary. The total distance was probably no more than five hundred yards, and it never occurred to me to arrange to go by car. We had, however, only walked halfway across Whitehall when I realized that he was in some physical distress. As always seems to be the case in Whitehall, every taxi that passed was engaged, but we eventually secured one and arrived at the meeting only a minute or two late. This was the first indication I had had that Seretse was himself a victim of the complaint which had struck down his uncle.

The next day the Secretary of State, together with Seretse and Ruth Khama and a large number of others, including myself, attended a memorial service for Tshekedi Khama at St Martin-in-the-Fields. The following day Vera and I saw the Khamas off at London airport on what turned out to be a triumphal return to Bechuanaland. One can only regard the subsequent twenty years during which Sir Seretse led his country with wisdom and restraint, as a remarkable bonus for the whole of southern Africa as well as for his many personal friends. His death in 1980 was widely mourned.

CHAPTER 10

THE FEDERATION UNDER FIRE

EARLY IN JANUARY 1959, Lord Home sent for me. David Cole, who was then his Principal Private Secretary, showed me into the splendid room in the Downing Street office which, since the beginning of the century, had been occupied successively by Secretaries of State for the Colonies, for the Dominions and for Commonwealth Relations. Ten years earlier I had myself been familiar with it as Assistant Private Secretary to Mr Noel-Baker. I was slightly baffled to find the room apparently empty. Assuming that he was in the lavatory next door I walked slowly across the room, half wondering if I should retreat and try again later. I nearly jumped out of my skin when his head suddenly popped up from behind his enormous desk. 'Oh, come in, David,' he said. 'I didn't realize you were there. I am just practising a trick I picked up from Pandit Nehru, but I'm afraid I still haven't quite got the knack.'

He sat down at his desk and placed on it a handful of lumps of sugar which he had been engaged in retrieving from the floor. He kept one in his hand, leaned back in his chair and opened his mouth. From the level of his lap he flicked the lump of sugar towards it. The lump hit his nose and fell on the floor. The second attempt was successful and the sugar went neatly into his mouth. 'Nehru can do that with peanuts,' he said. 'He's absolutely infallible. Next time I see him I want to be able to show him that I can do it too. Have some tea?'

Lord Home then explained that ministers had been considering how to make progress to resolve the increasing friction between the Federation of Rhodesia and Nyasaland, and the governments of the two northern territories. As I knew, Dr Banda was at that moment on his way back to Nyasaland from the All-African Peoples' Congress in Accra, and preparations were being made by his supporters to give him a hero's welcome as the long-awaited saviour of his country. As a result of this emotional build-up, the security situation in the territory was deteriorating rapidly, and the Governor, Sir Robert Armitage, had asked the Colonial Secretary for a preliminary round of constitutional talks, to include Dr Banda, to start in late February. Although these would not amount to a formal constitutional conference, the talks could be expected to arouse the deepest misgivings in the Federation. Ministers had accordingly decided to send Lord Perth, then Minister of State in the Colonial Office, to hold exploratory talks in both Zomba and Lusaka in mid-February. In order to reassure the Federal authorities that their views were not being ignored, the Colonial Secretary had agreed that after his talks in the two northern capitals Lord Perth should visit Salisbury to put the Federal Government in the picture. Since he would be accompanied on his visits to Zomba and Lusaka by Colonial Office officials, Lord Home felt that I, as head of the CRO Department concerned, should join the party for the visit to Salisbury.

From that moment on I found that I was having to concentrate almost exclusively on Federal and Southern Rhodesian affairs; somewhat to my regret the High Commission Territories work was increasingly taken over by others.

The security situation in Nyasaland deteriorated even more quickly than had been expected. The famous 'meeting in the bush' of the Nyasaland African National Congress leaders on 25 January was subsequently to become one of the main subjects of investigation by the Devlin Commission. The Nyasaland Government were responsible for the maintenance of law and order in the territory, but preliminary reports of this meeting, the accuracy of which was not at the time fully assessed, reached the Federal authorities on 10 and 18 February. Sir Roy Welensky, the Federal Prime Minister, believing that a co-ordinated campaign of murder and terrorism was about to be launched, called the three territorial heads of government (the Governors of Northern Rhodesia and Nyasaland and the Prime Minister of Southern Rhodesia) to a meeting in Salisbury under the chairmanship of the Governor-General, Lord Dalhousie, at which the possible declaration of an emergency and the provision of Federal troops in support of the civil power were discussed. Although Welensky later stressed that 'this meeting took no major policy decision – it had no power to do so',[1] there is no doubt that the Federal Government made it clear that they would intervene if this should prove necessary.

The proof of the pudding was in the eating. A few days later, at 8 a.m. on 26 February, Sir Edgar Whitehead declared a State of Emergency in Southern Rhodesia. In his supporting broadcast he gave his reasons for the decision and explained the action already taken. In particular, he said that steps had been taken to control or prohibit public meetings; powers had been taken to detain people without trial for one month, and certain organizations, including the Nyasaland ANC, the Southern Rhodesian ANC, the Zambia National Congress and the Northern Rhodesian ANC were henceforth banned in Southern Rhodesia. Sir Edgar ended:

It is a very ancient tradition of the British people that Governments should defer action against subversive movements until actual rioting or bloodshed has occurred. My Government does not subscribe to this tradition. I do not think it would be an exaggeration to say that the security forces have always been a little in advance of the subversive elements in Southern Rhodesia.

The following month the Governor of Nyasaland also declared a State of Emergency, and Dr Banda, with over a thousand of his supporters, was arrested. The Federal Government made available certain forces from Southern Rhodesia to arrest the Nyasaland leaders, including the Rhodesian African Rifles, the 1st (Mashonaland) Battalion the Royal Rhodesian Rifles and 'powerful units of the RRAF'. On 24 March the Colonial Secretary announced the appointment of a Commission of Inquiry under a High Court judge, Sir Patrick (later Lord) Devlin, to look into the whole affair.

Lord Perth arrived in Nyasaland on 14 March. I left London a few days later, and arrived in Salisbury on 18 March to stay with Mr Rupert Metcalf, the British High Commissioner. This was to be the first of many flights I made to Salisbury over the next few years. The following day Lord Perth, accompanied by Mr James Morgan, my opposite number in the Colonial Office, also arrived at Salisbury. Rupert Metcalf met Lord Perth and his party and I joined them at Government House, where we attended a short preliminary meeting with Lord Dalhousie, the Federal Governor-General. From there Metcalf took Lord Perth to a *tête-à-tête* luncheon with Sir Roy Welensky. James Morgan and I had lunch with Federal officials at Meikle's Hotel, in the course of which James brought them up to date on the progress of the talks in Zomba and Lusaka.

After lunch we joined Lord Perth and the High Commissioner for a meeting with the full Federal Cabinet, at which Lord Perth explained the Colonial Secretary's proposal to establish a Royal Commission on the future of the Federation. This was not well received; Sir Roy subsequently commented that he and his ministers put forward no fewer than eight points of substance in arguing against this proposal, which

... was to dominate our relationship with the UK Government for many months ahead, and did more than anything else, in the end, to undermine my confidence in their good faith and integrity. We made our views known from the beginning, and we held them to the last. The British Government put on a great show of candour and consideration; it took us a long time, and we had to go through a great deal of disillusionment, before we faced the fact that from moment to moment we never knew where we were with them.[2]

In this account Welensky glossed over the fact that several of the Federal Cabinet's objections were, in fact, subsequently met. When the Monckton Commission was eventually set up, it did *not* have the status of a Royal Commission, which would have given it far greater authority than in fact it possessed, and the Federal Government were permitted not only to nominate members to it but also to attach to it a senior liaison officer to keep them informed of the progress of its deliberations. It is, moreover, fair to comment that the views of successive British Governments over the years were at least as consistent as Welensky's: they based their policy on the valid assumption that, at the end of the day, the Federation could only survive if it won the acquiescence and co-operation of its constituent territories. It was not enough to argue blandly that because the Federation had been created by a British Government it had the inalienable right to demand that successor British Governments should maintain it in being.

If, as he said, Welensky never knew where he stood with HMG, it was, I fear, because he persuaded himself, in spite of the evidence to the contrary, that a Conservative government must eventually come to the support of the Federation, no matter how great the opposition from black opinion in the two northern territories and, indeed, the rest of the continent. In reaching this conclusion he was actively misled by the self-styled 'friends of Rhodesia' in Britain. These people either misread the prevailing historical trend, later to be formulated in Mr Macmillan's 'winds of change' speech in Cape Town, or were determined, against all the odds, to frustrate it. By their uncritical support of successive white regimes in Rhodesia, they undoubtedly contributed to the progressive hardening of attitudes which culminated in UDI and the tragic civil war of the 1970s. I shall return to them in due course.

I must at this point put in a word about James Morgan, who was then head of the East and Central African Department of the Colonial Office. James had served with the King's African Rifles in East Africa during the war and had a far deeper and more practical experience of Black Africa and African advancement than I had. To those who did not know him well, he sometimes appeared to be an old-fashioned, even blimpish figure. (He was affectionately known by some of his colleagues on the Monckton Commission as 'the General'.) But underneath his occasionally pompous exterior, he hid a splendid, sometimes impish, sense of humour combined with enormous reserves of humanity and good sense. During the next four or five years I was to work almost continuously in double harness with him and came to regard him as one of my closest friends. Although we did not always agree, our disagreements were invariably educative and usually fruitful.

Lord Perth's party left Salisbury by BOAC Britannia on Saturday 21 March. Lord Perth was due to report to his ministerial colleagues at a meeting arranged for 10 o'clock on Monday morning. He had hoped to make use of the aircraft's scheduled stop at Nairobi to bring the Governor, Sir Evelyn Baring, up to date on his talks, but we heard that Baring was on an up-country tour and did not expect to return until late that night. Lord Perth did, however, arrange to meet the Chief Secretary, Mr (later Sir Eric) Griffith-Jones, for a talk in the VIP room at the airport.

We were still deeply engaged in our discussion with Griffith-Jones when we realized that we had been in the airport building for over an hour, and should already have been called to resume our flight. It turned out that there was a major fault on our aircraft and we were unlikely to be able to take off that night. Griffith-Jones got in touch with Government House, and Lady Mary Baring kindly offered us hospitality for as long as we might need it. All this took time, however, and not long after we arrived at Government House Sir Evelyn returned from his safari. Almost simultaneously we became aware that there was crisis in the air. Charles Douglas-Home, then Sir Evelyn's ADC and later his biographer, told us in confidence that news had just been received from the prison camp housing Mau Mau detainees at Hola in the Northern Province that several prisoners had died in suspicious circumstances and that an enquiry was being put in hand.

Fortunately for us, Sir Evelyn was a person who could apparently switch off his anxieties at will and deal with a new subject as if it were the only thing in the world that concerned him. Although he had to absent himself from time to time to deal with developments in the Hola crisis, we had a fascinating evening. The problems facing the African colonial territories, and particularly the Mau Mau rebellion in Kenya, were clearly all too relevant to developments in the Federation. Sir Evelyn was not given to personal bitterness, but he did not dissociate himself from the widely held belief that his predecessor, Sir Philip Mitchell, had consistently ignored the growing volume of intelligence concerning Mau Mau 'oathings' which had been coming forward in the months before he retired. By the time Baring arrived in the country, a full-scale rebellion was already under way.

Lord Perth arrived back in London convinced, as was virtually every official visitor at that time, that if the Federation were to have any chance of survival, major concessions to political advancement in the two northern territories would have to be made. He reported accordingly to his colleagues, recommending, notwithstanding Sir Roy Welensky's opposition, the establishment of a high-level Commission of Inquiry. In domestic political terms one of the subsidiary aims of such a commission would, of course, be to resolve the growing conflicts in British official and parliamentary attitudes towards the future of the Federation.

Action on Lord Perth's recommendations was, however, of necessity held up while the Government awaited, and then considered, the report of the Devlin Commission on the much more limited subject of the disturbances in Nyasaland. Unfortunately its criticisms of the security action taken in Nyasaland did little to resolve the conflicts at Westminster, which themselves reflected the growing tensions on the ground between black and white and, less directly, between the Federal and territorial governments. It was not until 21 July 1959, therefore, that Mr Harold Macmillan announced the setting up of an elaborate two-stage investigation, with both stages of which, as it turned out, I was to be closely involved.

The first stage was the establishment of a preparatory committee of officials, drawn from all the five governments concerned – the British Government, the Federal Government and the three territorial governments – whose task would be to examine and report on the relationships between the Federal and territorial authorities, particularly in regard to the division of powers between them.

The second stage would be the appointment of a high-level Advisory Commission with the following terms of reference:

In the light of the information provided by the Committee of Officials and of any other information the Commission may require, to advise the five governments, in preparation for the 1960 Review, on the constitutional programme and framework best suited to the achievement of the objects contained in the Constitution of 1953, including the Preamble.

The committee of officials was chaired by Mr Burke (later Lord) Trend, who was then Third Secretary in HM Treasury and was shortly to become Secretary to the Cabinet. James Morgan and I became members *ex officio*, and Sir Ralph Hone, a CRO legal adviser and former Governor of British North Borneo, looked after the legal aspects. The Federal Government appointed the Secretary for Internal Affairs, Mr A.D. ('Taffy', later Sir Athol) Evans as their senior representative on the committee. He was supported by Mr Yates, the Attorney-General, and two or three other officials. The three territories were represented at a correspondingly senior level.

In broad terms the Federal Government were responsible for inter-territorial matters, including defence, foreign relations and economic affairs, while the territorial governments were mainly responsible for domestic matters, particularly those directly affecting the blacks, ranging from agriculture and roads to health and (black) education. In practice, however, there were a number of controversial areas where powers conflicted or overlapped. The fact, for example, that white education, which was a Federal subject, involved an enormously greater *per capita* expenditure than black education, which was dealt with by the territories, was a particular and understandable source of dissatisfaction. Another was the belief that Salisbury, as the economic centre of the Federation, was able to attract finance for development far more easily than either Lusaka or Blantyre, even though a substantial proportion of the Federation's foreign exchange earnings was derived from the revenues of the copper mines in Northern Rhodesia.

The United Kingdom members of the committee of officials began meeting in London in early September, and on 17 September we flew to Salisbury to join our Federal and territorial colleagues. There, after two or three plenary sessions to work out our method of operation, we divided into subcommittees. After about ten days of intensive discussion and drafting James Morgan had to return to London; the rest of the UK team spent the next ten days touring in Northern Rhodesia and Nyasaland, where we had talks with the Governors, senior officials and leaders of the main political parties.

In the course of this tour those of us who were new to the territories found time to see something of the tourist attractions of the Federation. Some of us flew to the Victoria Falls in one of the Piper Aztec aircraft of the Northern Rhodesian Government Flight, and from there went on to spend a night at the Ngoma game camp in the Kafue National Park. While we were waiting in a very battered grass-rooted 'basha' for our baggage to be collected from the aircraft, the game ranger in charge of the camp apologized for the state of the hut with the classic remark, 'I'm afraid the terminal building was eaten by an elephant last night.'

On our way from the airstrip to the camp the ranger took us on a short detour, telling us that we might see some game on that particular track. Sure enough, within a matter of minutes we came upon a large, if somewhat elderly, black-maned lion lying almost alongside the track. We were naturally thrilled, and an orgy of photography took place from the closest possible range. A couple of years later, visiting the same camp with Vera and the children, I was amazed to find the same lion in almost exactly the same place. I only then discovered that this particular lion was almost completely blind and had only been kept alive for the past five years, mainly as a tourist attraction, by being provided with a twice-weekly haunch of venison.

During the Northern Rhodesian leg of the trip, the committee had talks with the recently appointed Governor of Northern Rhodesia, Sir Evelyn Hone, and his officials in Lusaka. Hone had taken over at a difficult time. Although he was a man of strong personal convictions, his calm and restraining personality did much to keep the temperature down in the years that followed. Unless he had succeeded in winning and retaining the confidence of the political leaders, it is difficult to believe that Zambia's transition to independence could have taken place as smoothly as it did.

After leaving Lusaka we visited the Provincial Commissioners at Livingstone and Kasama. The latter was Robin Foster, whom, with his characterful wife Madge, Vera and I were to get to know well, first as Chief Secretary of Nyasaland in Zomba, and later in the Pacific as the last Governor and first Governor-General of Fiji.

From Kasama we flew over some very wild country in the north-west of Northern Rhodesia to Mzuzu in the northern province of Nyasaland. One of the features of this area, which was highly conspicuous from the air, was the traditional system of agriculture under which circular areas of forest in the vicinity of villages were burnt down in rotation to form gardens. Millet and cassava were sown in the ashes. This avoided the need to plough, and provided good crops, but at great expense in terms of the conservation of primary woodland. The removal of the slow-growing hardwoods in particular tended to leave lower quality secondary growth when regeneration took place.

From Mzuzu we travelled south, visiting the highly successful rice co-operative at Kota Kota. This flourishing project was managed by a German wartime detainee, Dr Popper. His special contribution had been to stimulate rice production by establishing as part of the co-operative a retail shop in which the growers were encouraged to spend their earnings on consumer goods. Apart from necessities, the shop contained a number of relatively sophisticated items such as modern cookers, radios and even cameras. This enlightened approach resulted in an extraordinary increase in productivity in the co-operative and the emergence of a uniquely prosperous and ambitious community. Although Popper himself was subsequently compelled to resign from the co-operative by political pressures, the lessons he taught were not forgotten. I like to believe that his experiment played a part in the remarkable agricultural development which has characterized the Malawi economy in recent years under Dr Banda's leadership.

In Zomba we had talks with the Governor, Sir Robert Armitage, who was still smarting from the criticisms contained in Mr Justice Devlin's report, in particular the allegation that Nyasaland was being run as a police state. As Africa has good reason to know, the dividing line between security and repression is often a finely drawn one; in the light of later events elsewhere it is difficult to believe that the Nyasaland Government went very far, if at all, across the line at that time.

Back in Salisbury, we met both the Federal Prime Minister, Sir Roy Welensky, and the Prime Minister of Southern Rhodesia, Sir Edgar White-head. We also undertook a tour of Southern Rhodesia, paying visits to some of the Tribal Trust Lands as well as to Bulawayo, Umtali and the Kariba Gorge. From Umtali we visited the famous Leopard Rock Hotel in the Vumba district, which looks directly over the border with Mozambique and to which Sir Edgar delivered milk from his farm when he relaxed from the affairs of state. At Kariba we saw the great dam and hydroelectric project in the early stages of their construction.

After an interval of about three weeks in which the delegations drafted their various contributions, the Federal members of the committee joined us in London. Our meetings took place at Lancaster House. The process of consolidating our various drafts was by no means straightforward, and was not made easier by the mutual suspicion with which some of the components of the team viewed one another. In a letter which Taffy Evans, the senior Federal representative, wrote to Welensky's Private Secretary, Stewart Par-ker, on 10 December 1959[3] he referred to the 'undisguised and continued hostility' with which the Northern Rhodesian delegation viewed the Federal Government. He also alluded to the fact that Nyasaland was demanding a 'new look' constitution. But what obviously worried him most was that, for reasons of their own, the Southern Rhodesians were liable to join forces with the other two territories, so that his team frequently found themselves in the position of 'the Federation v. the rest'.

There was an element of truth in this, though the fact that the Federal Government at that stage seemed to hold most of the cards provided some justification for the territories' hostility. There were, moreover, particular subjects which, for no very apparent reason, aroused the deepest passions. One of these was the unlikely matter of road–rail crossings. In the two Rhodesias, though not in Nyasaland, railways were a Federal subject. Roads, on the other hand, were the responsibility of the territorial govern-ments in all three territories. Who should be responsible when one crossed the other? Bridges were relatively simple; when a road bridge was constructed over a railway line it was still essentially a road. Equally, when a bridge carried the railway over a road, it could usually be treated as an integral part of the railway line. But what happened at a level-crossing? Should Rhodesia Railways be made responsible for installing warning signs and lights merely to deter careless motorists from crashing into their trains? Yes, argued the territories. But was the position different when the railway line was already in position when the road was built? The arguments seemed to go on *ad infinitum*.

As chairman, Burke Trend displayed unfailing tact and patience and quickly developed an encyclopaedic knowledge of the facts. Reading our report again recently, I was relieved to find that neither the hours of acrimonious debate spent on relatively trivial subjects, nor the mutual suspicions which often permeated the discussions, were reflected in the report as published. At the same time I was amazed to discover how large a volume of work we had managed to get through in a relatively short time. Our findings were eventually printed in the form of two thick appendices[4] to the report of the Monckton Commission, which was published almost a year later. One of these contained a factual survey of developments in the Federation between 1953 and 1959, including an account of how the various functions of government worked. The second suggested possible constitutional changes, including a redistribution of functions between the Federal and territorial governments designed to meet the requirement that matters affecting the daily lives of ordinary people should wherever possible be the responsibility of the territories.

While our work was going on, decisions were being taken elsewhere about the membership of the Commission which was to form the second phase of the enquiry. This had originally been conceived as a Royal Commission. But, as recorded earlier, this proposal encountered strong objections from the Federal Government and was eventually dropped. An alternative suggestion, that the commission might be composed entirely of members of the Privy Council, would effectively have excluded black participation and was ruled out for that reason. It was not until November that Lord Monckton of Brenchley was appointed to head an Advisory Commission whose main task would be to prepare for the review of the working of the Federation.

Welensky had only been persuaded to agree to the establishment of any commission at all with the greatest reluctance. Mr Julian Greenfield, the former Federal Minister of Law, in his autobiography, *Testimony of a Rhodesian Federal*,[5] deals with the Commission in a chapter entitled 'Monckton's Hopeless Report'. He comments that the only reason why the Federal Government submitted to its being set up at all was that 'Lord Home told us politely but firmly that if we did not agree the UK would hold an inquiry directed to the situation in the two northern territories, in which we would have no voice. This we thought would be just as dangerous if not more so than the general inquiry Lord Home was asking us to agree to.'

Having reluctantly accepted the Commission's establishment, Welensky attempted to lay down as a precondition that it should not be permitted to consider the break-up of the Federation or the secession of any of its member territories. This condition was not explicitly acceptable, but his aim was broadly shared by the British Government, who genuinely wanted the Federation to survive if at all possible. This desire was underlined in a private letter[6] from the Colonial Secretary to Sir Roy Welensky, written from Nyasaland on 9 February 1960, shortly before his visit to Salisbury to discuss Dr Banda's release from prison. In this letter, Mr Macleod had written:

... I do assure you that I am and always have been a believer in Federation and I do not like to think what would happen to Nyasaland, in particular, if the Federation broke up. Indeed in a sense the proposals we are in conflict about do stem from our urgent desire to keep Nyasaland linked to the Federation. It is my belief at least that this can only be done if they are given swiftly an imaginative measure of constitutional advance.

The arguments kept coming back to the fundamental and inescapable question – *could* the Federation continue in being against the wishes of the inhabitants of its constituent parts? To any impartial outside observer the answer could only be no. It was for this reason that the Colonial Secretary had insisted on the inclusion of the words, 'including the Preamble' in the Commission's terms of reference. The Preamble, though arguably not having the same legal force as the body of the Constitution, incorporated several significant assumptions on which the Federation was established; without which, indeed, the territories would probably never have agreed to join together at all. For Southern Rhodesia, for example, it stipulated, 'whereas Southern Rhodesia should continue to enjoy responsible Government'; and for the two northern territories, 'whereas Northern Rhodesia and Nyasaland should continue, under the special protection of Her Majesty, to enjoy separate Governments so long as their respective peoples so desire'. In relation to the Federation itself it stipulated, 'whereas the association of the Colony and territories ... would conduce to the security, advancement and welfare of all their inhabitants, and in particular would foster partnership and co-operation between their inhabitants and enable the Federation, when those

61

inhabitants so desire, to go forward towards the attainment of full membership of the Commonwealth'.

Note the constant harping on the wishes of the people; it was to these, above all, that the constitutionally prescribed Federal review would have to address itself before either the status of the territorial governments could be changed or the ultimate independence of the Federation itself be proceeded with. Thus the Preamble clearly foreshadows the condition which was later to become crucial in the context of the independence of Southern Rhodesia – no independence before majority rule (NIBMAR).

CHAPTER 11

THE MONCKTON COMMISSION

ON 24 NOVEMBER 1959 Lord Monckton's appointment as Chairman of the Commission was announced in Parliament; the same day he invited Mark Tennant, an Under-Secretary in the Ministry of Labour whom he had selected as his Secretary-General, James Morgan and myself to meet him for lunch at the headquarters of the Midland Bank, of which he was chairman. There we discussed the establishment and functions of the secretariat, of which we were to form the senior UK component. This was my first experience of the style in which the chairman of one of the big clearing banks operated, and I was suitably impressed.

Although the names of most of the members were announced on the same day, the final composition of the Commission was not settled until shortly before Christmas. One of the difficulties was the reluctance of the Labour Party to take part;[1] another was the continuing argument with Federal ministers about the inclusion of any individual who might at any time have expressed doubts about the Federal set-up. Eleven of the eventual twenty-six members of the Commission were drawn from the United Kingdom; two, a Canadian and an Australian, from the 'old' Commonwealth, and thirteen from within the Federation. Of the last, four were nominated by the Federal Government and three each by the three territorial governments. For the first time in a body of this kind five of the members were black.

Sir Donald MacGillivray, who had recently retired from the Colonial Service following a testing period as High Commissioner in the Federation of Malaysia, was appointed Deputy Chairman; another distinguished former colonial servant, Sir Charles Arden-Clarke, the last Governor of the Gold Coast and first Governor-General of the independent Ghana, was a member. Among the members appointed from the United Kingdom were four Privy Councillors: Lord Crathorne, a former Conservative Minister of Agriculture; Lord Shawcross, a leading QC and former Labour Attorney-General and President of the Board of Trade; Sir Lionel Heald, MP, also a leading barrister and former Conservative Attorney-General, and Lord Molson, who had

63

recently relinquished the post of Minister of Works. Other United Kingdom members were drawn from a wide spectrum of people with experience of Africa and of politics, including Mrs Elspeth Huxley, the author, Mr Aidan Crawley, the political commentator and former MP, Professor D.T. (later Sir Daniel) Jack of the University of Durham, and the Right Reverend Dr R.W.T. Shepherd, the retiring Moderator of the Church of Scotland, who had spent many years as a missionary at the Lovedale Mission in the Ciskei, South Africa.

On the Federal side were Mr A. E. P. (later Sir Albert) Robinson, a leading Rhodesian businessman and Chairman of Central African Airways, who, shortly after the completion of the Commission's work, became Federal High Commissioner in London. Another Federal nominee was Mr Hezekiah Habanyama, an African from the Gwembe district of Northern Rhodesia, who had qualified on a local government course at Bristol University, had wide practical experience of the problems of local government in his home area and, in particular, played a leading role in the politically difficult task of resettling the inhabitants of some of the villages due to be submerged under the vast lake created by the Kariba Dam. Mr R. M. (later Sir Robert) Taylor, a former colonial civil servant who until recently had been Federal Secretary of Finance, was also nominated by the Federal Government. He later became well known in the City of London as chairman or deputy chairman of several leading companies. The fourth Federal member, Sir Victor Robinson, had recently retired as Federal Attorney-General.

Prominent in the Southern Rhodesian team was Mr Justice (later the Rt Hon. Sir Hugh) Beadle, who subsequently performed an ambivalent role as Chief Justice of Rhodesia after the unilateral declaration of independence. Also nominated by Southern Rhodesia were Chief Simon Sigola, representing the Council of Chiefs, and Mr Geoffrey Ellman-Brown, a businessman and retired politician. Although Chief Sigola was somewhat handicapped by his lack of fluency in English, he was a man of integrity who played a useful part in making the Commission aware of the attitudes of the more conservative African elements in Southern Rhodesia.

Two other African members were outstanding. Mr Laurence Katilungu, from Northern Rhodesia, was associated with the African National Congress and was probably the most politically articulate. Sadly he lost his life a few months later in a road accident in the Katanga Pedicle. If he had lived he might well have played a significant role in later events in Zambia. From Nyasaland, Mr Manoah (Wellington) Chirwa, a former Federal Member of Parliament, also made a useful contribution.

The Commission also had a large supporting staff. Under the Secretary-General were three Assistant Secretaries: James Morgan and myself from the United Kingdom, and Frank Wisdom, of whom more hereafter, from the Southern Rhodesian public service. The administrative and secretarial staff, which included an information officer, numbered between fifteen and twenty and were drawn from the Commonwealth Relations Office, the Colonial Office and the Foreign Office.

The staff began to assemble at 12 Chester Terrace, Regent's Park, early in January 1960. The first weeks involved us in a range of diverse, sometimes bizarre, problems. We became involved in lengthy discussions with the Treasury on the commissioners' – and our own – conditions of service; there were few, if any, precedents for a body of forty or fifty people, including civil servants and private individuals, many of them not resident in the United Kingdom, getting together for a period of six to eight months, a fair proportion of which would be spent overseas. There were constant arguments about the scales of honoraria and allowances, and who should be entitled to what. One of the secretariat's more difficult tasks was to explain to the commissioners the distinctly idiosyncratic rules governing the entitlement of these allowances; for example, the question of what items of clothing were – or, more important, were not – eligible for the tropical kit allowance to which they were entitled. Each item had to be accounted for. It was not easy to explain to an outraged former minister of the Crown that he was allowed to claim a refund on a tropical-weight suit, but not, for some reason best known to the Treasury, on a light-weight dressing gown. It was, perhaps, salutary to all concerned that the sort of rules which civil servants tend to become conditioned to accepting were energetically questioned by some of the very people who in other circumstances might have criticized the expenditure as extravagant.

Apart from the task of organizing the Commission as a whole, the secretariat also had to adjust to working with each other. Frank Wisdom, who was the only member not based in the United Kingdom, probably had the most difficult task of settling in, especially since the rest of us had got to know each other before he joined us. I know that at times he felt that the home team had taken decisions on which he ought to have been consulted. Fortunately, although Frank was – and is – a delightful and modest man, he was well capable of standing up for himself. Although it was not known to us at the time, he had featured obliquely but recognizably in the account of the pre-war white Rhodesian society immortalized by his first wife, the author Doris Lessing, in her novel *Martha Quest*.[2] He and his second wife, Dolly, became close friends of Vera and myself when the work of the Commission was over, and have remained so ever since.

We had only about five weeks to complete the preparatory work before leaving for the Federation, where it had been agreed that the Commission would meet in full session for the first time. It did not, however, assemble in Salisbury, where, it was felt, the territorial members might feel too much under the shadow of the Federal Government. A BOAC Britannia aircraft was chartered to take us to Livingstone in Northern Rhodesia; from there we crossed the Victoria Falls Bridge to set up a temporary headquarters at the Victoria Falls Hotel, where the other members of the team were awaiting us.

The first few days, which were mainly spent in working out a programme, demanded the full measure of diplomatic skill for which Lord Monckton was renowned. This was the first occasion on which a multi-racial team had got together in the Federation to do a job on equal terms. Even before we left London, we had had to take special steps to ensure that there would be no difficulty in securing hotel accommodation, especially in Southern Rhodesia, in which blacks and whites could live and work together. Somewhat surprisingly, the Victoria Falls Hotel, which was run by Rhodesia Railways, was already permitted to accommodate guests of all colours; but in Salisbury a brand-new hotel, the Jameson, had to be approached to apply for a multi-racial licence. This was readily granted, but for a time an unfounded rumour circulated among our black colleagues that it would only be valid for the period of the Monckton Commission's visit and would thereafter be withdrawn. This caused some consternation until it was categorically denied by the Southern Rhodesian Government.

At the first plenary meeting of the Commission on 16 February, a critical discussion took place on the terms of reference. Early in January, long before we left London, Lord Shawcross had stated in a television interview that he would feel free to consider the possibility of secession; predictably, this had been challenged by Sir Roy Welensky as a breach of an understanding given to him by HMG. This question had been simmering ever since; it was indeed crucial to the credibility of the Commission. The chairman in particular found himself on highly delicate ground, having to steer a course between the Federal Government's insistence that secession was not within the competence of the Commission even to discuss, and the reluctance of the black members to take any part in an exercise that could be represented as underwriting or perpetuating the Federation they hated. Lord Monckton, therefore, solemnly appealed to all members of the Commission that they should make no statements to the press except through the official press officer, and even then only after consulting him. This request was eventually accepted by all the commissioners.

Unfortunately, unknown to the chairman, Mr Chirwa had been button-holed by a reporter the previous evening. Even before the meeting ended the radio news from both London and Salisbury was carrying his statement to the effect that he had only joined the Commission in order to advocate the break-up of the Federation. It took all Lord Monckton's tact to smooth this over. Taffy Evans, the Federal liaison officer, received an immediate demand from Sir Roy Welensky to seek an explanation from the Commission, and accusations of bad faith were levelled against Mr Chirwa by some of his colleagues. It was only after he demonstrated conclusively that the interview had taken place before the chairman's meeting that tempers began to cool.

This is not the place to embark on a blow-by-blow account of the Commission's work, though no detailed account by a participant has, to my knowledge, been published. It would make interesting reading. (Apart from the Commission's report, which does not contain much local colour, and a valuable, but necessarily brief account in Lord Birkenhead's biography of Lord Monckton,[3] the only literary reference to it of which I am aware occurs in highly fictional form in Elspeth Huxley's light-hearted novel, *The Merry Hippo*.)[4]

In general, it is fair to say that the Commission carried out its task with energy and despatch. During our three months in the Federation, and leaving aside the journeys of some five thousand miles each way between Europe and central Africa, I personally clocked up nine thousand miles of travel within the Federation, mainly by air and road, and listened to evidence from well over two hundred witnesses.

During our tours gathering evidence, the Commission usually split into three groups, under the chairmanship of Sir Donald MacGillivray, Sir Charles Arden-Clarke and Lord Crathorne. I was secretary to the group led by Sir Charles Arden-Clarke. Lord Monckton himself, with a small group including Lady Monckton and the Secretary-General, travelled from one group to another to keep informed of any problems which arose and of the general tenor of the evidence being received. This division of labour enabled the Commission to meet many more people than would otherwise have been possible in the time available, though we came together in full session to hear evidence from some of the more significant witnesses. The itineraries of the various groups were well advertised, and individuals as well as organizations were invited to give evidence. Substantial numbers, both black and white, responded to this invitation.

In the process of hearing evidence, not all of which was either relevant or well thought out, the commissioners quickly began to know and respect one another. In one of the earliest interviews given by our group, an elderly white lady embarked on a highly intemperate tirade against the alleged irresponsibility and immorality of the Coloured community in Northern Rhodesia. She seemed to be totally oblivious (or perhaps she wasn't) of the fact that the group listening to her included a black Commissioner, Manoah Chirwa. Although Sir Charles Arden-Clarke was growing increasingly embarrassed at her outburst, which went on for about a quarter of an hour non-stop, he did not interrupt. At the end, Chirwa, with studious politeness, asked the only question. 'I was very interested in what you had to say, madam. I am sorry that you do not like the Coloured community. But I would like to ask you just one question. You say you disapprove of miscegenation; so do I. But to whom would you attribute responsibility for the existence of the Coloured community - the blacks, or the whites?'

Since it is a matter of common knowledge that over the years the vast majority of mixed marriages - and mixed sex in general - has taken place between white men and black women, this polite but devastating question left the lady unable to answer. She burst into tears and abruptly departed. Chirwa was as embarrassed as the rest of us, but our admiration for him rose sharply.

At the end of our first week, Lord Home passed through Salisbury on his way home after accompanying Mr Macmillan on the visit to South Africa in the course of which he made his dramatic speech to the South African Parliament drawing attention to the wind of change blowing through the continent. Lord Home was naturally anxious to have a first-hand account of how the Commission's work was going, especially since Sir Roy Welensky was already complaining bitterly of attitudes taken up within the Commission, particularly in relation to the possibility of secession.[5] He requested that Lord Monckton meet him in Salisbury to bring him up to date, and as the CRO representative I went with him. This visit was not well regarded by certain of the commissioners, nor indeed by Frank Wisdom, who was initially inclined to regard it as confirming his suspicions of a British conspiracy, but the meeting was a useful one. The Secretary of State was accompanied by Sir Henry Lintott, the CRO Deputy Secretary concerned, and by Mr Duncan Watson, representing the Colonial Office. I was able to report to them on the prevailing atmosphere of suspicion, making it clear that I did not take the accusations too seriously; conspiratorial attitudes were in any case very much in evidence on the Federal side also. Indeed, a constant flow of information –

sometimes pure speculation – about the Commission's activities was finding its way to Welensky, who was only too ready to put the worst interpretation on what he heard. From Lord Monckton's point of view, the meeting with Lord Home was also valuable in confirming that the Secretary of State had full confidence in the way in which he was carrying out his task.

From Livingstone, the Commission travelled north to Ndola, where the Salisbury party rejoined them. Almost immediately Lord Shawcross, who had arrived in Northern Rhodesia a few days late because of a slipped disc, had to go into hospital for treatment. Several of us visited him there. It quickly became clear that there was no hope of his making a sufficiently speedy recovery to enable him to take part in the rigorous touring programme ahead. He was flown home at the end of February and did not take any major further part in the activities of the Commission.

A few days later Sir Henry Lintott visited us at Ndola to bring Lord Monckton up to date on the developments in Nyasaland. I went to the airport to meet him, and was surprised to find a large crowd, including several African choirs, also meeting the aircraft. I met Lintott at the foot of the steps, and as we were walking across the tarmac to the terminal building I commented on the harmonious singing of the choirs, saying that I hoped he was impressed by the welcome we had arranged for him. 'I'm afraid you can't get away with flattery,' he answered. 'Billy Graham is on this flight too. We've had angels formating on the wingtips ever since we left Salisbury.'

After spending a few days taking further evidence on the Copper Belt, Sir Charles Arden-Clarke's group flew to Barotseland. This fascinating territory comprised the extreme western areas of Northern Rhodesia bordering on Angola, including the Zambezi flood plain from the border with the Congo (Zaire) southwards to the Caprivi Strip in South-West Africa (Namibia). Our first stop was at Balovale, an attractive district headquarters situated on a slight rise overlooking the majestic breadth of the Zambezi. That evening I was amazed to see a vast throng of hawking tern-like birds – thousand upon thousand of them – feeding on an immense hatch of insects and flying ants. No one I met could tell me what they were; I only deduced years later that I had been watching a 'swarm' of black-winged pratincoles, a migrant species which particularly like to follow swarms of locusts.

From Balovale we flew south down the flooded Zambezi valley to Mongu, the administrative capital of Barotseland. There we were joined by the chairman and his team to be conveyed in the royal barge to Lealui for a meeting with the Litunga, or Paramount Chief of Barotseland, Chief Mwanawina Lewanika III. Traditionally, the Litunga moves by barge from Mongu to

Lealui each year when the floods fall: this is a ceremonial and tribally signifi-cant occasion on which the barge is propelled by a team of paddlers consist-ing of elders of the Lozi (Barotse) people; one theory has it that the ceremony is related to the water processions held in ancient Egypt, from where it is believed the Lozi originally migrated. However this may be, the journey of some seven miles by water, sometimes following well-defined channels and at others crossing expanses of open water a mile or more wide, is both colourful and romantic.

The state of quasi-independence from Northern Rhodesia which Barotse-land then enjoyed no longer exists under the Republic of Zambia. At that time the Litunga was regarded by his people as having royal status inferior only to that of the Queen. Even his ministers approached him on their hands and knees; every remark he made was greeted by subdued clapping from a kneeling position to indicate approval and respect. Chief Mwanawina made strong representations to the Commission that the status of Barotseland should be safeguarded in any recommendations they might make on the future of the Federation. Lord Monckton listened to what he had to say, but could clearly make no commitment in advance of the Commission's con-sideration of the evidence as a whole. The problem for the Lozi was not, of course, the attitude of the Federal Government: Godwin Lewanika, the Litunga's nephew, was a Federal Member of Parliament and was in close touch with the United Federal Party establishment in Salisbury. It was rather that the Northern Rhodesian political parties, particularly the United National Independence Party (UNIP) led by Mr Kenneth Kaunda, were in-stinctively and understandably opposed to the feudal and traditionalist sys-tem maintained in Barotseland. Unfortunately for the Litunga, the parallel with the princely houses in independent India was all too close. There was little doubt that once Zambia became independent, the writing would be on the wall for the independence of Barotseland.

As soon as the taking of evidence in the rural areas of Northern Rhodesia was complete, the Commission reassembled in Lusaka to hear the views of those political leaders who were prepared to meet them, and to obtain the comments of the Governor and his senior staff. The secretariat and most of the commissioners stayed at the newly built Ridgeway Hotel, an attractive modern building constructed round an ornamental pool and rock garden. The only trouble about the pool was that it had been invaded during the rains by a plague of frogs, which croaked unceasingly all day and – less acceptably – all night. After a number of complaints from insomniac guests, the man-agement had the brilliant idea of introducing four baby crocodiles, purchased from a local crocodile farm, which they calculated would eat the frogs. And eat them they did. Each night the volume of croaking decreased; on about our fourth night there was only one audible survivor, and the next night the silence was complete. By the time we left, the crocodiles were still there, and presumably getting hungry. I never heard what eventually became of them; happily they were still too small to eat the guests.

Before we left Lusaka, Elspeth Huxley and I were invited to spend a night at the Lochinvar ranch in the Kafue flood plain. This contained the largest surviving herd of red lechwe, a small and elegant antelope whose existence was already threatened by the inroads of farming in the area. We were also taken to see the experimental Anglo-American Corporation's polder scheme. This had been developed as a market-garden to supply much-needed fresh vegetables to Lusaka. The land was contoured with great precision and used gravity irrigation to bring the water of the Kafue River on to a large area which could previously not be farmed. Although it called for relatively heavy capital investment and careful management, it was expected that the high price of vegetables in Lusaka would make it a valuable and rewarding training ground for African farmers, who were encouraged to cultivate the land as tenants with the option of buying their plots if all went well. After independence, however, the scheme was overtaken by the construction of the Kafue barrage, which put both the polder area, and much of the habitat of the red lechwe, under permanent water.

After our period of concentration in Lusaka, the Commission once again broke up into three parties to visit Nyasaland. The membership of the parties had been shuffled, but I remained with Sir Charles Arden-Clarke. Our party flew direct to Mzuzu, and from there we followed much the same route down Lake Nyasa as the Trend Committee only four months previously. This time, however, we also visited the headquarters of the Central Province at Lilongwe, where we saw something of a Provincial Commissioner's office in action and took evidence from a number of people. A senior officer from the Provincial Secretariat, Mr Peter Swan, had been attached to us as liaison officer for this leg of our trip, and from Lilongwe he took my secretary, Barbara Pearson, and myself with one or two others to Salima on Lake Nyasa, where we had an enjoyable Sunday sailing and water-skiing on the lake. I say water-skiing; in fact others water-skied. I never managed even to stand up on my skis before ignominiously falling off.

While we were taking evidence at Lilongwe, another small party including Dr Shepherd, the ex-Moderator of the Church of Scotland, travelled north to Nkata Bay, with the intention of visiting the famous Church of Scotland

Mission at Livingstonia. This mission, which had for long provided a centre for African nationalist activities in Nyasaland, opposed the presence of the Commission in Nyasaland and had advised the local people not to have anything to do with it. It was not surprising, therefore, that the elders of the mission declined to give evidence to Dr Shepherd. But what was deeply wounding to him was that they refused him any access to the mission at all: it seemed unnecessarily humiliating that the most recent head of their own church should be forced to leave without being permitted to visit one of the most famous of its overseas establishments. This decision was all the more bitter because Dr Shepherd had himself spent many years of devoted service in a Church of Scotland Mission in South Africa with a very similar history to that of Livingstonia. It is sad that, when devout men decide to stand on their principles, charity often seems to go out of the window.

The whole Commission reassembled at Blantyre on 28 March at what turned out to be an historic moment. Mr Iain Macleod was at that moment in Salisbury to inform Sir Roy Welensky of his intention to release Dr Banda in the next few days, a step which he regarded as essential if peace in the territory was to be restored. Sir Nigel Fisher, his biographer, records[6] that the issue of Dr Banda's release had led to almost the only serious disagreement between Macleod and Mr Harold Macmillan. At his meeting with the Federal Cabinet in Salisbury in January, the Prime Minister had been told by Sir Malcolm Barrow, who was himself a large landowner in Nyasaland, that ten thousand Africans would die in riots if Banda were released. Subsequently, Welensky sent a formal request to London that the decision should be deferred until after the Monckton Commission had reported. This suggestion appealed to Mr Macmillan, who, on his return to London, asked the Colonial Secretary to agree to it. Macleod was reluctant to do so and made clear that he was prepared to support his refusal by resignation if necessary. Nigel Fisher ends his account of this confrontation by saying that once the two men had talked it out Macmillan accepted Macleod's decision and gave him his full support.

On 31 March 1960, Mr Macleod, accompanied by Mr Duncan Watson, who had taken charge of the Central African Department of the Colonial Office on James Morgan's appointment to the Monckton Commission, arrived at Chileka airport. He came direct from a meeting with Sir Roy Welensky at which, in spite of the latter's continued objections, he finalized the arrangements for Dr Banda's release from Gwelo prison.

That evening, James Morgan and I were put in the picture by Duncan Watson, in a somewhat conspiratorial meeting in my bedroom in Ryall's

Hotel in Blantyre. I well remember that as we passed Chileka at about 8.30 the next morning on our way to take evidence at Cholo, we saw the aircraft containing Dr Banda, a Dakota of the Royal Rhodesian Air Force, making its final approach to land. A remarkable feature of the Doctor's return was that, although not a word had been released officially, crowds were already gathering around the entrance to the airport and along the road to Zomba. But the blood-bath threatened by Sir Malcolm Barrow totally failed to materialize. After a year of virtual rebellion in the protectorate, Macleod succeeded in bringing Banda back into a political dialogue.

On our departure from Nyasaland the Commission flew direct to Bulawayo, deliberately leaving Salisbury as our last port of call. A dramatic external event took place on 9 April while we were staying at the Victoria Hotel, Bulawayo. During the afternoon I had to go back to my hotel bedroom to change. On the way I met the middle-aged (white) lady who was the housekeeper in charge of our floor of the hotel. She was in a state of great agitation and called out to me, 'Have you heard? They've got him, they've got that wicked man.'

I hadn't the faintest idea what she was talking about, and persuaded her to start again. 'It's Verwoerd,' she said. 'It's on the radio. They've shot him at the Rand Show in Johannesburg.'

The news certainly came as a shock, especially since it followed hot on the heels of the Sharpeville riots. It even seemed possible that a revolution might be on its way in the Union. It soon emerged that Verwoerd was not dead; but in retrospect I found the violence of the lady's reaction illuminating. It became easy in Europe in the years following UDI and the subsequent build-up of guerrilla warfare to think of Rhodesia as the last home of reaction and racial conflict, and of South Africa as a country where progress towards the elimination of racial discrimination was at least being discussed. But at that time the boot was entirely on the other foot. A widespread consciousness seemed to be emerging in Rhodesia of the need to press ahead towards a truly multi-racial state, and there was a strong feeling among the more liberal Rhodesians that South Africa's increasingly repressive policies were damaging Rhodesia's chances of finding a peaceful solution to her own problems.

From Bulawayo some of the Commission spent Good Friday, 15 April, visiting the grave of Cecil John Rhodes in the Matopos, and on Saturday most of the Commission flew to Wankie to take evidence and to visit the colliery. In the process we managed to have Easter Sunday as a holiday in the Wankie National Park, where the tourist season had not yet begun and where the main camp was reserved for us for the night. At first light on

Sunday morning a number of us were taken out in the chief ranger's Land-Rover to see game; I caught my first fleeting glimpse of a leopard and we managed to put up a small flock of ground hornbills. Like many other large and heavy birds they are immeasurably more beautiful on the wing than on the ground, where their flashing white primary feathers are invisible. One of them, which staggered into the air directly across our bows, narrowly avoided a collision with the Land-Rover. If it had hit us I am not sure which would have come off worse.

Back in Wankie later that morning we heard evidence from several witnesses, and were taken round a small section of the colliery. The Commission came away greatly impressed with the efficiency of the mine, where the main seams of coal are up to forty feet thick, and where heavy earth-moving equipment is used underground in a way which until recently would have been inconceivable in most mines in the United Kingdom. They also came to appreciate the importance to the company of the Federal connection, which enables Wankie coal to be extensively marketed on the Northern Rhodesian Copper Belt.

After a brief visit to Gwelo we finally arrived in Salisbury on Wednesday, 20 April. Although we made a number of further visits to Southern Rhodesian centres outside Salisbury, the Jameson Hotel was our main home for the next three weeks. Our arrival created something of a stir, since it was the first time that blacks from within the Federation had been allowed to stay in a five-star hotel in the capital. It later became official British Government policy wherever possible to patronize hotels where segregation had been abolished, and from then on all British official visitors stayed at either the Jameson or the Ambassador, whose proprietor decided to follow the Jameson's lead. Thus by its very presence the Commission did something to change prevailing attitudes.

Shortly after we settled in, Manoah Chirwa invited two Nyasaland friends, both nurses working in a hospital at Durban, to dine in the hotel, and asked James Morgan and myself to join them. This was the first time that I had met attractive and articulate African women on an equal social footing. Knowing that they came from the Union of South Africa I asked them, rather presumptuously I realized in retrospect, whether it was not splendid that things had changed so far in the Federation that we could now be sitting and eating together in a first-class restaurant.

Their reaction was not at all what I had expected. After a pause for thought, both of them came up with the same answer. Yes, it was nice being treated as human beings in a civilized hotel. But this did not mean that it was easier for a black to live a civilized life in the Federation than in South Africa. How many hotels were there in Southern Rhodesia which now admitted blacks? Perhaps four. In Durban there were none. But at least you knew where you were there. Until *all* hotels were multi-racial it would not be easier for blacks to obtain what they regarded as their right; there would always be an area of embarrassing uncertainty. In any case, they could certainly not afford to stay at the Jameson. In short, window-dressing was not enough. This conversation taught me a lesson that I never forgot.

During the final phase of our work in Salisbury, a measure of consensus began to emerge within the Commission. Although the white Federal members remained as convinced as ever of the need to maintain a ban on the right to secede, they came for the first time to accept that without a fundamental change in attitudes, especially among the whites, the Federation would not survive. Among the converts was Judge Beadle; I noted at the time that he seemed to have seen the light on the road to Damascus. To those who heard it, the weight of the evidence had become irresistible.

During our last week in Salisbury we were under some pressure for time. Queen Elizabeth the Queen Mother was expected in Salisbury on Thursday, 12 May 1960, on her way to Kariba to open the new dam, and for practical as well as political reasons it had been decreed that we must leave before she arrived. Friday, 6 May, was set as the final date for the receipt of evidence. I spent our last Sunday with the High Commissioner and Dorrie Metcalf at Mirimba House, partly relaxing and partly exchanging my impressions of the Commission's work for Rupert Metcalf's latest news on developments in Nyasaland and in London. Two days later the United Kingdom members of the Commission and the staff left for London.

CHAPTER 12

A DEAFENING SILENCE

AFTER A SHORT BREAK, the members from the Federation joined us in London, and the Commission reassembled in a rather drab building, Cornwall House, near the southern end of Waterloo Bridge. (For me this had the real compensation of being within five minutes walk of Waterloo Station, but some of the commissioners regarded it as being distinctly too spartan.)

We took a limited amount of new evidence, much of it from industrial and mining companies based in London. But our main task was now the preparation of the Commission's report. We started, as is the normal procedure in Whitehall, with draft chapters prepared by the secretariat, work on which had already begun before we left Salisbury. This did not, however, suit some of the commissioners, who perhaps felt that our efforts were designed to paper over the cracks rather than to resolve the genuine differences between them. Drafting subcommittees were therefore formed to produce chapters within a framework agreed by the Commission as a whole.

While this was going on, the Federal liaison officer was attempting to keep in touch with the progress of work, and was sending almost daily bulletins to Welensky and the Federal Cabinet in Salisbury.[1] Reading these reports twenty years after the event it is interesting to discover how little firm information appeared to have reached him, even from the Federal members of the Commission, whom Welensky expected to maintain a Federal party line. A recurring theme in Evans's reports was, 'I am still at a loss to know what sort of lead Monckton is planning to give.'

The fact was, of course, that Lord Monckton, being deeply conscious of the breadth of the chasm he had to bridge, was deliberately refraining from giving too firm a lead himself. Nevertheless, the consensus within the Commission which had begun to develop in Salisbury was steadily strengthening. In the middle of July, Mr Julian Greenfield was sent to London, nominally to discuss the 1960 Federal review conference with Lord Home, but mainly to try to find out what was going on. It is not clear from his autobiography how much he managed to discover. But it may be significant that on 21 July Evans wrote[2] to Mr A.E.P. Robinson, Mr R.M. Taylor and Sir Victor Robinson, the three white Federal nominees, pointing out that it had not been intended that the review conference should be used for the purpose of considering secession, but rather that it should consider possible lines of constitutional advance, ways of rectifying defects in the machinery of government, and a possible redistribution of functions.

From this it seems likely that Greenfield had guessed that the Commission would attempt to get round the problem of giving the territories the right of secession by referring it forward to the review conference. It was perhaps only to be expected that the letter was *not* addressed to the fourth Federal nominee, Mr Habanyama.

On the afternoon of 22 July 1960 I had an unexpected telephone call from David Cole, whose term as Private Secretary to Lord Home was about to end. He asked if Vera and I could attend a farewell dinner party for his wife and himself which Lord and Lady Home were giving two days later at Dorneywood, then the Commonwealth Secretary's official residence. The guests were almost all to be from the CRO, so it was in the nature of a family party. We accepted with enthusiasm, though I was a little surprised at the extreme shortness of the notice. However, when we arrived at Dorneywood David took us on one side and told us that the news was about to break that Lord Home was himself leaving the CRO on transfer to the Foreign Office. Lord Home confirmed this during the course of dinner. Sad as we in the CRO were to see him go, his promotion was clearly a matter for congratulation. Lord Home tells in his autobiography[3] of the outcry which broke out the following week in the House of Commons and the press at the decision to appoint as Foreign Secretary a member of the House of Lords, but this quickly evaporated when the session ended a week or two later.

The Commission had hoped to finish its work by the beginning of August, and the Scotts were booked for a family holiday in Majorca starting on 14 August. But it became clear by the end of July that if there were to be any hope of the Commission achieving a unanimous report, more time was needed. Our holiday was postponed and work went on throughout August. A number of changes were made to the draft, mainly as a result of representations by the black members of the Commission, designed to modify the political powers of the Federation and to make it more acceptable to the territories. It eventually became clear, however, that at least two, and possibly more, of the black commissioners would find it impossible to sign a majority report which recommended that *any* nucleus of a Federal Government should remain in being, even though its powers would be severely curtailed. After a final urgent attempt to reach a compromise, it was reluctantly accepted that a minority report was unavoidable. This faced several of the commissioners with a very difficult decision. In the end only Manoah Chirwa and Hezekiah Habanyama felt themselves compelled to subscribe to a minority report, though a number of others entered reservations in relation to particular recommendations.

It is not easy to summarize briefly the 103 recommendations of the report,[4] particularly in view of the numerous reservations of detail. The tone was, however, set in the summary of conclusions:

Federation cannot, in our view, be maintained in its present form. On the other hand, to break it up at this crucial moment in the history of Africa would be an admission that there is no hope of survival for any multi-racial society on the African continent, and that differences of colour and race are irreconcilable. We cannot agree to such a conclusion ...

More specifically, its second recommendation said:

If some form of federal association is to continue, Africans must in the immediate future have a much higher proportion of seats in the Federal Assembly.

In short, hope was fading unless the urgent need for major surgery were accepted by governments.

The Commission finally completed its work at the end of August 1960, and on Friday 2 September, the Secretariat went to London airport to say goodbye to the members from the Federation. By then the Commission had been working together for seven months and, although we had had our differences, the parting came as quite a wrench. The printing of the report was expected to take several weeks, and in the meantime it was agreed that nothing should be said to the press on its substance. Advance copies were, however, made available on a confidential basis to the governments concerned.

Behind the scenes the reactions of Federal ministers to their first sight of the report were violent. The Secretary of the Federal Cabinet was asked to prepare a commentary which was given restricted circulation to Cabinet Ministers on 15 September.[5] This paper concluded:

Perhaps the most suitable name for the report is the Monckton Commission (Interim Appeasement) Report. It is a very inadequate document to have come from as august a body of planners. Its recommendations rest mainly on opinion and very little on fact. The proposal that parity of representation in the Federal Parliament would promote confidence and stability is puerile ... [it] would be nothing but an uneasy and short-lived resting place before an all-black government.

If the Commission's main conclusions are accepted, the end of the Federation will become inevitable within a decade. Its disintegration will be accompanied by weak and inept administration, economic crises and mounting racial tensions probably culminating in widespread violence ... Better face reality now and save what is possible for Southern and Northern Rhodesia.

A few days later the Federal Secretary for Defence made a different comment in a minute dated 21 September:[6]

There will be a general idea that if Southern Rhodesia cuts away from the North it will have got rid of 'deferred African nationalism' and there can be a return to 'the good old days'. Nothing could be more incorrect. The racial policies of Southern Rhodesia are in the eyes of the world not dissimilar to those of the Union. It is left alone for the time being because it is linked with the two northern territories 'in the greatest deliberate racial experiment of all time'. If it cut loose it would ... come under the same remorseless pressures from UNO ... which hack away at the Union today.

Of these two comments, that of the Secretary of Defence shows the greater sense of realism. The Cabinet Secretary's advice that, if the Commission's conclusions were accepted, the end of the Federation would become inevitable within a decade cannot be disproved; but the implied converse, that if the conclusions were *not* accepted it might survive, was all too quickly demonstrated to be false.

Back in London, the work of the Secretariat was not entirely finished, but Mark Tennant had kindly agreed that on the following Sunday, 11 September, I should depart, come what may, for our deferred holiday. The delay had meant that both the boys would go back late to school, but in the circumstances their headmasters had raised no objections, and certainly neither Robert nor Andrew did. I was by then feeling much in need of a rest, and on our arrival in Majorca I made it clear that, although it was up to them how many English papers Vera and the children read, they were not to show them to me. Just before lunch on Sunday, 18 September, however, while we were relaxing on the beach at Puerto de Soller after a swim, Robert came over from the hotel carrying a copy of that morning's London *Sunday Times*. Wearing a rather portentous expression he sat down beside me and said, 'I know what you said about not wanting to see the papers, Dad, but I really think you ought to see this.'

'This' was a long front-page lead, obviously based on an authoritative leak from Salisbury, indicating that Welensky had seen a copy of the report, and that he intended to reject it in its entirety. Greenfield records[7] that Welensky was finishing a holiday at the Cape when the report reached Salisbury.

Greenfield flew to meet him at Johannesburg station so that Welensky could look at the report on the short train journey from there to Pretoria, where he and Lady Welensky had been invited to dine with Dr Verwoerd, who had by now recovered from his wound. Between Welensky's return to Salisbury and the report's publication on 11 October, there was a series of increasingly heated exchanges between him and Mr Macmillan, which are recorded by the latter.[8] On the day of publication Welensky made a broadcast rejecting the Commission's recommendations, and in particular denouncing their acknowledgment of the territories' right to secede.

This was, in effect, the end of any hope that the Federal Government might accept the report. Mr Macmillan's own view was that it need neither be accepted nor rejected by HMG. He regarded it as a further contribution to the solution of the problem, but felt that it would be valuable mainly as a contribution to the review conference, to which all were committed. From United Kingdom ministers, therefore, there was a deafening silence. Unfortunately, Welensky failed to appreciate that in terms of the art of the possible, the Monckton solution offered probably the last hope for the Federation's survival. His rejection of the report effectively sealed the Federation's fate; there was never again a reasonable chance of salvaging anything useful from the wreckage.

Nearly twenty years later, in the garden of our official residence in Cape Town, I asked Sir Roy why he had decided so implacably to reject the Monckton Commission's recommendations. He thought for a moment, and then said, 'David, I think I was badly advised.'

I did not think I could leave it there; after all, he had been Prime Minister. So I asked, 'Who by?' Again he thought. 'I suppose mainly by my officials.' This seemed to be said with less conviction, and having subsequently had a chance of reading Sir Athol Evans's voluminous bulletins from the Victoria Falls and from London I find it difficult to believe that the advice contained in them did more than reinforce doubts about the outcome of the Commission's report which already existed in Welensky's mind. Nor do I believe that the Federal members of the Commission in any way misled him. In fact, A.E.P. Robinson and Bob Taylor had written him a joint letter[9] from London at the end of August containing a reasoned explanation of their decision to sign the majority report. In it they said, *inter alia*:

We have, we believe, achieved much in the final result, but we acknowledge that we have failed to produce support for some important current views of the Federal Government either because other arguments prevailed or because we received evidence and legal advice that made it necessary for us to seek new solutions for some of our problems.

In short, they too had seen the writing on the wall.

So, where did this bad advice come from? In my view it came primarily from the right-wing members of the Conservative Party to whom I have referred earlier. Throughout his premiership Welensky was engaged in a highly confidential personal correspondence with three or four senior members of the right wing of the party, all former British ministers. His perfectly legitimate aim was to win support for his cause. He had come to believe over the years that successive British Governments, and in particular Mr Macmillan himself, were unfairly biased in favour of what he regarded as the unreasonable political aspirations of 'power-hungry politicians' in the two northern territories, and against the genuine political and economic advantages of the Federation.

Unfortunately, he allowed himself to be unduly encouraged in this belief – as later did the leaders of Southern Rhodesia both before and after UDI – by an unrepresentative clique of back-room Tory figures in Britain who led him to believe that he enjoyed far wider support from the Conservative Party as a whole than was in fact the case. By their flattery of the local boy made good, the boy who had 'swum bare-arsed in the Makabusi',[10] they ensured that he would fight their battles for them, to the point of reason and beyond.

Mr Macmillan was, of course, well aware of what was going on. He himself quotes from his diary of 24 March 1961:[11]

I tried very hard to persuade Sir Roy that about the only friend of Federation is Her Majesty's Government. The Socialists and the Liberals here are against it. All the Africans in the three territories are against it ... Why does Sir Roy insult Her Majesty's Government; quarrel with me and my Ministers; incite my Party to revolt; stir up Lord Beaverbrook, etc., etc.? If Her Majesty's Government fails, they will not be succeeded by Lords Salisbury and Lambton. His only friends who have any effective strength will have gone ...

In the light of the correspondence, I would question whether it was solely, or even mainly, Sir Roy who was inciting the Conservative Party. The boot was on the other foot.

I am not a subscriber to the conspiracy theory of history, and I do not suggest that this was a sinister plot with some well-defined ulterior motive. I believe rather that the people concerned were, in the main, simple old-fashioned reactionaries who were reluctant to accept that the way of life which was slowly beginning to elude them at home could not somehow be preserved, as it were in aspic, in the last remaining old-fashioned colony. Lord Salisbury himself was doubtless influenced by a sort of feudal attitude towards his family estates in Rhodesia and towards the city named after his grandfather; this could be summed up in a sentence which he sometimes used – 'my people expect me to support them'. In the end, however, by encouraging their Rhodesian friends and clients to resist all compromise, these people ensured not only the destruction of the Federation they purported to defend; they came very close to destroying finally the prospects of the whites in Southern Rhodesia itself. They were not, as Lord Salisbury said of Mr Iain Macleod, too clever by half; they were just not half clever enough.

Fifteen years later, when I was Ambassador in South Africa, I found it significant that when these particular people visited South Africa on their way to Rhodesia, they almost invariably made their arrangements through the Rhodesian diplomatic representative in South Africa, my friend Air Vice-Marshal Harold Hawkins, rather than through the Foreign and Commonwealth Office or myself. Fortunately, my relations with Hawkins were such that he usually kept me informed of their movements.

I returned to London in late September to help complete the anticlimactic task of preparing for publication the volumes of evidence given to the Commission. On 3 October James Morgan gave a small lunch party at his club to say good-bye to Frank Wisdom. It was a sad and rather sentimental occasion; we had no idea then how much we should continue to see of each other over the years ahead.

My preoccupation with the Monckton Commission had distracted my attention from developments currently taking place in the Union of South Africa. Dr Verwoerd, possibly triggered by what he regarded as an unfair attack on South Africa in Mr Macmillan's 'wind of change' speech at the beginning of the year, decided to call a referendum to settle an issue which had long been dear to the Afrikaner community: whether or not South Africa should declare itself a republic within the Commonwealth. He chose his time well. Many South Africans, even among the English-speaking community, had come to see the Crown as a divisive symbol in the special circumstances of South Africa. The referendum which was held in October resulted in a substantial majority in favour of introducing legislation to make South Africa a republic. It was understood that the question of continued Commonwealth membership was a matter for the Commonwealth to decide; although the admission of India in similar circumstances provided a favourable precedent it was realized that in South Africa's case the answer could not be regarded as a foregone conclusion. Nor can it be assumed that in his heart Dr Verwoerd desired it.

During my absence from the CRO my job as head of the Central African and Territories Department had been filled, but for the next few weeks I was fully occupied with preparations for the Federal review conference. A special interdepartmental committee of officials, the Rhodesia and Nyasaland Committee, of which I was a member, had been set up to co-ordinate the work. By late October this committee was meeting almost daily. It was also concerned with providing ministers with material for the debate on the Address from the Throne, in which the future of the Federation was a major issue.

The Prime Minister opened the debate, which, he recorded, was well received at home. But, 'as I expected, Welensky ... does *not* think my speech fair and will reply next week ...'[12] Welensky had at first proposed that the earlier exchange of telegrams between himself and Mr Macmillan on the question of secession should be published, but he later withdrew this request. Lord Salisbury nevertheless chose precisely this moment to revive the charge of 'bad faith' against HMG in a letter to *The Times*.

On 16 November 1960 there was a full-scale debate on the Monckton Commission in the House of Lords on a motion by Lord Listowel. I attended the debate in the official box, mainly to be on hand to brief the Duke of Devonshire, one of our junior ministers, who was speaking. Lord Salisbury did not attend, though the Government were well aware of the danger of his leading a right-wing revolt. The standard of debate was exceptionally high, even for their Lordships' House. Above all others the speech I remember was that by Lord Hailsham, who wound up for the Government. His peroration included a witty but profound historical analysis of the human problems facing colonialism in retreat. The parallel he drew between the Roman occupation of Britain and the white settlers in Rhodesia was resented at the time in Salisbury, but it is so relevant to what has happened since that it is worth quoting:[13]

There are a lot of ghosts in British history, and I think one is wise to remember them ... I sometimes see the ghost of a military tribune of Claudius's army standing on the coast of Kent. He must have said, must he not, as he saw our bewoaded ancestors, the subjects of Boudicca, 'What have these people ever done to further human progress? Here are we, with all the might of Rome behind us, with Latin and Greek literature enriching our school days, with our technical know-how, our great wealth, and our immense civilization. What have we to do with these people, except to teach them the things we know?'

The Romans came here and they brought civilization. It did not last, because it found no lasting root at that time in the hearts of the people. I think, on the whole, the sainted Pope was wiser when he saw up for sale in the slave market in Rome the two golden-haired boys, and said, '*non Angli sed angeli*'. But I have no doubt that some of the bystanders there said, 'How very charming those children are. One must remember, however, that when they are grown up they will be just buck Anglo-Saxons.'

One could add, taking the parallel on a century or two, that many of the Roman settlers who decided to remain when the legions finally left Britain at the end of the fourth century AD, doubtless said to themselves, 'We understand these people. They are quite incapable of governing themselves. Although they will never admit it, in their hearts they know they are better off working for us than trying to farm this land on their own.' It is a sad fact that, almost to a man, woman and child, the Romans who stayed on and tried to make a go of it were eventually either compelled to leave, or remained, butchered, in communal graves.

The Federal review conference assembled at Lancaster House on Monday 5 December. A full account of its proceedings is contained in Mr Macmillan's autobiography.[14] It ended without a breakdown, but only just. Mr Duncan Sandys in his winding-up speech proposed that the conference should be adjourned in order to get on with the territorial reviews, leaving it to be reconvened at the right time in the light of progress made in the latter. This was accepted, but in the event the Federal conference never met again.

During the conference, parallel talks had also been taking place with Sir Edgar Whitehead, who had formally requested that the Constitution of Southern Rhodesia should be revised, with a view to transferring to Southern Rhodesia the powers still vested in the British Government. A Southern Rhodesian Constitutional Conference was accordingly convened in London after the Federal conference, with the intention that it should reassemble in Salisbury early in the New Year.

At this juncture I was for a few weeks taken off the Rhodesian desk altogether in order to take over part of the work of the West African Department, which was under considerable pressure following the achievement of independence by Nigeria on 1 October. My work there forms no part of this story, but immediately before Christmas I was told that I was being posted to Salisbury in March 1961 as Deputy High Commissioner under Rupert Metcalf. Vera was particularly pleased at the prospect of seeing the Federation for herself; not for the last time in our career she had a chance of catching up with places I had been visiting in the course of a home posting.

CHAPTER 13

LORD ALPORT'S
SUDDEN ASSIGNMENT

MR DUNCAN SANDYS flew to Salisbury in early January 1961 for the second stage of the Southern Rhodesian Conference, and by 7 February had secured agreement on a new Constitution by Sir Edgar Whitehead, on behalf of the Southern Rhodesian Government, and by Mr Joshua Nkomo, representing the Southern Rhodesian African National Congress.

The new Constitution did not immediately give Southern Rhodesia the wide range of additional powers Sir Edgar was seeking, but provided a carefully balanced package under which black representation in Parliament would be immediately increased and a progressive, but still qualified, franchise introduced. Under this franchise, the number of Africans on the common voters' roll would steadily increase with advances in wealth and education. It was calculated that a black majority on the voters' roll would be achieved within fifteen, or at the most twenty, years – in other words, at the latest by about 1980.

While the conference was still in progress, Dorrie Metcalf was taken ill and had to be flown home for emergency surgery. Rupert Metcalf himself was not in the best of health and at short notice it was decided that he should be brought home and that he should be succeeded as High Commissioner by Mr Alport, the Minister of State, who at the same time was promoted to a Life Peerage. The wider implications of this appointment are set out in Lord Alport's own memoir,[1] but at a domestic level the decision also had implications for Vera and myself. Among other things, it was clear that the importance of the post and the status of the High Commissioner had been significantly upgraded by the change. An ex-Minister of State would presumably be in a position to operate a hot line to his Secretary of State in the way a career diplomat could not. This would also have an effect on the role of his deputy. For all I knew, he might even want the post filled by someone of his own choosing. But even if he wanted me, it looked as if there might be a practical problem. Vera and I, with Andrew, were booked on RMS *Pendennis Castle*, sailing for Cape Town on 2 March. Since the Alports had received even less notice of their posting than we had, they might reasonably expect us to cancel our coveted sea passage to prepare the ground for the new High Commissioner.

It was with some trepidation, therefore, that I sought an interview with the Minister of State the day after his appointment had been announced. I had, of course, worked closely with Mr Alport for the past eighteen months, but being his deputy in an overseas post was altogether another thing. While I was waiting for his previous visitor to depart, I sounded out his private secretary, Mr J.B. Unwin, a fairly new Assistant Principal in the Common-wealth Office, on what the minister's plans were likely to be. What I heard greatly reassured me. In particular, Unwin told me that he himself would be coming to Salisbury as Lord Alport's private secretary – an appointment which would have been unheard of for a career head of mission in a medium-sized post. He also said that Lord Alport was planning to travel to Salisbury ahead of his family to case the joint, as it were, and to have preliminary talks with the Federal and Southern Rhodesian Governments on the basis of which he would prepare a working brief for approval by his ministerial colleagues.

When I was finally ushered in, Lord Alport could not have been more friendly. He confirmed that he expected to fly to Rhodesia on 2 March, the very day on which we ourselves were due to sail. He planned to spend only about four weeks in Salisbury on the first visit, however, and was content that we should stick to our travel plans. This would mean that I would take charge of the mission almost as soon as we arrived, while he returned to London for a final ministerial briefing before collecting his family, whom he also proposed to bring back by sea. I was very happy to fall in with this arrangement and expressed suitable appreciation of the fact that our plans could remain unchanged.

Three weeks later we left Southampton. During the voyage the only cloud in the sky was the political news which trickled through to us from London. A few days before we were due to arrive at Cape Town, the Commonwealth Prime Ministers assembled at Lancaster House for the second Common-wealth Conference in a year. From the little we had heard, things did not seem to be going well at it, especially for South Africa.

Before flying up to Salisbury, we had arranged to spend a night each with two sets of friends in Cape Town; the first with Rex and Mardee Wilson, and the second with Rupert and Lorna Shephard. To both we had written that we intended to keep off politics, and that we hoped to spend our time with them catching up on family affairs. As soon as we docked on the morning of 16 March 1961, however, we were greeted on board by John Morrison, an old CRO friend who had the previous week been promoted to the peerage as Viscount Dunrossil following the unexpected death of his father, a former Speaker of the House of Commons. John's first question was whether we had heard that morning's radio news. When we said that we hadn't, he told us that it had just been announced from London that Dr Verwoerd had decided to take South Africa out of the Commonwealth, following what he regarded as unacceptable interference in South Africa's internal affairs by the rest of the Commonwealth.

That was good-bye to our peaceful two days. We were invited to lunch by the High Commissioner and Lady Maud, after which I spent some time in the office being brought up to date on the latest developments. We also met my predecessor in Salisbury, Godfrey Bass, who had just arrived from Rhodesia to take up his appointment as Minister in the High Commission to South Africa and deputy to Sir John Maud. The evenings with the Wilsons and the Shephards were deeply charged with politics and we didn't get to bed much before 4 a.m. on either night. There was a widespread feeling in South Africa that Verwoerd had done the only possible thing by withdrawing from the Commonwealth, though the English-speaking community in the Cape were uncomfortably aware of the implications of the decision for South Africa's external relations, particularly those affecting the United Kingdom.

On Saturday morning we were poured in a state of exhaustion onto an aircraft for Johannesburg. In those days there were still no jets on the domestic services in South Africa, and the seven hours or so it took us to get to Salisbury provided a much-needed opportunity to adjust our thoughts to the new job. On arrival we were taken straight to Mirimba House, where Lord Alport had invited us to stay until our heavy baggage arrived. Here we were greeted by Brian Unwin; Lord Alport himself returned later that evening from his first visit to Nyasaland, where he had been making his introductory calls on the Governor and Dr Banda.

For the next few days I was kept very busy meeting members of the office and generally getting myself dug in. Lord Alport was due to make his initial call on Sir Humphrey Gibbs, the Governor of Southern Rhodesia, in Bulawayo on 22 March. This, we belatedly discovered from Unwin, was also his birthday. We therefore decided that we must drink his health in a glass of champagne before he left. Our own heavy baggage, and with it our drinks supply, had still not arrived, so we arranged with Unwin that he should raid the High Commissioner's cellar, to which he had the key, to 'borrow' a couple of bottles, which we could replace as soon as our own supplies arrived. Lord Alport was suitably touched at the thought; we did not tell him until after his return from London, when we had replaced the bottles, that we had been toasting him in his own champagne.

At the end of the week Lord Alport returned to London, taking Unwin with him. A few days later we moved into the Deputy High Commissioner's official house, Wahroongu (meaning 'foreigners' in Seshona), about a mile from Mirimba. I started on the necessary task of making my calls on ministers, both Federal and Southern Rhodesian, and on other significant personalities such as the Chief Justice and the Vice-Chancellor of the University. I also took the opportunity to renew acquaintance with a number of old friends from my earlier visits. These included Frank Wisdom, now reinstalled in the Southern Rhodesian Public Service; Taffy Evans and Hugh Parry, both Permanent Secretaries in the Federal civil service, and Bob Taylor, now taking over as Chairman of Central African Airways from A.E.P. Robinson, who had just started work as Federal High Commissioner in London.

Salisbury was not an easy place for a British diplomat to work in, and it was a bonus for me that so many of the people I had to deal with, sometimes in circumstances where our official aims were diametrically opposed, were by now personal friends with whom I could talk relatively freely. They on their side recognized that, notwithstanding my official position, at least I was not a complete stranger to the local scene. Our two countries certainly needed all the mutual understanding we could achieve; sadly, at the end of the day it was not enough.

Although the British High Commission in Salisbury was directly responsible for conducting HMG's relations only with the Federal and Southern Rhodesian Governments, Lord Alport quickly realized that it was essential for us also to work in the closest possible collaboration with the Governors of the northern territories. It was only too obvious that, unless we did so, Welensky would persevere in his efforts to drive a wedge between the Departments of State concerned in London, the Commonwealth Relations Office and the Colonial Office. Lord Alport rightly felt that as High Commissioner he must be seen to represent the whole of the British Government rather than just one ministry. This was all the more necessary because of the almost pathological distrust which had developed between the Federal Prime Minister and the Colonial Secretary.[2]

Only a few weeks earlier, following disagreements over the Northern Rhodesian Constitution, Sir Roy had launched a characteristic attack on Mr Macleod in the Federal Parliament, in the course of which he said:

To all this must be added the deterioration which there has been in the affairs of those territories for which the present Colonial Secretary has been responsible since he took office in 1959.

He calculates that the winds of change are blowing irresistibly in one direction and that it is the better part of discretion to go along with them. May I say that he calculates without the people of Rhodesia and Nyasaland, who have seen from pretty close range what havoc those winds can wreak in a place like the Congo, and who are detemined to moderate their force.

Brave words! But whose calculation was, in the end, the more accurate?

The following week-end was Easter; as soon as it was over, in line with the new policy, I paid a short visit to Northern Rhodesia to resume my contacts with the administration and to make my number with the Governor. On 5 April Vera and I flew to the Copper Belt, where over the next two days we called on the District Commissioners and visited the mines at Mufulira, Chingola and Luanshya. It was an interesting thought that if it had not been for the war I might well myself have been working on one of them as an engineer.

From the mines we visited Ndola, where we met the civic authorities and were conducted round the copper refinery; thence we travelled south to Lusaka. Here we stayed with Martin Wray, the Chief Secretary, who with his wife, Joy, were old friends from the High Commission Territories. On Saturday I had a meeting with the Governor, Sir Evelyn Hone, which was also attended by Trevor Gardner, the Secretary of Finance, and Brian Tucker, a United Kingdom civil servant from the Ministry of Power, who was spending five years on secondment to the Northern Rhodesian Government and was concerned with constitutional matters. Gardner had been a member of the committee of officials and had also been the Northern Rhodesian liaison officer with the Monckton Commission. For the next two years he and Tucker and I were to be constantly associated on the various constitutional developments in the Federation as they affected Northern Rhodesia.

Brian Unwin arrived back in Salisbury on 26 April 1961 in order to supervise the arrangements for the High Commissioner's return, and came to stay with us until he could find himself somewhere to live. Lord and Lady Alport, together with their three children and their nanny, arrived two days later. I see from my diary that immediately after his return Lord Alport held an office meeting at 9.30 a.m. on Saturday to bring the staff up to date on his talks in London; this was before the introduction of the five-day week, at least for those of us serving overseas.

The following week the Alports left for Bulawayo, to attend the opening of the annual Trade Fair, at which Great Britain was represented for the first time by a permanent pavilion. An impressive exhibit had been arranged by the Central Office of Information, and members of the staff of the High Commission took turns in manning it. Vera and I travelled down by car at the beginning of the second week. After a couple of days in attendance at the pavilion, in the course of which we took the Governor of Southern Rhodesia and Lady Gibbs round the exhibits, we moved on from Bulawayo to Fort Victoria. There we visited the Zimbabwe ruins, the mysterious atmosphere of which never failed to impress. There is great argument about the origins of this fascinating complex, but modern carbon-dating techniques seem to indicate an age of between eight hundred and a thousand years. The civilization which constructed it, and which presumably also built the vast area of agricultural terracing in the mountains of the Eastern Highlands, has vanished. But the evidence of gold refining, and the elegant stone carvings found at the site, suggest a marked degree of sophistication.

Our visit to Fort Victoria also coincided with the opening of the Kyle Dam, a sort of mini-Kariba designed to provide hydroelectric power and irrigation for the rapidly developing citrus and sugar-growing projects in the southern low-veld area. The dam itself was an impressive structure, and the surrounding country, apart from the weather, strongly reminiscent of the Highlands of Scotland.

After our return to Salisbury I became involved with Lord Alport in a concentrated and interlocking series of negotiations. In the light of the increasingly violent criticism beginning to be expressed by Mr Joshua Nkomo and the Rev. Ndabaningi Sithole of the National Democratic Party (which had been formed out of the ashes of the banned African National Congress), Sir Edgar Whitehead had decided to call together the participants of the February constitutional conference to prepare for the implementation of the new Constitution. The reconvened conference met in a sour atmosphere. The British Government was represented by Lord Alport, who records in his memoir[3] how his solitary attempt at reconciliation was rebuffed by Mr Nkomo. Before the end of the first day, the NDP delegation repudiated their earlier acceptance of the new Constitution and walked out of the conference. This decision to back-track on his earlier agreement was extremely damaging to Mr Nkomo's credibility with the whites, and gave the right-wingers just the excuse they needed to maintain in the future that 'these people' (the blacks) 'cannot be trusted'. From then on, Southern Rhodesia was on a descending spiral of mistrust.

On the morning that the Southern Rhodesia meeting opened, Brian Tucker came down from Lusaka for preliminary talks with me on the parallel proposals which were beginning to take shape for amendments to the Northern Rhodesian Constitution. It would in due course be necessary to discuss these proposals with the Federal Government before they could be implemented. It became my task to act as a sounding-board – even occasionally as devil's advocate – on whom officials from the two northern territories could try out their ideas in terms of the atmosphere in Salisbury.

For tactical reasons it was of course essential to ensure that the content of these talks, which were necessarily highly confidential, should not become public knowledge prematurely. Sir Roy Welensky had already let it be known that the discussions in Gwelo gaol between Dr Banda and his legal adviser, Mr Dingle Foot, although theoretically privileged, had been deliberately eavesdropped by the Federal authorities. We were, therefore, at all times conscious of the possibility that a Federal bugging operation might also be mounted against us. For this reason we constantly changed the venue of our talks in Salisbury on the assumption that they could not be listening to us everywhere all the time. This particular round of talks was, in fact, held in our house in Highlands, much of it in the garden.

One immediate result of the breakdown of the Southern Rhodesian talks was that Sir Edgar Whitehead invited Mr Duncan Sandys, who had presided over the earlier phase of the constitutional conference, to visit Salisbury for further discussions in the light of Mr Nkomo's change of mind. Mr Sandys took advantage of this invitation to have talks also with Sir Roy Welensky and Federal ministers. At the same time, Lord Alport, initiating a pattern which was to be followed more than once in the years ahead, invited the Governors of the two northern territories to Salisbury for a tripartite conference of British representatives, at which matters of common concern could be discussed with the Commonwealth Secretary.

This was not my first experience of working with Mr Duncan Sandys, nor was it to be my last. Ministers, like everybody else, have their own ways of operating: Mr Sandys's way tended to be one of attrition, based on the assumption that if one went on hammering away long enough, in the end something had to give. This was often effective, particularly when what was at stake was the achievement of some tangible British objective. But it was sometimes counter-productive. Compromises arrived at in the early hours of the morning, possibly involving difficult constitutional decisions which nevertheless might have lasting effects on the lives of a great many people, were less likely to stick if on reflection the other party felt that he had been over-persuaded, perhaps when he was already half asleep. Mr Sandys himself had tremendous stamina. He was quite capable of negotiating until 2 a.m.

and then taking his own team off to his room for a further hour's discussion on the tactics for tomorrow. I sometimes wondered how the people who worked for him permanently managed to survive at all. But it is only fair to say that when a negotiation had gone right he would often relax with a warm and warming grin which would allow everything to be forgiven.

The concept of the Governors' conference was not new to the Federation; such a meeting had, indeed, been held under the auspices of the Governor-General only a year earlier to discuss the disturbances in Southern Rhodesia and Nyasaland. A conference held under Federal sponsorship had awkward political implications for the Governors, however, since it was liable to attract hostile criticism both at Westminster and in the northern territories themselves. Any suggestion at such a conference that the Federal armed forces might, for example, intervene in support of the territorial authorities (who were specifically responsible for law and order) could easily be interpreted as Federal interference in the domestic affairs of the territory.

On the other hand there were also problems in holding such a conference under the sponsorship of the British High Commissioner. Apart from anything else, it removed a useful – in practice almost the only – forum for contact between the Governors and Welensky, with the result that misunderstandings which already existed tended to grow and fester. The following year, writing to one of his right-wing friends in London,[4] Sir Roy commented on the change of relationship which had taken place. After some highly critical personal observations he wrote: 'Since his [Lord Alport's] arrival here . . . I have had almost no contact at all with the Governors of the two Northern Territories; he has taken that over completely.'

The Governors, for their part, although finding it politically easier to deal with the High Commissioner than with the Federal Prime Minister, also had their reservations about the new arrangements. In particular, they feared that Lord Alport, as a former Commonwealth Relations Office minister, might come to be regarded by the British Government as a sort of overlord interposed between them and the Colonial Secretary, and that this might lead to the emergence of a pro-Federal bias in Whitehall. In practice, this fear was not justified; Lord Alport, even though he had undoubtedly arrived in Salisbury as a firm supporter of Federation, became aware at a very early stage that drastic action involving some transfer of power to the territories would have to be taken if the Federation were to be saved.

No one was better aware than he of the knife-edge on which he walked. I remember one day commenting to him on the fact that something he had said had gone down very well with, if I remember correctly, Mr Joshua Nkomo.

'That's very worrying, David,' he said. 'The best we are entitled to hope for in this job is parity of disesteem. Once either side gets the idea that we are the cat's whiskers, we've had it.' I found that this was a fair comment on much of the rest of my professional career as the servant of successive British Governments in southern Africa. Parity of disesteem was an equally essential part of our negotiations many years later with the South African Government on Namibia. In the latter context I remember repeating Lord Alport's words to Don McHenry, subsequently United States Ambassador to the United Nations, in 1978. 'I'd say that was the story of our lives,' was his comment.

A few weeks after Mr Sandys's visit, Diana joined us from Bristol University. She followed the route we had come by; she even came in the same mailship, the *Pendennis Castle*, to Cape Town. An unaccompanied nineteen-year-old girl was an unusual phenomenon on a ship mainly patronized by the rich and elderly. 'It was marvellous,' she said, 'I had my meals in the First Class, but I was always asked to the Tourist Class dances. And if I didn't like somebody I could always escape from him back to my cabin.'

Although by that time Brian Unwin had found himself a flat of his own, he had formed the habit of looking in on us at fairly frequent intervals. He confessed to us later that he had been dreading Diana's arrival because he thought it would make it more difficult for him to go on treating us as a casual stopping-off point. However, on the second evening after she arrived we asked him in to supper, and the night after that he asked her over to see his new flat. By the time they had been out together for eight nights in a row it seemed clear that any misgivings about the new arrival had been dissipated.

CHAPTER 14

CRISIS IN KATANGA

LOOMING OVER THE constitutional squabbles within the Federation, an even more immediately serious situation was, in 1961, developing across the border in the Congo, notably in the Province of Katanga, which shared with Northern Rhodesia the enormous copper deposits along the Zambezi-Congo watershed.

I am not concerned with the details of the events leading up to the United Nations intervention in Katanga, but only with those aspects of them which concerned us in Salisbury. It is, however, worth recalling that a year earlier, on 30 June 1960, the Belgians had precipitately – many would say irresponsibly – withdrawn their administration from the Congo, leaving that vast country to find some kind of *modus vivendi* without the help of any of the transitional constitutional precautions which had been taken in former British colonies making their own leap to independence. A central government of a sort was set up under President Joseph Kasavubu, a former civil servant under the Belgian administration. Within a matter of days the Army mutinied, the general fabric of government effectively collapsed and the majority of the prosperous Belgian trading and mining communities unceremoniously disappeared, virtually overnight. The only part of the Congo where some sort of order was maintained was Katanga. There, on 11 July 1960, with powerful support from the Belgian mining corporation, Union Minière, Mr Moise Tshombe, the Provincial President, proclaimed Katanga's independence from the rest of the Congo and appealed to the British and Federal Governments, among others, for military assistance.

This help was not granted, nor did either country officially recognize the independence of Katanga, though Welensky tried strenuously to persuade the British Government to accord it some kind of *de facto* recognition. Not only were the Katanga mines a source of strategic materials, particularly copper and cobalt, vital to the West, but they also represented the main source of wealth of the Congo as a whole. If they were to be detached from the control of the central government in Leopoldville, the loss of revenue

94

would further impoverish other parts of the country, which would consequently become even more fertile soil for the spread of Communism than it was already. It was for this reason, as well as to pre-empt a great-power conflict, that the United Nations had concerned themselves so closely with events in the Congo in the year following the Belgian withdrawal.

A fascinating personal account of events in Katanga during this period, including an inside report on the United Nations operations to remove the mercenaries and to arrest Mr Tshombe and his close associates (Operations *Rumpunch* and *Morthor*) is contained in Mr Conor Cruise O'Brien's book *To Katanga and Back*.[1] This was published in 1962, in the heat of the public attacks on Mr O'Brien which followed his recall from UN service and his resignation from the Irish Foreign Service.

I have never met Mr O'Brien, but I am an admirer of his writing and believe that if ever I did meet him I should like and respect him. His account is patently honest, in the sense that he includes in it a number of things that must have been as hard for him to write as they undoubtedly were for the UN Secretariat to read. But re-reading it today, almost twenty years after the events it portrays, I find it as hard as I did then to understand how the United Nations could have allowed themselves to become as deeply involved in the internal conflict as they did. Operative paragraph 4 of the Security Council Resolution (S/4426) of 9 August 1960, as Mr O'Brien freely acknowledges, specifically reaffirmed that the United Nations force in the Congo 'will not be a party to or in any way intervene in or be used to influence the outcome of any internal conflict, constitutional or otherwise'.

On 21 February 1961, however, a much stronger Resolution (S/4741) was passed by the Security Council which, *inter alia*, authorized the Secretary-General to take vigorous action, *including the use of force if necessary* (my italics), to remove the mercenaries, and it was this resolution that Mr O'Brien was sent to Katanga to enforce.

On 11 July, shortly after Mr O'Brien's arrival, a ceremony to mark the first anniversary of Katanga's 'independence' was held in Elisabethville. This was accompanied by the opening of an International Trade Fair, in which a number of Belgian and Federal companies and organizations took part. This fair was reported by the Federal Government's representative[2] as making 'an important contribution to the mood of exuberant self-confidence' which prevailed in Katanga at that time. But storm clouds were threatening. On 2 August, President Kasavubu was replaced in Leopoldville [Kinshasa] by a new government under M. Adoula, with considerable support from the Communists. At the same time a dramatic change began to emerge in United

Nations policy towards the Katanga Government. Whereas hitherto, with the sole exception of the Korean War intervention, United Nations forces had always been used exclusively for peace-keeping operations, as opposed to active military involvement, orders apparently now went out that the United Nations forces were to intervene directly in support of the central government.

Operations *Rumpunch* and *Morthor* followed. Conor Cruise O'Brien makes an interesting, and I think revealing, reference to his personal attitude in writing of his decision to arrest Munongo, Tshombe's unattractive 'Minister of the Interior':

The thing to do with Munongo, in my opinion, was not to investigate him impartially, or to punctuate [sic] his titles. The thing to do was to get him behind bars, thus depriving the European die-hards of Elisabethville of 'their' African and their control of the police apparatus.[3]

This statement perhaps reflected the understandably emotional reactions of an intellectual who suddenly found himself faced with the need for decisive action. All of us at one time or another have felt the urge for dramatic action, but for the diplomat it is usually an urge to be resisted. The unresolved question in all of this is the extent to which O'Brien's actions at the time were blessed with the authority of the UN Secretary-General, Dag Hammarskjöld, who played his cards notoriously close to his chest: after what turned out to be the fatal flight from Ndola, would he have supported O'Brien's actions or did he intend to rebuke O'Brien for exceeding his instructions? O'Brien clearly expected the latter,[4] and I have no reason to question this expectation.

In his own memoir,[5] Lord Alport gives a graphic account of his part in arranging the meeting between the UN Secretary-General and Mr Tshombe which was to have taken place at Ndola airport on 17 September 1961. To complement his report and that of Mr O'Brien it may even at this late stage be useful to give a brief personal account from a totally different angle of the background to the tragic events of that night.

August and September were the months when our children were on their school holidays. Lord Alport had therefore arranged that he and I should stagger our own periods of leave so that both of us could have some time away with our children. We had gone first, combining business with pleasure on a tour which took us first to the now completed Kariba Dam and thence up the Northern Rhodesian shore of Lake Kariba to the Victoria Falls, the Wankie National Park and the Matopos, and from there back to Bulawayo and Salisbury. On the way we spent a day in the Gwembe district, where our old friend from the Monckton Commission, Hezekiah Habanyama, met us and took us first to visit the Gwembe-Tonga Tribal Authority and then to meet his wife and family at their home at Chipepo, close to the shore of Lake Kariba. It was an outstandingly pleasant and relaxed occasion.

A day or so later at the Victoria Falls I had an unexpected telephone call from the High Commissioner asking me to join him at a meeting with the Governors of Northern Rhodesia and Nyasaland at Lusaka on 6 September. He added that Duncan Watson was flying out from the Colonial Office to attend the meeting. This involved some rearrangement of our plans, but I found that by cutting out one of our nights in the Wankie Park I could catch a direct flight from Bulawayo to Lusaka on the evening of 5 September.

On my arrival at Government House, Lusaka, Lord Alport briefed me on the progress of the meeting. In June, with the grudging agreement of the Federal Government secured after some four months of detailed and often acrimonious consultation, the British Government had published proposals for a new Constitution for Northern Rhodesia. These consultations, and the delay they had involved, had aroused the suspicions of Africans in the territory, who regarded the June proposals as back-tracking from the earlier ones in response to Federal pressure. There had been serious disturbances in Northern Rhodesia in July and early August, and doubts were being expressed in London whether the proposals would not now have to go further to meet African aspirations. Political advancement could, after all, only come about on the basis of a Constitution in which the Africans were prepared to acquiesce, and the landslide victory of Dr Banda's Malawi Congress Party in the recent Nyasaland elections was likely to stimulate further pressure in Northern Rhodesia. Duncan Watson had accordingly been sent with a message from Mr Iain Macleod telling the Governors – and Lord Alport – that the Northern Rhodesian proposals would have to be looked at again.

Lord Alport, with justification, feared that this would put him into a difficult position with Welensky, who could be expected to protest forcibly that HMG were once again going back on their agreement with him and that to give way in the face of violence would set the worst possible precedent for the future of the Federation. He also feared that the need to explain this likely Federal reaction to the Governors would evoke the accusation that the High Commissioner was adopting a pro-Federal attitude. He recognized, however, that for better or worse there was little chance of persuading the British Government to reverse their decision. Lord Alport recorded that this 'led to a very embittered discussion at the conference before we parted'.[6] It was because I had been involved in the earlier discussions on the Northern

Rhodesia Constitution that he had particularly wanted my presence and support at the meeting.

On the evening of 6 September I flew back to Salisbury, and the following morning went on to Bulawayo in order to pick up the family from the Matopos. In the meantime Lord Alport had been instructed to see Welensky to explain the change of policy to him. I did not attend that meeting, but I know that Alport came back from it sore and battered, having faced more than the usual stream of accusations of perfidy and bad faith for transmitting a decision which, as Welensky may or may not have guessed, had been taken in London in the face of his (Lord Alport's) strong opposition.

On 11 September the Alport family in their turn left Salisbury for a holiday in the Eastern Highlands. No sooner had they left than I had a telephone call from our own Secretary of State, Mr Duncan Sandys, telling me that there was increasing anxiety in London about the deteriorating situation in Katanga and that Lord Lansdowne, a Parliamentary Under-Secretary of State in the Foreign Office, was being sent to the Congo to obtain a first-hand report on conditions there. He would, if possible, look in on Salisbury in the course of his tour in order to bring us up to date on what he elicited. I passed this on by telephone to Lord Alport at Troutbeck, suggesting, however, that there was no need for him to interrupt his holiday until we had firm news of Lord Lansdowne's movements. I added that we were keeping in close touch with Denzil Dunnett, the British Consul in Elisabethville, and were arranging as and when necessary to pass on to London messages received from him through our local channels.

It may be worth digressing slightly at this point to comment on the complicated and highly inefficient communications system which we were operating at that time. It has to be remembered first that there were no fewer than three separate ministries involved in London, each having their own separate channels of communication. British diplomatic staff in the Congo, that is the ambassador at Leopoldville and the consul at Elisabethville, reported to the Foreign Office, the ambassador direct by diplomatic wireless service and the consul mainly through commercial Post Office circuits. The High Commission at Salisbury reported on a separate – and incompatible – cypher channel to the Commonwealth Relations Office, also using diplomatic radio. If we needed to communicate with, say, Leopoldville, or wished to repeat there a telegram we were sending to London, it had to be transmitted first to the CRO, from where it was passed to the Foreign Office for distribution to Foreign Office departments and re-encyphering. Only then could it be re-transmitted as a FO telegram to Leopoldville. At best this took several hours;

at worst, when traffic was heavy, it could take up to two days. Finally, the Governors of Northern Rhodesia and Nyasaland had their own channels to the Colonial Office. This often resulted in delays in circulating their telegrams to other departments in London, but it was not so hard for us since the High Commission did in fact share a compatible cypher system with the Governors, so that a telegram from, say, Lusaka to London could be repeated direct to Salisbury and Zomba without the need to re-encypher.

An additional complication was the fact that at times of crisis the Post Office link with Elisabethville was subject to interruption precisely when we were likely to need it most. To overcome this difficulty we had come to a confidential arrangement with the Federal Power Corporation and the mines, so that in case of necessity urgent messages could be transmitted down the power cables from Kariba to Elisabethville. This link was achieved by what seemed an almost magical technique whereby tiny telegraph voltages were superimposed on the massive 133,000-volt power-transmission system. Messages sent through this channel were regarded as confidential, but they were also accessible to the Federal Government and, presumably, to the Union Minière and through them to the Belgian Government.

Early on the morning of 13 September we received a message reporting that before dawn United Nations forces had taken over the post office and other key buildings in Elisabethville, and that Tshombe had disappeared. I passed this message immediately both to London and to Lord Alport at Troutbeck, who decided that he must return forthwith to Salisbury. He also asked me to warn Neil Ritchie, one of the High Commission First Secretaries, to hold himself in readiness to fly up to Katanga if, as seemed likely, it should be necessary to make contact with Tshombe. In fact, Tshombe, having evaded the United Nations detachment sent to arrest him, made contact with Dunnett later that morning and with his help left Elisabethville. Thereafter he went into hiding. Ritchie was instructed if possible to locate his place of retreat and to stand by in Northern Rhodesia to establish a link with him as soon as we had anything to say. How he did this is set out in Lord Alport's own account.[7]

In the meantime, largely as a result of pressure from the British Government, Mr Dag Hammarskjöld decided to fly from New York to Leopoldville to assess the position for himself and, it was hoped in Salisbury, to reassert his authority over his representatives in the Congo. These appeared, at least to observers from the Federation, to be exceeding their authority by abandoning their traditional peace-keeping role and embarking on aggressive military operations in support of the Adoula Government. Lord Lansdowne had a useful meeting with Hammarskjöld on his arrival at Leopoldville, as a result of which the Secretary-General agreed to meet Tshombe at Ndola the same, Sunday, afternoon.

In Salisbury, 17 September was being celebrated as Battle of Britain Sunday. Lord Alport, who had expected still to be out of Salisbury on holiday that day, had asked me to represent him at the service of remembrance at the cathedral, after which Vera and I, accompanied by Brian Unwin and Diana, had planned a picnic lunch at one of the local dams. In fact, while the service was still in progress, Lord Alport had been contacted by Lord Lansdowne and had made arrangements with Welensky to use a RRAF aircraft to take him to Ndola in order to meet Hammarskjöld and to stage-manage the meeting between him and Tshombe.

I knew nothing of all this until I emerged from the cathedral at about 11.45, but Vera, realizing that we were not going to be able to have our planned picnic, hastily scooped up the lunch which had been prepared for us and offered it to Lord Alport and Brian to take with them on the aircraft. In exchange, Lord Alport invited us to Mirimba House to eat the lunch then being cooked for him. He also asked Vera if, in the absence of Lady Alport, who was still at Troutbeck with the children, she could hold herself responsible for preparing Mirimba in case Lord Lansdowne and his Private Secretary arrived that night. He might, or might not, be back in time to greet them himself.

During the afternoon and evening I was fairly constantly in touch with Lord Alport through Brian Unwin at Ndola airport. Shortly after they arrived there, Tshombe and his immediate entourage also turned up in two light aircraft, but there was as yet no sign of either Mr Hammarskjöld or Lord Lansdowne. Eventually I received a message from Leopoldville saying that Lord Lansdowne had taken off, and that it was believed that another aircraft containing the Secretary-General and his staff would be leaving shortly. I passed this on to the party at Ndola, who were having increasing difficulty in persuading Tshombe to wait.

Lord Lansdowne eventually arrived at Ndola at about 10.40 p.m. His arrival was simultaneously confirmed to me by the regional air traffic controller at Salisbury airport tower, who also told me that he had been in contact with Hammarskjöld's aircraft. At about half-past eleven I rang Brian once more to find out whether Lord Lansdowne was still expected to come on to Salisbury that night. Brian confirmed that the Minister expected to take off from Ndola in the next few minutes, but that Hammarskjöld had still not arrived.

I met Lord Lansdowne at Salisbury airport just before 2 a.m. on Monday, 18 September 1961. I was, incidentally, deeply shocked at the condition of the aircraft in which he arrived: a clapped-out DC6 freighter, registered in Belgium, which seemed to be stripped down to the bare essentials and tied together with bits of string. The Minister was accompanied by Michael Wilford,* a friend from our days in Singapore where we had served together as First Secretaries. Vera had herself made up the beds at Mirimba and was waiting for us when we got back to the house. We dumped the luggage, and while she was showing Lord Lansdowne his room, Michael and I stood for a moment chatting in the hall. While we were talking I became aware of a peculiar scratching sound which appeared to be coming from a large chest in the hall. At first I thought there might be a mouse behind the chest, and began to pull it out to investigate. But I then realized that the noise was coming from inside one of the air travel bags which we had just put down. I immediately assumed that there was some sort of hostile device hidden in the bag and picked it up to throw it out onto the lawn. As I did so, however, Wilford and I simultaneously realized that the scratching concealed the faint sound of a human voice, and we both burst into laughter. It was Lord Lansdowne's transistor radio, which had somehow switched itself on inside the bag. After a tense day this false alarm left us feeling silly, but also a trifle shaken.

In the morning there was still no news of Hammarskjöld's aircraft. Although the air traffic authorities were convinced that it had been over Ndola at about midnight, the exchange of information with the pilot had been highly ambiguous; it was clear that he was worried about the security of the flight and it was still thought possible that he had decided at the last moment, for some unexplained reason, to divert to some other airfield, or had possibly even returned to Leopoldville. As the night wore on, however, it became increasingly certain that he had not arrived anywhere else, and at first light instructions were issued to initiate a general search.

During the morning I took Lord Lansdowne to call on Sir Roy Welensky. Although it was useful for the Federal Prime Minister to learn at first hand of the efforts being made to persuade the United Nations Secretary-General to institute a cease-fire, the conversation was inevitably overshadowed by the uncertainty over Hammarskjöld's whereabouts. Around noon I heard that Lord Alport was on his way back to Salisbury, where he was due to land at about 2 p.m. We therefore agreed to have an early lunch so that Lord Lansdowne could meet the High Commissioner briefly before taking off on

* Sir Michael Wilford, GCMG, HM Ambassador, Tokyo 1975–80.

his own return to Leopoldville. When we arrived at the airport at about 1.45 we were met by a member of the High Commission staff with the shattering news that the wreckage of Hammarskjöld's aircraft had been located in the past few minutes and that it seemed almost certain that the Secretary-General was dead.

Later that afternoon Lord Alport returned to Ndola, picking up Sir Evelyn Hone, the Governor, at Lusaka on the way. The events of the next few days are recounted in some detail in *The Sudden Assignment*,[8] including the extraordinary manœuvrings of a junior member of the United Nations staff from Elisabethville to try to obtain Mr Hammarskjöld's brief-case. I was only marginally involved, but with many others was later called on to give evidence to the United Nations enquiry.

That night I was woken by the telephone beside my bed ringing at about 1.30 a.m. There was a call from New York for Lord Alport. Would I take it? I tried to have the call switched to the Provincial Commissioner's house at Ndola, where I knew Lord Alport was spending the night, but I was told that they had tried the number already without success. At that moment a foreign voice told me that the United Nations Secretariat were on the line, and that Mr Andrew Cordier would like to speak to me. I was still only half awake, but my immediate reaction was to hope inwardly that he would not expect me to speak French. However, the voice was unmistakably American. He began by telling me that, although there was no Deputy Secretary-General who could take over from the late Mr Hammarskjöld, he (Cordier) was in overall charge of the African operations and as such was taking the initiative in trying to follow up the Secretary-General's efforts to secure a cease-fire. Could I bring him up to date on the latest position?

I told Cordier that before Lord Alport had left for Ndola the previous afternoon he had instructed a member of his staff to keep in touch with Tshombe, and that the latest news from Leopoldville was that the United Nations command there were trying to set up a new meeting. If such a meeting could be arranged, he asked me, what were the chances of Tshombe being willing to attend? I said that I did not know, but that since Tshombe had come to Ndola to meet the Secretary-General I assumed that he would be prepared to come back to talk to somebody else. Good, Cordier said. But how did I regard the overall situation? I said that I had very little to guide me on the situation in Katanga, but I knew that the Federal authorities were as anxious as we were to get the talks back on the rails, and that, always provided that Tshombe was willing to play ball, I regarded the present position with guarded optimism.

At that point the conversation ended. When I turned on the BBC news at 8 a.m. the next morning, the first item, inevitably, concerned the aftermath of the Hammarskjöld disaster. A press statement had been issued in New York a few hours earlier, saying that the UN Secretariat was examining ways of reopening the talks to establish a cease-fire, and that, in spite of the tragedy of the Secretary-General's death, they regarded the present position 'with guarded optimism'. 'So *that's* how history is made,' I said to Vera. A few days later Lord Alport confessed to me that when the call had first come through to Ndola he was still up, talking to the Governor and the Provincial Commissioner. When he heard that a certain Monsieur Cordier wanted to talk to him from United Nations headquarters, he, like me, had assumed that he was French. 'Ah,' he said, 'David will deal with that.'

In the atmosphere of hysteria which followed the crash, wild accusations were being bandied about to the effect that the aircraft had been shot down by a Katangese Fouga jet and that either the Federal or the British Government, or both, had been involved in a sinister plot to murder the Secretary-General. It was, therefore, very much in the interests of both of us that a technical enquiry should establish the medical facts about the accident as soon as possible. With the full approval of the Federal Government, Squadron Leader P.J. Stevens, RAF, a specialist in aviation and forensic medicine from the Accident Investigation Branch of the Air Ministry, was made available as a member of the medical investigating team within hours of the news becoming known. I met Stevens on his arrival at Salisbury airport on the morning of Wednesday, 20 September, and, after giving him lunch in Salisbury, saw him off on a flight to Ndola. His assistance in the examination of the bodies and the aircraft later proved invaluable in determining that the aircraft was in a normal descent attitude when it hit the tops of the trees, and that the deaths of all on board were solely the result of the impact.

CHAPTER 15

FIRST GLIMPSE OF
EAST AFRICA

IN THEIR DIFFICULT and honourable task of arranging the transfer of power from white to black in the former colonial territories some of the Governors concerned took an intensely protective line towards the emerging black governments, whom, perhaps naturally, they tended to regard as their personal protégés. One curious example of this affected me directly.

In the somewhat insulated atmosphere of Salisbury Lord Alport and I were very conscious that, apart from our close and regular contacts with the Governors of Northern Rhodesia and Nyasaland, we were in the nature of things increasingly out of touch with developments in West and East Africa, where independence was fast becoming a reality. West Africa was altogether too far out of our orbit. But it happened that for practical reasons we were involved in a fortnightly diplomatic courier service to East Africa, calling at Dar es Salaam and Nairobi. Towards the end of 1961, therefore, not long before Tanganyika was due to celebrate her independence, I suggested that on one of these runs, in order to get some first-hand knowledge of what was going on, I should myself act as Queen's Messenger. This proposal was welcomed by Lord Alport and cleared with the Commonwealth Relations and Colonial offices, both of whom felt that it had positive advantages.

To our astonishment, when the suggestion was put to Dar es Salaam, the Governor turned it down flat, arguing that 'his' Prime Minister, Mr Julius Nyerere, would take the strongest exception to a visit by anyone connected with the Federation. Even when Lord Alport pointed out in a bluntly worded telegram that the Deputy British High Commissioner was a servant of HMG and not of the Federal Government, he remained adamant.

Fortunately, the Kenya administration did not suffer from the same sensitivities, and welcomed the idea that I should visit Kenya. I therefore cut out my planned visit to Dar es Salaam and flew direct to Nairobi. I was so irritated by the Governor of Tanganyika's negative reaction, however, that when I was asked to fill in the immigration form before landing at Embakazi (Nairobi) airport I answered the question, 'Have you ever been declared a prohibited immigrant in any of the East African Territories?' by writing, 'Yes, Tanganyika.' It was not strictly true, since the Governor's views had been expressed only in a confidential telegram, but I much hoped that this would lead to my being officially questioned on landing. I looked forward to pointing out that I was probably the first senior British official ever to be denied entry to a British protectorate by order of Her Majesty's Representative in the territory.

Disappointingly, but perhaps predictably, the result was exactly nil. It was clear that, as I have often suspected, no one bothered to read the form. If they had, the East African authorities could scarcely have admitted a self-confessed prohibited immigrant without at least asking him some questions. I have, of course, met President Nyerere a number of times since then. He is far too sophisticated to believe that a civil servant's loyalties were likely to depend on the particular country in which he found himself posted, and I suspect that if he had been consulted at the time he might even have asked to see me himself.

Although a visit to Dar es Salaam at that juncture would have been useful, my talks in Nairobi fully justified the journey. I was able to meet and talk to a number of political figures, including the late Mr Tom Mboya, Sir Michael Blundell, Mr Bruce Mackenzie and Sir Eric Griffith-Jones. Blundell, who had been a pupil of my father's at Wellington College before emigrating to Kenya, was then doing his second stint as Minister of Agriculture. Both then, and later when I was serving in Uganda, he was generous with his time and gave me a great deal of useful background information.

Sir Donald MacGillivray, who had been deputy chairman of the Monckton Commission, also invited me to visit him. The MacGillivrays had an attractive house and a small farm in the Aberdares not far from Gilgil, and I found it both pleasant and illuminating to see at first hand how a Kenya settler household lived. On my way back from Gilgil to Nairobi I caught a taxi-bus – an estate car fitted out with an extra row of seats to take eight passengers – and was interested to find myself at close quarters with two or three black businessmen, and a couple of black housewives going in to Nairobi to do their shopping. This could never have happened in the Federation – what a lot the whites would have learned if it had.

Shortly after I got back to Salisbury it was announced that Mr Iain Macleod was being replaced as Colonial Secretary by Mr Reginald Maudling. This news was warmly welcomed by Federal ministers, who took a strongly personalized view of the influence individual British ministers were able to exercise on the overall course of events. They found it impossible to appreciate that governments of whatever political colouration were subject to a wide range of internal and external pressures which effectively limited their freedom of action. Even if it were true, which was by no means self-evident, that Mr Macleod had been moved from the Colonial Office because of his abrasive effect in the Federation, it was inevitable that his successor would still have to face the international facts of life. Welensky later quoted[1] Iain Macleod's farewell message to him as containing an assurance that the British Government were firm believers in the future of the Federation. He went on to comment that Mr Macleod was still Leader of the House of Commons and Chairman of the Conservative Party eighteen months later when his colleague, Mr Butler, communicated to him (Welensky) the British Government's unilateral decision to dissolve the Federation. Why should he have regarded those two statements as mutually contradictory? It was the limitations of the art of the possible, not the decisions of one British minister or another, which destroyed the Federation.

So it was that at the beginning of December 1961 Mr Maudling, in Welensky's words,[2] 'bustled cheerfully round the Federation'. In due course, as Welensky also noted, Maudling went back to London without having committed himself in the slightest. The principal subject he was discussing was whether or not the Northern Rhodesian constitutional proposals should be reopened. Predictably, he came to the conclusion that they must be – just as Mr Macleod would have done.

But Northern Rhodesia was not the only source of friction between the British and Federal Governments; grave embarrassment was also being caused by the support the Federal Government was continuing to give to the cause of Katangese secession. Lord Alport records that he had learnt on 12 December that the airfield used by Tshombe at Kipushi, which lay across the border between Northern Rhodesia and Katanga, had been considerably improved, adding that this was 'a fact of which Welensky was, I am sure, ignorant'.[3] However that may have been, the United Nations were unlikely to take an equally charitable view and the British Government had no wish to be branded as guilty by association. As a result of the pressure brought on the Federal Government by Lord Alport over Christmas, the use of Kipushi as a transit point for mercenaries joining Tshombe was stopped, but the atmosphere was not entirely friendly as a result. I remember turning up with Brian Unwin at Welensky's house late on Christmas Eve for a meeting with the Prime Minister arranged by Lord Alport, to discover a full Cabinet meeting in progress. Our arrival was greeted with considerable embarrassment since, unknown to us, Lord Alport had been told a few minutes earlier by Welensky's private secretary that the meeting had been cancelled on the ground that Welensky was suffering from a migraine. As Lord Alport pointed out, the tragedy was that basically the British Government's aim in Katanga was not very different from that of Welensky; unfortunately, however, we were far more vulnerable to American and Third World charges of bad faith than he was. The fact that only a year later Tshombe was translated to Kinshasa as Prime Minister of a united Congo Republic demonstrated *ex post facto* that neither of us had been backing entirely the wrong horse.

One couple whom we got to know well at this stage were Mr and Mrs Nathan Shamuyarira. Nathan, who is now (1980) Minister of Information in the Zimbabwe Government, was then editor of the *Daily News*, a newspaper primarily aimed at the black population of Rhodesia. As such he was a respected and influential personality in the African community. For precisely the same reason he was highly suspect to many Europeans. Our friendship with the Shamuyariras gave us a greatly enhanced insight into African thinking at a time when most white Rhodesians were still relying on their servants for understanding of a black point of view.

Another family friendship which developed at this time was with Mr John Wilfred, the Commissioner for India, his wife Flora, and their attractive daughter Shanti, who was a fellow student with Diana at the University College of Rhodesia and Nyasaland. John did not have an easy job: the Asian community in Rhodesia was highly articulate and intelligent, as well as being commercially successful, and they were regarded with great suspicion by many of the white Rhodesian establishment. Leaders of the community such as Mr Suman Mehta, who later identified himself with Mr Joshua Nkomo's ZANU Party, were close friends of the Wilfreds and quickly became friends of ours also. In the process, the High Commission acquired a good channel of communication with one of the more radical groups, which proved of considerable value in our political reporting. It happened also that the South African Commissioner, Tasie Taswell, was a friend of ours from our South African days; we thus had useful contacts at both ends of the political spectrum.

CHAPTER 16

MR BUTLER TAKES CHARGE

IN FEBRUARY 1962 Mr Duncan Sandys paid his second visit to the Federation. Lord Alport has commented on the somewhat abrasive manner in which he opened his talks with Federal ministers; it is clear that the impatience Mr Sandys displayed on that occasion reflected a growing disquiet about Federal attitudes that was developing within the government in London. From Salisbury, he travelled to Lusaka and Zomba. In his autobiography, Mr Julian Greenfield[1] asserts that while Mr Sandys was in Nyasaland 'he gave Dr Banda to understand that secession was on the way, a fact of which R.A. Butler subsequently informed Welensky'. Welensky himself makes the same point in his own account, and asks the question: 'Did the British Government, as far back as February 1962, come to an agreement with Banda behind my back, while they were still negotiating with me? This is something I still do not want to believe.'[2] Whether he believed it or not, it seems unlikely that Mr Sandys made much more than a general statement to the effect that he accepted that Nyasaland could not be kept in the Federation indefinitely against the wishes of the people.

When Mr Sandys returned to Salisbury, he had a fairly traumatic meeting with Welensky, which he opened with a report on his visit to Nyasaland. Welensky was accompanied at the meeting by Julian Greenfield and Taffy Evans, and Mr Sandys by Lord Alport and myself. In the course of this meeting the two Federal ministers continued to argue strongly that the British Government must tell Dr Banda once and for all that they were irrevocably committed to supporting the Federation and that under no circumstances could Nyasaland be granted the right of secession. Mr Sandys argued equally strongly that it was sheer illusion to believe that the Federation could be kept together by force against the wishes of the majority of its inhabitants. In the end, exasperated by what he clearly regarded as the lack of realism being displayed by the Federal representatives, Mr Sandys used the famous words reported by both Welensky and Lord Alport, 'But you must understand, Roy, we British have lost the will to govern.'

There is no doubt that this particular choice of language made a profound effect on all his hearers. I know it did on me. Julian Greenfield, as Welensky reported, responded immediately and icily, 'But *we* haven't.'

This exchange was followed by an embarrassed silence. It was, in fact, a moment of truth, even though Sandys and Greenfield were to some extent at cross-purposes. Mr Sandys may well have intended to imply that he personally dissociated himself from the sentiment he expressed, or at least to suggest the unspoken qualification 'against the wishes of the people'. But Greenfield and Welensky took the statement entirely at its face value. In retrospect, Greenfield should, perhaps, have been challenged on his reaction. Although Rhodesians might have had the will to govern Nyasaland and Northern Rhodesia, it was obvious that in the last resort they did not have the means. Successive British Governments deserve more credit than they have usually been given for ensuring that Malawi did not become our Vietnam.

Lord Alport's account[3] sets out the comings and goings of the next few weeks. On 27 February 1962, Welensky, with the full support of the Federal Cabinet, flew to London to make his point yet again and at the highest level. Mr Macmillan saw him, but without enthusiasm. Having got nowhere by orthodox methods, Welensky used what he clearly regarded as a trump card by threatening to resign and call a general election. Sandys tried hard to talk him out of this on the ground that it would achieve nothing. Lord Alport, who reinforced this argument when Welensky returned to Salisbury, commented that many people in Britain, who were not unfriendly to Welensky or the Federation, were getting bored with his importunities. They were also, no doubt, irritated by his habit of arriving in London and attempting, not without some success, to appeal over the heads of ministers to a wider public. In the end this did not do him much good, but there is no doubt that it caused the Conservative government considerable embarrassment, especially with their right wing.

Welensky stuck to his guns, however, and four days after his return offered the Governor-General his resignation and advised him to dissolve Parliament. As if in response to this, but probably in fact following a decision which had been made in principle some time earlier, Mr Macmillan announced on 18 March that Mr R.A. Butler, then Home Secretary, was to assume unified responsibility for Central Africa, taking over Southern Rhodesian and Federal affairs from Mr Sandys, and Northern Rhodesian and Nyasaland matters from Mr Maudling. Under Mr Butler a small new department, the Central African Office, was set up, with staff drawn mainly from the CRO and the CO. Its Secretary was Mark Tennant, the former Secretary-

General of the Monckton Commission. He was supported by a specialist staff headed by Rupert Metcalf, the former High Commissioner, and Duncan Watson of the Colonial Office, both having first-hand experience of the Federation and the territories. In order to extract the maximum advantage from the change of management, Lord Alport immediately suggested that he and the two Governors should be called to London for consultations. This advice was accepted, all the more readily since Mr Butler rightly felt that he could not visit the Federation himself until the Federal general election was out of the way.

Although in one sense the Federal election was a non-event, it had a profound effect on what happened later. The most important single factor was that Mr Winston Field, the leader of the opposition Dominion Party in the Federal Parliament, decided to boycott it altogether, preferring to keep his powder dry for the Southern Rhodesian elections which were due to take place later in the year. It is true that in the immediate result Welensky, whose United Federal Party gained fifty-four out of the fifty-nine seats in the Federal Assembly, could claim a landslide victory and the fullest support for his stand *vis-à-vis* the British Government. But in the slightly longer term, by allowing the Dominion Party to concentrate their electoral efforts on Southern Rhodesia, Welensky opened the way for the victory of the Rhodesia Front later in the year, and for the eventual unilateral declaration of independence by Mr Ian Smith.

Once the election was out of the way Mr Butler lost no time in making a major policy statement. This was carefully balanced. It began by acknowledging that 'Dr Banda and the Malawi Party in Nyasaland, supported by a firm mandate at the last election, are not prepared to remain in the *present* [my italics] Federation.' But this was qualified by going on to affirm that 'HMG think it right that before any firm conclusion is reached about Nyasaland's withdrawal ... there should be a full examination both of the consequences of withdrawal for Nyasaland and also of possible forms of association with the other two Territories.' Finally a bow in the direction of Welensky and the Preamble to the Federal Constitution: 'It remains the view of HMG that there are great advantages for all the peoples of Central Africa in a continued association of the three Territories.'

Mr Butler's statement also contained a sentence which affected me directly though I did not know it at the time. In order to carry out the promised examination of the consequences of Nyasaland's withdrawal, he proposed to appoint a small team of advisers to make recommendations to him personally; the names of the team were announced some weeks later. Sir Roger

Stevens, a Deputy Under-Secretary of State at the Foreign Office, was appointed leader; Arthur Brown, Professor of Economics at Leeds University, was economic adviser, and Sir Ralph Hone, constitutional adviser. The fourth member was myself.

Mr Butler arrived in Salisbury on 11 May. After a preliminary round of talks with the Federal Government, he went on to Nyasaland for three days. When he left Zomba he was able to announce, not that Nyasaland would be permitted to secede, but that Dr Banda and his ministers had agreed to an examination of the consequences of secession. His visit to Nyasaland was followed by five days in Lusaka, where he had 'warm and cordial' conversations with Mr Kenneth Kaunda. Finally he returned to Salisbury for a further three days of talks with the Federal and Southern Rhodesian authorities.

Although this visit reached no firm conclusions, nor indeed was it intended to do so, it resulted in a surprising improvement in the atmosphere, in Salisbury as well as in the territorial capitals. Sir Roy Welensky issued a friendly statement when Mr Butler left, which concluded:[4]

For some time ... the Federal Government have urged the Government of Great Britain to make a full examination of what the consequences of the secession of Nyasaland would be, and we welcome the Secretary of State's decision to have this examination made. The Federal Government is glad to note the statement made by Mr Butler that no decision has been made other than to undertake an appraisal of the situation by means of a committee of advisers.

There was a slight potential embarrassment in my nomination as a member of the team, since I was still Lord Alport's deputy and by implication the advisers were to operate independently of the High Commissioner. However, Lord Alport accepted that one of my tasks would be to keep him informed of the progress of the team's activities, and that he would be in no way committed to any conclusions we might reach. He accordingly raised no objection to my taking part.

The team assembled in Salisbury in mid-July 1962. On the afternoon of his arrival Sir Roger Stevens made courtesy calls on Sir Roy Welensky and Sir Edgar Whitehead. The next morning we all had a meeting with Taffy Evans in order to give him some idea of our programme and method of proceeding.

The same day – 17 July – we flew to Blantyre and thence were driven straight to Government House, Zomba. That night, the Governor, Sir Glyn Jones, who had taken over from Sir Robert Armitage the previous year and was known locally as 'Malawi Jones' from his undisguised commitment to early independence for the territory, laid on a dinner party for us at Government House. This was attended by Dr Banda and by the United Federal

Party leader, Mr Blackwood, and got our mission off to a highly auspicious start. Roger Stevens later recalled that the speeches went on until well after midnight.

We spent our first two nights at Government House; thereafter, in order to avoid any suggestion that we were being unduly influenced by the Governor, we moved to offices in the Old Residency, where we set up a sort of advanced headquarters. During the next few days we met most of the Malawi Party ministers and had a long session with Dr Banda in Blantyre; on 21 July Dr Banda gave a huge dinner in our honour at Limbe, attended by several hundred people. Our schedule of engagements with the Malawi Party were largely in the hands of Mr Aliki Banda, a leading member of the youth wing of the party, who was responsible for editing the party newspaper and was perhaps Dr Banda's closest personal aide. With his agreement we decided that a return of hospitality would be appropriate and we invited Dr Banda and some of 'my boys' - the collective name he gave to his young ministerial nominees - to an informal dinner party. To our amazement we discovered that there still did not exist in Zomba a single restaurant at which we could legally entertain a racially mixed party. We were, moreover, warned that if, for example, the local United Federal Party representatives heard of our plans they might well report them to the police as an intended breach of the law. We therefore made our arrangements in some secrecy, though the Governor was, of course, well aware of what was intended and entirely approved. He did, however, warn us that the Kamuzu did not normally accept private invitations, and might well decline ours.

The dinner was arranged to take place at the Kuchawi Inn, a popular and spectacular resort high up on the slopes of Zomba Mountain. Even when we arrived to greet our guests we could not be absolutely certain that Dr Banda would turn up, though we were reasonably confident that some of his associates would. After about twenty minutes of anxious waiting we saw the lights of a procession of cars coming up the mountain road towards the hotel. When they arrived, we found that everyone who had been invited had come, with the Doctor last, as befitted the leader of his country. It was an historic occasion, at which each side was able to convince the other of their goodwill. It also turned out to be an excellent party, at which both sides enjoyed themselves. Speeches were ruled out of order; after dinner cigars were passed round and James Morgan introduced our guests to a silly game using the aluminium containers as rocket projectors. Dr Banda himself did not take part, but his young ministers-designate were delighted to relax in a multi-racial atmosphere after the tensions of the previous year.

During our week in Nyasaland we also had long discussions with the leaders of the United Federal Party and with officials, in particular Henry Phillips, Minister of Finance, and Hugh Norman Walker, Secretary to the Treasury, both of whom, though sympathetic to the idea of independence, were acutely conscious of the economic and financial problems which Nyasaland would face without support from the rest of the Federation.

After this first round in Nyasaland we returned to Salisbury. On the Monday morning Roger Stevens and Arthur Brown left to spend a day at the Kariba power station and dam; Ralph Hone and I caught up with them on the Tuesday when we all reassembled at Lusaka. Here the pattern of interviews was repeated, though sadly Mr Kenneth Kaunda was unwilling to see us. Much of what we heard was new to Stevens and Brown, but for Hone and myself it was the third time round the course: occasionally I felt that if one of our witnesses forgot his lines I could complete his evidence word for word. Fortunately I was never tested.

A week later we again visited Nyasaland, and once again called on Dr Banda at his residence at Blantyre. Although he was entirely friendly to us, he made no secret of his detestation of 'that wicked Federation'. We were also subjected to long diatribes from two of his ministers: Mr Orton Chirwa, a lawyer who had been leader of the Malawi Party in Dr Banda's enforced absence, and Mr Henry Chipembere, a notably tough character. (It is interesting to note in retrospect that both men were later found guilty of plotting against Dr Banda.) At the end of the week we again returned to Salisbury, this time for a series of briefing sessions with the Southern Rhodesian and Federal authorities.

Having been subjected to a very similar range of evidence, it was not surprising that our conclusions closely paralleled the findings of the Monckton Commission two years earlier. To me it was significant, however, to see how far public opinion, especially among the blacks, had hardened in the intervening period. In particular, it was becoming widely accepted that Federation had operated principally, if not exclusively, to the benefit of the Europeans; not least it had favoured investment in Southern Rhodesia at the expense of the northern territories. In the light of the evidence presented to us we could not fail to endorse the view that in the last resort Nyasaland could not be kept in the Federation by force. We also accepted that if the two Rhodesias were to be kept together there would have to be an extensive redistribution of powers from the Federal to the territorial governments.

At this point there was a break in the proceedings, during which Roger Stevens returned to London to discuss with Mr Butler a preliminary outline of our proposals, and Arthur Brown to Leeds to prepare an economic section. During this lull, Vera and I took the children around the three territories for a three-week game-watching holiday by car. Early in September the three UK-based members of the team returned to Salisbury and we all did a final round of visits. We ended with an intensive week checking our factual information with the Federal Government before returning to London to report to Mr Butler.

Unfortunately we were hampered in making constructive recommendations by the rigid line being taken by Sir Roy Welensky. This is exemplified by his own account in the final chapter of his autobiography, under the title, 'Federation Destroyed'. Sir Roy argues forcefully,[5] but in legalistic rather than political terms, that HMG's insistence that any settlement of the Federation's problems must depend on the consent of the inhabitants, as laid down in the Preamble to the Constitution, was only part of the requirement. He insisted that the consent of the three territories *and of the Federal Government* (my italics) was necessary for any major alteration of the Constitution. He thus in effect demanded for his government the right to veto any recommendation for Nyasaland's secession no matter what the practical consequences might be.

The advisers, on the other hand, like the Monckton Commission before us, were convinced that the force required to keep Nyasaland, and ultimately Northern Rhodesia, in the Federation against the will of their elected representatives would be unacceptable to public opinion in Britain, as well as to the rest of the world. If the Federation were to survive in any form, it would have to justify its own existence. Neither Britain nor the world owed it a living.

We accordingly recommended that HMG should in due course put forward proposals for a new form of primarily economic association between the two Rhodesias, with which Nyasaland might be more or less loosely connected. Such an association could, we felt, incorporate a common market with defined common services, including a single customs service, continued mobility of labour between the territories, and perhaps a common monetary policy. We also pointed out the advantages of co-ordinating the commercial aspects of foreign affairs, as well as external defence. Finally we put forward suggestions for possible arrangements for the transitional period before the new association could be set up, including the winding up of those Federal functions which would no longer be applicable to the new association.

The Monckton Commission's report in 1960 had been published and then pigeon-holed. Ours never saw the light of day. In *The Sudden Assignment*

With James Morgan in
Northern Rhodesia, 1959.

The Monckton Commission, Victoria Falls, February 1960.

Vera and I at the Bulawayo Trade Fair with Sir Humphrey (*right*) and Lady Gibbs
(*second from left*), 1961.

Lord and Lady Alport leaving Salisbury at the end of their tour of duty, 1963.

Robert, Andrew and Diana in Salisbury, 1962.

Three generations of Scotts, Salisbury, 1962. *Left to right:* Vera, my mother Mrs Barbara Scott, Diana and myself.

Lord Alport meeting Mr Butler (*right*) at Salisbury airport, 1962, (Andrew behind).

Greeting members of the advisory team on the future structure of the Federation of Rhodesia and Nyasaland, 16 July 1962. *Left to right:* Professor A.J. Brown, Sir Roger Stevens and Sir Ralph Hone.

The end of the Federation, Victoria Falls Conference, July 1963.

Vera and I (*right*) with the Ugandan Minister of Foreign Affairs, Mr Sam Odaka, and the Canadian High Commissioner, Miss Meagher (*left*), at a party to celebrate the Queen's Birthday, 1969.

ABOVE LEFT In conversation with Jayant Madhvani, Jinja, 1969.

ABOVE RIGHT Brian and Diana Unwin.

LEFT Dr Milton Obote, President of Uganda, says farewell to members of the diplomatic corps at Entebbe before leaving for the Commonwealth Presidents and Prime Ministers Conference, 4 January 1969.

BELOW Michael Fairlie.

Presenting my credentials to the South African State President, His Excellency Dr Nicolas Diedrichs, with the Secretary of Foreign Affairs, Mr Brand Fourie (*right*), 17 March 1976.

Vera and I with Mr and Mrs Pik Botha (*right*) at the Queen's Birthday party, Cape Town, 23 April 1978.

Dr David Owen and Mr Don Jamieson, the Canadian Foreign Minister, being greeted by Mr Pik Botha on arrival at Waterkloof Airbase, Pretoria, after visiting Windhoek, 1978.

Vera with Ann and Nicholas Monsarrat, Gozo, January 1978.

Lord Alport commented,[6] 'The report they eventually produced is still a bit of a mystery and I cannot remember whether I ever read its final version.' On the face of it, this does not seem to be much of a tribute to the way in which I carried out my liaison function. The explanation is that, with characteristic caution, Mr Butler had made it clear in a note to Sir Roger Stevens[7] that he wanted to keep things fluid for the time being, and wished to avoid even giving the impression that an actual report had been handed in, whether it be described as interim or not. With regard to our preliminary proposals, he commented that the emphasis of our recommendations seemed to be to wind up the Federation through a Commission to be appointed from June 1963. Since he regarded it as his duty to retain the confidence of the Europeans and to help provide a future for them as well as for the preponderating Africans, he did not want the emphasis to be on liquidation of the Federal set-up but rather on the construction of some alternative. But he added that he would regard it as no breach of faith in his dealings with Sir Roy if he were to lead him towards an alternative system, however different from the existing one.

This idea of a Commission to replace the Federal Government also features in Mr Butler's reference to our recommendations in *The Art of the Possible*.[8] Curiously enough, the advisers themselves did not regard the establishment of a Commission as a central feature of our recommendations, but primarily as a transitional device. Sir Roger Stevens, who was by then Vice-Chancellor of Leeds University, queried the version contained in *The Art of the Possible* in a letter to Mr Butler dated 17 October 1971,[9] in which, *inter alia*, he wrote:

... as I recall the position, we made a positive recommendation that, after Nyasaland's right of secession had been granted and after the N. Rhodesian and S. Rhodesian elections had been held, viz. in January 1963, HMG should call a Conference to which the two Rhodesian Governments and the Federal Government should be invited, specifically to consider the situation created by Nyasaland's secession. Our *expectation* was that this would result in the demise of the Federal Government through action taken by the two Rhodesian governments and not as a result of any initiative by HMG; our *hope* was that out of a conference which had just reached this conclusion – and perhaps at no other time and no other way – some willingness to search for the terms of a new association between N. and S. Rhodesia might emerge.

We therefore suggested ... that HMG might tentatively propound the desirable ingredients of such an association, ask the Governments concerned to go away and think about it ... and then come back in, say, six months to a further Conference at which (with luck) the seal might be set on the new association. Whether in the event any of this would have happened ... is doubtful; but anyway I think not only that this is what we recommended after much heart-searching, but also that it was our key proposal, elaborated in some detail.

By contrast, the proposal for a Commission ... was as I remember both subsidiary and tentative in our final report. ... I think we should have fallen down badly on our job of advising you if all we had recommended formally in the end (as your account might be held to imply) was a Commission (constitution and function unspecified) to replace the Federal Government.

In his reply, dated 23 October 1971,[10] Mr Butler commented that Stevens's letter gave a fuller account of the advisers' advice than his book, and that he wished he had sent him the chapter before publication. 'I could make some adjustments which would set the record straight quite easily, but this would depend on the second edition ... I feel you realize that I did justice to my advisers but that the justice should have been tempered with accuracy.' A year later the point was, in fact, cautiously referred to in Mr Butler's revised preface to the Penguin edition of *The Art of the Possible*.[11]

CHAPTER 17

ELECTION IN
SOUTHERN RHODESIA

THE ADVISERS SPENT the second half of September and the first half of October 1962 in London completing their report, an abridged version of which was presented to Mr Butler in mid-October. This period in London contained a personal bonus for me, since Vera and I had been asked earlier in the year by the Master of Haileybury if we would allow Robert to stay on for an additional term to be head of the school for the College's centenary celebrations. We had naturally agreed, and the Master, Mr Christopher Smith, invited me to stay with him for a week-end in October to have a chance of seeing Robert in action. It was a good week-end, which I would not willingly have missed.

As soon as I returned to Salisbury, Lord Alport himself left for London in order to bring himself up to date on the First Secretary of State's thinking on the advisers' recommendations and on his own parallel ideas for a 'composite approach'.[1] This latter would have involved a resumption by Britain of direct responsibility for certain Federal functions, including defence, at the moment Nyasaland was permitted to secede. His proposals were not accepted, however, and Lord Alport came back from London with what Welensky described as 'very grave news'; in effect that the British Government accepted the principle of Nyasaland's withdrawal from the Federation without qualification and that this would be announced before the start of the Nyasaland Constitutional Conference in November. As a result of pressure by Sir Roy Welensky, this announcement was deferred until after the Southern Rhodesian elections in December. This was the final moment of truth.

In the meantime, Sir Edgar Whitehead had unexpectedly decided that he would personally attend, and speak at, the debate on Southern Rhodesia in the United Nations Committee on Colonialism in New York in mid-October. He took this decision in the full knowledge that the Southern Rhodesian general election was due to take place only a few weeks later. Although on his return he had every reason to be pleased with his reception in the debate, the fact that he appeared to be giving preference to the United Nations over his own constituents did him great harm with the voters. There was a clear parallel here with General Smuts's attitude towards the 1948 general election in South Africa: both men failed to comprehend that their own priorities were not shared by their electorate. Whitehead's absence from the country during the run-up to the dissolution of Parliament, combined with his increasing blindness and deafness, prevented him from detecting the growing backlash against his own modestly liberal – but uncompromisingly expressed – views, especially his commitment to repeal the Land Apportionment Act. By contrast, the Rhodesian Front opposition exploited every opportunity to capitalize on the fear of many ordinary white Rhodesians, especially those at the lower end of the wages structure, that their jobs would be threatened by black advancement.

Nevertheless, the extent of the Rhodesian Front landslide came as a shock to most outside observers, including, one must admit, the British High Commission. It taught me a healthy lesson on the danger of attempting to prophesy the results of an election in an official despatch. One gets little credit for being right, but loses substantial credibility if one is seriously wrong.

Lord Blake comments[2] that the boycott organized by the Zimbabwe African People's Union (ZAPU) was decisive to the result of the election. Only a tiny proportion of the blacks qualified to register for the vote did so, and fewer still voted. He points out that if five thousand more 'B' roll voters had turned out for the United Federal Party, Whitehead would have won. 'In that sense Joshua Nkomo was the true architect of the victory of the Rhodesia Front.' In a deeper sense, however, Whitehead defeated himself. His undertaking to abolish the Land Apportionment Act was viewed with grave misgivings by many of the whites who had voted for him in 1958; at the same time the tough measures he had taken against the African Nationalist movements virtually ruled out the possibility that a substantial number of blacks would vote for him.

A direct consequence of the change of government was a dramatic shift in the official Southern Rhodesian attitude towards Federation and the Federal Government. Up to that time the two northern territories had made the running in favour of dissolving the Federation and achieving separate independence: now for the first time, though for different reasons, the Southern Rhodesian Government openly joined them. The northern territories regarded the Federation as tying them unwillingly to a white-dominated Southern Rhodesia; the new Southern Rhodesian ministers saw the Federation as providing, at best, a restraint on their own progress towards independence and, at worst, a dangerous link with two emerging black nations whose ultimate aim must be to seek black-dominated independence for the whole Federation. There was a growing public sentiment that if the two northern territories achieved independence it would be intolerable for Southern Rhodesia, by far the most sophisticated of the three, alone to remain a dependency.

Successive white governments in Rhodesia, ignoring the realities, tended to act as if they had the power as well as the will to settle their own future – and that of their black fellow countrymen – without reference to the rest of the world. On 23 November 1962, following the Nyasaland Constitutional Conference, Sir Roy Welensky told Mr Butler that he had no alternative but to tell the people of the two Rhodesias that he intended to use every available means of ensuring that HMG took no further action to break up the Federation, even if this involved a head-on clash between the two governments. 'I hope you will not think I am making idle threats,' he quotes himself as saying,[3] 'or indeed any threats at all. My responsibility is to the people of this country and I must put their interests ... first and foremost, and use what authority I have to protect them.'

In truth, however, he spoke only for his white constituents; alas, he had very few black ones. If, moreover, contrary to his protestations, he *did* intend to threaten HMG, the threat was proved within a year to have been an idle one.

Although they remained on reasonably good personal terms, the political gap between Field and Welensky rapidly widened. Sir Mark Tennant recalls that at a dinner party given by Lord Alport for Mr Butler during his visit to Salisbury in February 1963 Mr Butler asked Mr Field, in connection with some aspect of the possible break-up of the Federation, 'But what would Roy think about that?' Field significantly replied, 'I don't know. But, Secretary of State, does it matter what Roy thinks?'

The Rhodesian Front's platform for the 1962 election had been based on two main planks. First, they rejected 'the principle of subordination to any other Government', by which, on the reasonable assumption that the Federation's days were numbered, they meant the Government at Westminster. Secondly, they declared their intention to seek amendments to the 1961 Constitution on the grounds that without amendment it would bring about premature African dominance.[4] The first of these policies was highlighted by Mr Winston Field in his keynote speech in Parliament on 13 February. On 29 March in London, but urged on by Welensky, he wrote in uncompromising terms to Mr Macmillan,[5] saying, *inter alia*, 'I wish to state that the Southern

Rhodesian Government will not attend the [Federal dissolution] conference unless we receive in writing from you an acceptable undertaking that Southern Rhodesia will receive its independence concurrently with the date on which either Northern Rhodesia or Nyasaland is allowed to secede, whichever is the first.'

This undertaking was not given. Mr Butler pointed out that there were certain procedures to be gone through, including the convening of a conference to discuss financial, defence, constitutional and other matters 'which always have to be settled before self-governing dependencies are granted independence'. For several weeks, and several further exchanges of letters, Field stuck to his demand for 'unqualified recognition' of Southern Rhodesia's right to full independence. But on 15 June, to Welensky's chagrin, he finally accepted the logic that discussions on the terms on which Southern Rhodesia should proceed to independence were, in fact, necessary.

Winston Field was a man of integrity and considerable personal attraction. He was not, however, entirely at home as a politician and the Rhodesian Front's victory at the polls surprised him as much as it surprised Whitehead. He was in fact booked to undertake a tour of South America shortly after the date of the election, which had to be abruptly cancelled when he found himself Prime Minister.

Field had greatly mellowed by the time we got to know him, but as a young man he had a reputation for violent outbursts of temper. One of the stories he told about himself was that shortly after he had been commissioned into the Rhodesia Light Infantry in 1939 he had lost his temper with one of his sergeants and struck him on parade. Field was called before his commanding officer and told that in the normal way he would have been court-martialled. But in wartime conditions, and since in other ways he had the makings of a good officer, he would be given the alternative of transferring to the British Army with the prospect of early service in an active theatre. Consequently he found himself in one of the toughest infantry regiments in the British Army – the Durham Light Infantry – in which he served with distinction throughout the war.

Unlike most of his Cabinet colleagues, Field was essentially a pragmatist. In spite of his party's fears about the dangers of black advancement, he quickly reached the personal conclusion that, whatever posture the Southern Rhodesian Government might feel it necessary to adopt for their own internal purposes, it would nevertheless be greatly to their advantage to establish good working relations with their black neighbours. During the course of his first year in office he accordingly paid at least two unpublicized visits to Nyasaland for talks with Dr Banda, and established a friendly working relationship with him which would have stood Rhodesia in good stead if it had been allowed to mature.

CHAPTER 18

LORD ALPORT DEPARTS

LORD ALPORT MENTIONS[1] that after his return to Salisbury at the end of October 1962, he wrote to Mr Butler to raise the question of his own future. His initial two-year contract had another four months to run, but he records that his letter conveyed his feelings of disenchantment and was intended to give the Government an opportunity of replacing him if they felt that the public interest would be served by doing so.

Working closely with him as I did, I know that this letter was not intended – nor indeed was it taken – as an offer of resignation. It reflected, rather, a combination of frustration at the fact that his ideas, particularly his concept of the 'composite approach', were not being accepted or acted on in White-hall, and a growing awareness that, in loyally responding to a series of changing instructions from London, his relations with the Federal Cabinet were progressively deteriorating. A few weeks later, indeed, they reached a new low, following his press interventions in relation to the debate in the Federal Assembly on 19 and 20 December, and there were widespread rumours that he was about to be declared *persona non grata*.[2] About this time he made a comment to me which I often recalled during my own subsequent career: 'I don't believe in resigning; if they want to get rid of you let them sack you. But in the last resort, old boy, we all have to remember that the man on the spot is expendable.'

Sir Roy Welensky subsequently denied that any action to ask for Lord Alport's replacement was contemplated at that time, and the Federal Cabinet conclusions of the period confirm that the question was not raised formally until later. Welensky's papers, however, contain a letter written early in 1963 from one of the British ex-Ministers referred to earlier, saying that in his (Welensky's) place he would seriously consider declaring the High Com-missioner *persona non grata*. This was a fairly remarkable piece of advice from one of Lord Alport's former ministerial colleagues, who had moreover been his guest at Mirimba House only a few weeks before. This suggestion was actually discussed by the Federal Cabinet on 4 March 1963,[3] when it was agreed that before pursuing it further the matter should first be raised orally by Welensky with the First Secretary of State during his planned visit to London. There is no record of the outcome of any such discussion, or indeed of whether it took place at all.

I was, of course, wholly ignorant of these machinations at the time, though I, like many others, was surprised at the timing of Lord Alport's departure. In the event, his appointment was extended by three months, to early June 1963. Probably to his own relief this did not cover the final act of dissolution of the Federation, which took place at the Victoria Falls Conference at the beginning of July. But many who worked with him felt sad that the implication could be drawn that at the end of his tour of duty one more man on the spot had come to be regarded by a British Government as expendable.

The tempo of events began to accelerate as 1963 advanced. In March Mr Butler finally reached the conclusion that the Federation must be dissolved. In the same month he set up a committee in Salisbury - the Nyasaland Secession Working Party - under the able chairmanship of Sir George Curtis, who had recently retired from the post of Chief Land Registrar, to study the practical implications of secession. Sir George was assisted in this task by James Morgan, who thus once again became directly involved in the affairs of the Federation.

As part of the Federal Government's campaign to leave a viable association between the two Rhodesias after Nyasaland's departure, Sir Roy Welensky had been making some capital out of the desire expressed by the Litunga of Barotseland to seek separate membership of the Federation in order to protect Barotseland from what he regarded as the danger of left-wing domination by UNIP once Zambia became independent. Welensky was supported by Mr Godwin Lewanika, a Federal Member of Parliament and nephew of the Litunga. The Government of Northern Rhodesia had the previous year commissioned Mr R.S. Hudson, a former Secretary for Native Affairs, to report on the future constitutional position of Barotseland, but his report had already been to some extent overtaken by developments in the Federation. In order to obtain an up-to-date impression of local sentiment, therefore, Lord Alport agreed that I should do a short tour of the territory and report back. This idea was endorsed by Sir Evelyn Hone in Lusaka, who kindly offered to make a Piper Aztec aircraft of the Northern Rhodesia Government Flight available for the first part of the journey.

Vera came with me on this tour, the first leg of which took us to Solwezi, a small mining town at the extreme western end of the Copper Belt. From there we flew in appalling weather to Balovale, which I had previously visited with the Monckton Commission in 1960. We were in thick cloud and rain for most of the way, and the position was complicated by the fact that we were unable to raise Balovale on the radio. We could, however, hear continuous chatter from Kamina, the main United Nations airfield in the Congo, and at one point the pilot seriously considered diverting there. Before a final decision was necessary, however, we emerged into clearer weather and landed safely at Balovale.

During the morning I visited the local native authority headquarters while Vera was taken round the district hospital. In the afternoon we both paid a formal call on Senior Chief Ishindi at Makandakunda. As we were leaving, Chief Ishindi, who received us with some ceremony, presented us with a beautiful wooden carving of a bird, which we have treasured as a sort of household god ever since. Wherever we have travelled throughout the world we have never regarded ourselves as properly settled until our Lozi bird has been established in some suitably prominent position to protect the house. There is some family argument whether 'Bird' represents a cormorant or a vulture. I support the former theory – it certainly gives an impression of benevolence rather than one of predation – but I am in a minority. (My wife points out that cormorants are, in fact, more predatory than vultures and that the latter are beneficent, if not necessarily benevolent.)

After leaving Balovale we travelled south down the Zambezi valley on the scheduled Beaver service of Central African Airways. At Mongu, the administrative capital of Barotseland, we met a wide cross-section of the local establishment, both black and white; I also had discussions with the Resident Commissioner on the economic prospects for the territory, which seemed far from good.

From Mongu we crossed the Zambezi to Kalabo. This small settlement lies on one of the major tributaries of the Zambezi, the Luanguinga, which flows in from Angola. Before dinner, the District Commissioner showed us with pride a pair of spotted eagle owls which made a habit of roosting high up in a magnificent tree just in front of his house. Here again I had talks with the District Commissioner and the native authority.

The next day we flew back to Mongu and thence southwards. At Senanga, where we made a further stop, large sections of the runway were under water. In order to enable him to make up his mind whether it was safe to land, the pilot made a slow run down the strip at an altitude of about ten feet with his port wing low so that he could get a better view. He decided, against all appearances, that we could make it – and we did – but the spray thrown up was more appropriate to a float-plane than to one with wheels. Our final stop was at Sesheke, the southernmost district of Barotseland. Here the settlement faces across the Zambezi to the Caprivi strip in South-West Africa (Namibia); a few miles downstream is the mouth of the Chobe River, which provides the boundary between Caprivi and Botswana, then still the Bechuanaland Protectorate. At Katima Molilo, nearby, we visited the base of the Witwatersrand Native Labour Association (Wenela), one of several centres throughout southern Africa where African labour recruited for the Rand gold-mining industry was assembled and transported to and from the mines.

Our tour ended at Livingstone. The Zambezi was in flood, and for the first time we saw the Victoria Falls in their full majesty. Flying down the river, the 'smoke that thunders' could be seen from almost fifty miles away, and as we made our final circuit before landing the roar of the water could be heard even above the noise of the aircraft's engine. We returned to Salisbury the following day. Fascinating as the tour had been, I had to report grave doubts about the viability of Barotseland as a separate component of a revamped Federation.

On Friday, 7 June 1963, the Alports left by train for Beira, where they were due to catch a British India ship bound for London. The next day was the Queen's official Birthday, and I was launched into my new role as Acting High Commissioner by attending a military parade at 8.45 a.m., a reception by Mr Field at 10.15 and a garden party at Government House at 11.30. Whatever their relations with HMG, Rhodesians made a great deal of their loyalty to the Crown. At the Governor-General's party we met Mr George Ivan Smith, who had just been appointed by the United Nations as their representative in East Africa, with responsibility also for covering the Federation. He and his wife came to lunch with us the next day and soon became friends; it was only much later from Conor Cruise O'Brien's book that I learnt of George's bravery during the raid on the American Consul's residence at Elisabethville the previous year when he was acting as United Nations representative in O'Brien's absence.[4]

CHAPTER 19

THE END OF FEDERATION

THE VICTORIA FALLS CONFERENCE opened on Friday, 28 June 1963. My engagement book for the two preceding weeks records a constant stream of callers, all seeking information about the conference: the United States Consul-General, the editors of the main Salisbury newspapers, trade union leaders, leaders of the Southern Rhodesian African nationalist parties (including Mr Chikerema and Mr Nkala), the Japanese Consul-General, the South African Commissioner, to name only a few. At the same time I was having to attend meetings with Taffy Evans, once again the senior official on the Federal delegation; with Mr Field and with Sir Roy Welensky himself. In between times I was keeping in touch with the progress being made by Sir George Curtis and his Nyasaland Secession Working Party, which was highly relevant to the forthcoming conference on the Federation. For good measure, Diana's 21st birthday took place on 15 June and was duly celebrated.

Since Mrs Butler was accompanying the First Secretary of State, Vera came with me to the conference. In order to give ourselves a short break before it started, we decided to drive to the Victoria Falls via Kariba. James Morgan came with us and we all spent the morning of 25 June being taken round the vast underground generator hall before driving on up the lake to the Falls. The following day Mr Field and the Southern Rhodesian delegation arrived; in the afternoon Mr and Mrs Butler and the United Kingdom delegation landed at Livingstone, across the bridge in Northern Rhodesia. Sir Roy Welensky left his own arrival until the last possible moment, the evening of 27 June; the first plenary session of the conference took place at 10 o'clock the next morning.

Curiously enough, very little has been written about the conference by any of the participants. This may well be because Mr Butler played his cards so close to his chest that it was difficult, even for those who took part, to know for much of the time exactly what was happening. Communication was, moreover, made more difficult by the fact that Welensky had imposed on his own delegation a policy of non-fraternization with the UK team; although as the proceedings developed this was not observed to the letter, he maintained it rigidly in public. For the first few days, therefore, scarcely a word was exchanged outside the conference room between the delegations. For Welensky the conference represented the end of his dreams and his ambitions; this perhaps explains why it does not rate even a paragraph in his autobiography.

For Mr Butler personally, there is no doubt that the successful outcome of the conference was a triumph. He made no secret of the fact that he still felt strongly about his defeat by Mr Macmillan in the prime ministerial succession to Sir Anthony Eden in 1956. But he was looking to the future rather than to the past. Rhodesian affairs had not hitherto provided a reliable stepping-stone to political advancement at Westminster, and his acceptance of the Central African Office had clearly been something of a political gamble; if the appointment had not been accompanied by the title of Deputy Prime Minister it could scarcely have been attractive to someone whose political sights were still firmly fixed on the premiership. The conference could therefore in certain aspects be regarded as a make-or-break affair for him: provided it went smoothly, he was still in the race. If, on the other hand, it had led to an indecisive or turbulent result, then his chances of the succession had probably vanished once and for all.

As Mr Butler himself later emphasized,[1] the effort the British delegation had put into the preparation of the briefs played a significant part in the outcome. In the Central African Office he had an expert, articulate and hard-working team. Mark Tennant, the Permanent Secretary of the department, was thoroughly conversant with the political background through his experience as Secretary-General of the Monckton Commission; Duncan Watson, the Under-Secretary, had years of Colonial Office experience of Africa in both the political and security fields. Below these two was a small, highly competent team, including a senior Commonwealth Office legal adviser, Bill (later Sir William) Dale. As a result, Mr Butler came to the conference table far better equipped and supported than his Federal opposite number. (I have no personal inhibitions in saying this; although I was *ex officio* a member of the UK delegation, I had no part in the preparation of the briefs, which had been prepared in London.)

Having arrived at the point where the dissolution of the Federation was the only possible conclusion, it is probably fair to sum up Mr Butler's aims as follows:

(a) to ensure that the break was a clean one – in particular that the financial and political spin-off should not impair the launching of the future independent states of Malawi and Zambia – while trying to preserve the maximum degree of co-operation between the two Rhodesias;

(b) that the question of independence for Southern Rhodesia should not be dragged into the discussion, but should be left for settlement later; and

(c) that the British Government should not be left with sole responsibility for the defence of any or all of the emerging constituent parts.

The first of these aims was partly taken care of by the Nyasaland Secession Working Party. Although Nyasaland was represented at official level at the conference, they did not take an active part in the discussions. But, in common with the governments of Southern and Northern Rhodesia, they accepted Mr Butler's broad precondition of the conference, that the Federation should transfer its powers to the territorial governments in an orderly and speedy manner. Acceptance of this premise was indeed indicated by all concerned, including the Federal delegation, during the first plenary session of the conference, and its achievement was generally regarded as something of a miracle.

So far as the independence of Southern Rhodesia was concerned, Mr Field's presence at the conference provided some assurance that he accepted Mr Butler's priorities; only by continuing to demand independence as a condition of his own attendance could he have put the outcome seriously in doubt.

The third aim, that Britain should not be left carrying an open-ended responsibility for defence, in the event became the most difficult to secure. In particular, the demand that the bulk of the Royal Rhodesian Air Force should be handed over to Southern Rhodesia as a going concern caused long and anxious debate; eventually it was accepted by Northern Rhodesia as part of a package under which they would receive substantial defence aid, including some transport aircraft from the RRAF. The prospective acquisition of the armed forces provided a strong incentive to Southern Rhodesia not to rock the boat at the critical moment; with the benefit of hindsight, however, it is obvious that this powerful accession to Rhodesia's military strength made Mr Ian Smith's subsequent rebellion that much the more difficult to resist.

None of these aims was made explicit at the time; perhaps Mr Butler's greatest skill was in leading the protagonists from one limited objective to another without allowing them to look more than a single hurdle ahead. The negotiation of some form of association between the two Rhodesias was kept officially on the agenda until the conference was well under way; it lapsed only when it became obvious that Northern Rhodesia would have none of it, though it remained an aim of British policy. Sir Evelyn Hone's part in keeping the Northern Rhodesian delegation, led jointly by Messrs Kenneth Kaunda and Harry Nkumbula, on board for the full duration of the conference was a triumph of quiet diplomacy.

The conference formally ended on 4 July. Vera and I had returned to Salisbury the previous day, partly in order to meet our former High Commissioner, Evelyn Baring, now Lord Howick, who was visiting the Federation in his new capacity as chairman of the Colonial Development Corporation. He had been deeply concerned with economic development ever since, as High Commissioner in South Africa, he had played a vital role in the establishment, *inter alia*, of the Usutu Forests and irrigation schemes in Swaziland. In Nyasaland the CDC were engaged in several activities, including setting up a tung oil industry, and if only for that reason Lord Howick was closely interested in the outcome of the Victoria Falls Conference. During his visit we gave a dinner party to enable him to meet members of the local economic establishment; among our other guests was the Southern Rhodesian Minister of Finance, Mr Ian Smith, and his wife.

Almost immediately after Mr Butler's departure we had another visitor, Sir Patrick Dean, then United Kingdom Permanent Representative at the United Nations. Inevitably, much of Dean's work at the United Nations was concerned with the international pressures on southern Africa, and the Commonwealth Office had encouraged him to pay a visit to the area so that he could familiarize himself with the position on the ground before the opening of the General Assembly in September. Since part of his visit coincided with a week-end, Winston and Ann Field very kindly invited him, together with Vera and myself, to spend the Saturday and Sunday with them on their farm near Marandellas. This gave Dean an unrivalled opportunity to hear the Prime Minister's views at first hand and our talks confirmed my earlier impression of Field's realism and pragmatism. It also provided a relaxed interlude in an otherwise somewhat tense period.

On Sunday morning Field took Dean and myself for a drive round the farm, having in advance loaded the back of his Land-Rover with a large and heavy cardboard carton. Many of the farm roads were extremely rough, and as we were bouncing up a track towards his main water-storage dam, Field said, 'Guess what I've got in that box?' We naturally had no idea whatever. 'Actually, it's dynamite,' he said. 'I've just discovered that it's time-expired, and I imagine that by now it's thoroughly unstable. So I'm going to dump it in the dam.'

We expressed some disquiet, and mildly suggested that he might take the bumps a bit slower. 'Ah,' he said, 'this is in the nature of a diplomatic experiment. Just imagine what would happen if we all blew up. A lot of my colleagues would probably be quite relieved at my departure, but I'm sure they would put it about that the wicked British had engineered the assassination of their Prime Minister. But then,' he went on reflectively, 'I suppose it might be argued in Whitehall that the Prime Minister of Southern Rhodesia, with a somewhat quixotic disregard for his own safety, had prepared an elaborate plot to murder two of the senior diplomats involved in selling his country down the river – the Ambassador to the United Nations and the Acting High Commissioner in Salisbury. I wonder which story would be believed. One thing I'm certain of: nobody would regard it as a simple accident!'

Fortunately for all of us, the dynamite survived. Once it had been safely dumped, we had an enjoyable morning looking round the farm. When we got back to the house, Field took the opportunity of a pre-lunch drink to talk seriously. In particular, we discusssed the whole question of political development in Rhodesia in the light of what was by then a certainty – that there was no longer any question of salvaging the Federation. In the course of this conversation Field told us with great solemnity that, as we presumably knew, he was under pressure unilaterally to declare Southern Rhodesia independent. 'But I would like you gentlemen to know – and I am sure you will inform your Government – that so long as I am Prime Minister of this country that will never happen.' He paused, and then added, 'But if I did decide to go it alone, there is nothing you buggers could do about it.'

The first part of Field's statement was in fact a highly significant piece of information. He was not, of course, giving up the claim for Southern Rhodesia's independence; but he was saying that he would not take it without negotiation. It was, moreover, inconsistent with Mr Ian Smith's subsequent claim, reported by Lord Blake and others, that Mr Butler had conned Field and himself into attending the Victoria Falls Conference on the strength of a promise of independence for Southern Rhodesia as soon as the northern territories achieved theirs. Mr Butler himself has specifically denied that he gave any such undertaking; Field's words confirmed this. Consciously or unconsciously, however, the phrase, 'so long as I am Prime Minister', foreshadowed the night of the long knives in 1964, when Mr Smith and his cronies carried out the palace revolution against him as a preliminary to UDI.

By then I was in London and involved in other matters, but I still remember my surprise that Mr Field did not fight back by appealing to the country over the heads of the rebels. What I did not know – indeed at the time few people outside his immediate circle did – was that he was already under the influence of the heart condition which killed him a year or two later.

By now our time in Salisbury was coming to an end. The new High Commissioner, Mr Jack Johnston, arrived on 2 August. He was a career diplomat – later High Commissioner at Ottawa – and an old friend, and the hand-over went smoothly. The machinery agreed at the Victoria Falls Conference for working out the redistribution of Federal functions and assets was already getting into its stride; in August Sir Algernon Rumbold, earlier our Deputy High Commissioner in Cape Town, arrived with a small team to take charge of a committee dealing mainly with the financial implications of the breakup. I see from my engagement book that on 14 August a Mr Ken Flower called on me in the office; he was then deputy chief of the Federal Intelligence and Security Bureau (FISB) under Mr Bob de Quehen; fifteen years later I was to resume contact with him in South Africa in his capacity as chairman of the Rhodesian Joint Intelligence Committee. Ken is a great survivor; at the time of writing he is still one of the senior officials in Mr Mugabe's Zimbabwe.

While Andrew was still with us on holiday we managed to take a week off to visit the eastern districts of Southern Rhodesia and the neighbouring game reserve at Gorongoza in Mozambique. This was well known for its remarkable community of lions, which for reasons best known to themselves had colonized a disued rest-house. Lions could be seen lying and walking around not only in the downstairs rooms, but also on the roof, which they reached by climbing an outside flight of stairs. So domesticated did it all appear that we were not surprised to hear that, not long before, a German girl had leaned out of a car and patted one of the lions on the head. Unfortunately, the lion did not regard itself as domesticated, and the girl lost an arm.

We left Salisbury by train for Beira on the evening of Saturday, 9 November 1963. Diana was on the point of finishing her second year at the university and was anxious to stay on for a further year to complete her degree. We had every reason to believe that Brian Unwin was a factor in this anxiety, but although they had been 'going steady' for over two years we were still not sure of the outcome. Even when they announced that they would come down to Beira by car to see us off, not a word was said about the future. Jack Johnston gave a splendid buffet dinner party to send us on our way, from which the whole office moved in a body to the station for the final send-off. In the course of the proceedings Jack took us on one side and said, 'I know what you must be feeling about Diana. But don't worry. I'll look after her. And if I hear anything I'll let you know!'

The train pulled out of Salisbury station at 9.15. Twenty minutes later it stopped at Ruwa, the first halt on the line to Umtali. There on the platform, to our delight, were Frank and Dolly Wisdom to give us a special send-off of their own.

At Umtali we had to change in the early light of morning onto the Portuguese railcar which took us the rest of the way down to Beira. The first few miles down the escarpment was spectacular, but after that the route passed through low-lying sugar-growing areas containing little of scenic interest except for the long bridge across the Zambezi. Fortunately there was an excellent bar on the railcar, and by the middle of the morning we were sitting in air-conditioned comfort drinking beer. I had noticed earlier that we were keeping close to the road, and near a place inappropriately called Gondola we suddenly saw Brian's open Morris Minor running parallel with us along the road. Rather heartlessly we waved our beer mugs at it; Diana responded with signs indicating that they were dying of thirst.

The Union Castle intermediate-class mailship *Rhodesia Castle* was waiting for us at Beira, as were Diana and Brian. They accompanied us on board for dinner, at which we were made welcome by the chief steward, the redoubtable Mr Wigg. 'Father has asked me,' he began rather mysteriously, 'to find out whether you would care to join him at his table after we sail.' My computer creaked, but then clicked into action. 'Please thank the captain very much for his invitation, but we have had such an exhausting send-off from Salisbury that we were relying on the voyage to recover. We really would prefer a table for two if he will forgive us.'

Mr Wigg undertook to convey my message, though he was clearly somewhat put out by it. I think he regarded it as involving an element of *lèse majesté* which he found difficult to condone. But he was back shortly. 'Father quite understands,' he said, as one might of the Almighty. 'But he wonders if, when you have had a rest, you would join his table after Mombasa.' The faintest hint of the iron hand became discernible. 'I know he will be *very* disappointed if you can't.' We graciously acceded – and so it was. 'Father' turned out to be an excellent host, as well as a highly competent seaman.

We stopped for a day at Dar es Salaam, and this time were made welcome to a newly independent Tanganyika by Mr Stephen Miles, the Acting High Commissioner, and his wife. The next day we spent a few peaceful hours ashore in Zanzibar, where I believe ours was the last passenger ship to call before independence and revolution. I can still remember the extraordinary scent of cloves and spices which came to us across the sea while we were still five or six miles offshore. From Mombasa, where the ship was scheduled to spend three days, we paid a flying visit to Nairobi. There the decorations were going up for *uhuru*, due to be celebrated only three weeks later.

While we were in Nairobi, Mr Malcolm MacDonald, who was about to experience his metamorphosis from Governor to Governor-General, gave me a fascinating and prophetic two-hour briefing. In the course of it I asked him how he saw the prospects of stability in Kenya after independence. His reply astonished me, as no doubt he intended: 'Well, it depends entirely on how long Mzee [Jomo Kenyatta] survives. So long as he is with us the country will hold together. What happens when he goes is another matter.'

I made it clear that what he said amazed me. To someone who had spent the last three years living in Salisbury, his proposition sounded almost incredible: 'Wasn't it your predecessor who described Jomo Kenyatta as "the leader to darkness and death"?'

'You don't want to believe everything you hear,' was Malcolm's answer. 'But I can promise you that what I say is true. The only trouble is that no one knows exactly how old he is. He's probably nearer seventy than sixty. But he's a tough character and I would give him another five or six years, at least. And with luck that should be enough to get an independent Kenya onto a steady course.' In the light of later events, this was an astonishingly perceptive comment.

My most dramatic recollection of the rest of the voyage was of emerging from a cinema performance somewhere off Mogadishu, on a windless tropical night, to hear on a fellow passenger's transistor radio the shattering news that President Kennedy had been assassinated at Dallas. The impact was perhaps all the greater because of the incongruous setting in which we heard it.

A postscript to our tour of duty in the Federation reached us two months later at home at Guildford, when we had a telegram from Diana in Salisbury telling us that Brian was being posted to Ghana and that they hoped to get married in April during his home leave. We could not say that we were surprised – and I don't remember that my permission was asked. But we were delighted all the same.

PART THREE

UGANDA
1967–70

CHAPTER 20

RETURN TO AFRICA: MY OWN SUDDEN ASSIGNMENT

IN 1964, TEN YEARS after I had completed my six months at the Joint Services Staff College, I once again found myself on a course concerned with defence planning and strategy; this time for a year at the Imperial Defence College in Belgrave Square. At that time students were drawn only from the Commonwealth and the United States; later, under its new designation as the Royal College of Defence Studies, membership was extended to officers from other allied countries, including NATO and CENTO members. About a quarter are normally civilians. Amongst a number of fellow students who became close friends during the year was Leslie Harriman, a member of the Nigerian Foreign Service, who later became a colleague as Nigerian High Commissioner to Uganda and subsequently achieved international renown as Nigerian Ambassador to the United Nations and chairman of the Anti-Apartheid Committee.

In January 1965 I was posted as Deputy High Commissioner to Delhi, where for two-and-a-half years I worked under my second non-career High Commissioner, Mr John Freeman. This was an interesting and rewarding period and we confidently expected to remain in India at least until the end of 1967. So confidently, indeed, that Vera chose April of that year to have a routine, but fairly major, operation in the pleasant little hospital attached to the High Commission. This had tiresome complications, as a result of which she had to remain in hospital for five weeks. When she was finally discharged the doctors advised her to leave the heat of Delhi for a fortnight's recuperation at a hill station and to take things gently for the next six months.

Unfortunately, events did not take account of this advice. Three days after Vera was discharged John Freeman received a telegram from the Commonwealth Relations Office asking if he would be prepared to release me to take up appointment as High Commissioner to Uganda in three weeks' time. Although neither Vera nor I had any wish to leave India prematurely, the idea of a mission of our own appealed to both of us. The doctors reluctantly gave Vera permission to forgo her holiday on condition that I managed to

137

secure a short delay in the date of our departure. During the next two weeks, however, instead of being able to rest, she found herself setting up a sort of shop to dispose to our colleagues of a large stock of imported groceries bought to see us through a further nine months in India, and at the same time arranging for our effects to be packed for shipment via Bombay to Mombasa and Kampala. Within three weeks from the time the telegram had been received we were in London for a short period of briefing and reorientation.

During this period we had our first experience of the traditional audience with Her Majesty the Queen to 'kiss hands' on appointment as High Commissioner. This turned out to be a friendly and intimate occasion at which the Queen as it were sets her personal seal on the appointment. It is attended only by the Head of Mission and his wife (or, presumably, husband, though as yet no married woman has been appointed as one of Her Majesty's representatives overseas). In my experience these audiences have invariably demonstrated the extraordinarily detailed professional knowledge and interest which the Queen takes in diplomatic – and especially in Commonwealth – affairs. As a result of her informed and sympathetic discussion of our prospective posts we have always left these occasions encouraged and stimulated.

My predecessor in Kampala had been Roland Hunt, an old friend with whom we had served in South Africa and the Far East. He, poor man, had been withdrawn at short notice following objections raised by the Ugandan authorities to certain precautionary action he had felt it necessary to take to protect the local British community in the face of the prevailing state of lawlessness throughout the country. We therefore arrived with some apprehension, which the experiences of our first few weeks did little to dispel.

It had been arranged that I should present my letters of credence to President Obote about two-and-a-half weeks after our arrival. This was, however, knocked on the head by an event which took place in London only a few days after we reached Kampala.

In those days it was customary for the Chief of the Imperial General Staff, as he was still called, to hold a biennial conference attended by his opposite numbers, the Chiefs of Staff of all the armies of the Commonwealth. This conference went under the code name 'Exercise Unison'. As was usual, the senior officer in charge of the administrative arrangements held a press briefing some weeks in advance to explain the background to the conference and to announce the list of countries taking part. On this occasion there were only two prospective absentees, one of whom was Brigadier Amin, then commanding the Ugandan armed forces. In answer to a question, instead of confining himself to the fact that the Ugandan authorities had declined the invitation to attend, the officer concerned unguardedly, and inaccurately, replied that the two absentee countries had accepted arms from the Chinese; the clear, but groundless implication being that the British authorities had withheld invitations for this reason. This announcement received wide publicity, and not unreasonably President Obote blew his top, saying that, since the British Government seemed determined to maintain an attitude of hostility towards his regime, my presentation of credentials at that moment would be inappropriate and would be postponed indefinitely.

Sensibly, he did not carry this decision to the point where I was totally debarred from doing business with the Uganda Government. In particular, I was permitted to make my planned introductory call on Mr Sam Odaka, the recently appointed Foreign Minister. I was also, fortunately as it turned out, invited about five weeks later to attend a large luncheon party given by Brigadier Amin himself in honour of a visiting team of students from the current Imperial Defence College course. The lunch was a useful occasion and shortly afterwards, with 'Exercise Unison' behind us, I was invited to present my letters to the President.

In the light of later events it is interesting to recall that one of the IDC visitors was Brigadier Chandos Blair, formerly Amin's commanding officer in the Fourth (Uganda) Battalion, the King's African Rifles. Amin arranged a ceremonial parade of his old battalion at Jinja to greet Blair, a friendly gesture which did not escape notice in London; it was, significantly, Lieutenant-General Sir Chandos Blair who in 1975 flew to Uganda with a message to General Amin from the Queen to intercede for the life of the unfortunate, if deeply misguided, Professor Hills, then incarcerated in Kampala under sentence of death.

As we came to know Uganda better, one of the most pleasant aspects of the job was the friendliness and accessibility of some of the younger of President Obote's ministers. The fact that in many cases their wives also had good educational qualifications as teachers or nurses made possible a relaxed and constructive social relationship across the colour barrier which I have seldom encountered elsewhere in Africa. The Foreign Minister, Mr Sam Odaka, and his wife Margaret we counted as particular friends. Margaret had worked for six years as a staff nurse in a London teaching hospital, and indeed spent more of her adult life in England than in Uganda. Mrs Miria Obote had similarly lived for some time in London.

We did not manage to achieve an equally easy relationship with all the members of President Obote's administration. In the field of defence and security, in particular, there was a noticeable conflict between the three or four top personalities involved, none of whom was easily accessible to social contacts. Mr Francis Onama, the Minister of Defence, a tough, unprepossessing and uncommunicative character whose home territory (Madi) bordered on the Sudan, had an uneasy relationship with his nominal subordinate, Brigadier Amin, who came from the neighbouring West Nile district bordering on the Congo (Zaire). Both of them had reason to be jealous of Mr Akena Adoko (Langi), a kinsman of the President who, as head of the so-called General Service Department, exercised a shadowy but pervasive power throughout Uganda. He in turn was in some competition with Mr Erinayo Oryema, the (Acholi) Inspector-General of Police, who controlled the Special Branch and the CID. Of the four, the General Service Department, with its elaborate network of informers, both male and female, who were widely regarded as the President's eyes and ears throughout the country, was undoubtedly the most powerful and the most feared. It was typical of Obote's way of doing things that all four of these men were northerners, but that all four came from different tribes.

Life in Uganda between 1967 and 1970 was often pleasant, occasionally frightening, but never dull. My only previous experience of East Africa, apart from transit stops to and from Rhodesia, had been my brief visits to Nairobi in 1962 and 1963. Uganda was a new world to both of us. One of its greatest attractions was the easy access it offered to the magnificent Murchison and Queen Elizabeth National Parks. Both of these enormous, and at that time well-administered, nature reserves were full of wild life, including not only the more spectacular big game attractions – lions and cheetah, elephants and rhino – but an amazing range of birds and water life.

One of our favourite excursions became the launch trip up the young Nile from Paraa Lodge to the foot of the Murchison Falls. This stretch of river contains one of the largest concentrations of crocodiles remaining in Africa. These are largely supported by the population of Nile perch, some of them running to over a hundred pounds, which also provide splendid fishing. On one occasion we watched a troop of baboons scooping up crocodile eggs from a cache in the sandy bank, and eating them – not at all tidily. Surprisingly, none of the crocodiles lying around in the immediate vicinity took the slightest notice of this attack on their prospective progeny. In the ornithological line, a peculiar fascination of that stretch of water was the presence of a large flock of skimmers which frequented the sandbanks below the Falls. The tall and dignified goliath herons, the wood ibises and spoonbills were also a constant source of interest and pleasure. But, as always, the greatest joy was the harsh and ringing cry of the ever-watchful fish eagle, soaring or perched on a dead branch high above the river.

But I am running ahead. My first meeting with President Obote was when I presented my letters to him on 6 September 1967. Strangely, I can now recall absolutely nothing about that meeting, perhaps because, after my long wait, it was inevitably a somewhat tense occasion. As the months passed, however, I got to know the President well and developed a considerable respect and admiration for him.

Obote's early days as Prime Minister, before he became President, had not surprisingly involved him in constant friction with the then President, Sir Edward Muthesa. Sir Edward, better known as 'King Freddie', was the last – and least – in a line of absolute monarchs of Uganda's largest and most sophisticated tribe, the Baganda. The ruthless autocracy of Muthesa I, the first Kabaka who had contact with the West, is well set out in Alan Moorehead's admirable account of the early European exploration of Uganda and the Sudan in *The White Nile*.[1] Although Sir Edward had little of the strength or ruthlessness of his more notorious forebears, he found it difficult to renounce entirely his innate belief in the divine right of kings. It was perhaps inevitable that Obote took little time to reach the conclusion that there was no room in Uganda for both of them. In February 1966 he staged a *coup* to depose and exile the Kabaka, and thereafter proclaimed himself President in his place, though retaining for the time being the post of Prime Minister.

The *coup* itself was achieved with relatively little bloodshed. But when it was over, Obote took the opportunity to reconstruct his Cabinet, arresting five members in the process. They were still in gaol when we arrived in Kampala. An interim Constitution, establishing Obote as Executive President, was introduced in April 1966; a few weeks later the Attorney-General, Mr Godfrey Binaisa, who himself became President in 1979, courageously resigned in protest against the introduction, contrary to his advice, of legislation providing for preventive detention.

The debate in the Constituent Assembly was still going on when we arrived; the new Constitution passed into law on 8 September, two days after I presented my letters. In the course of the debate the Leader of the Opposition, Mr Abu Mayanja, introduced a number of amendments, some of which the Government accepted. Although through his party, the Uganda People's Congress (UPC), President Obote was in total command of Parliament, he did not entirely ignore the views of the Opposition; this may have been partly due to the impression made on him by the downfall of his Ghanaian mentor and exemplar, Mr Kwame Nkrumah. He was well aware that one of the major factors in Nkrumah's fall was his personal arrogance and his failure to keep in touch with reality.

Nevertheless, it was apparent to an outsider that in Uganda also the growing centralization of power was beginning to lead to a reluctance on the part of ministers and senior civil servants to take decisions without explicit approval from the President. Obote probably recognized that he was walking a knife-edge, but he may have hoped that this would become easier to tread as the years went by. I am sure that he aspired ultimately to achieve, like Kenyatta, the status of *Mzee*, the wise old man at whose feet the younger leaders of Africa would come and sit. The converse danger, that an excessively individualistic and secretive method of working might lead Uganda to regress to the Byzantine atmosphere of fear and distrust characteristic of earlier times, was demonstrated only too convincingly a few years later under Amin's presidency.

One of the principal aims of President Obote's policy was to strengthen the unity of the country by broadening the basis of tribal support for his government. Previously, under British administration, the Baganda had been used as the instrument of indirect rule; in the process of replacing Baganda ministers in his government by representatives of the mainly Muslim northern tribes, as well as by deposing the Kabaka, Obote had made enemies among the Baganda and among the other 'kingdoms' in the south and south-west of the country, whose rulers he also deposed. But the fact that the army had traditionally been recruited from the Muslim north made it easier for him to secure his position while at the same time achieving a genuine balance of tribal influence. One of his favourite slogans was 'We build a Nation', and he was well on the way to achieving this. By 1969, it was indeed calculated that there were more non-Baganda than Baganda living in Kampala, the historic capital of Buganda.

CHAPTER 21

EMBASSY IN RWANDA

SHORTLY BEFORE WE left London in July 1967, I was told that, in addition to holding the appointment of High Commissioner to Uganda, I was to be appointed concurrently non-resident Ambassador to the Republic of Rwanda. I have to confess that when I first heard of this unexpected extension of my parish I had to consult an atlas not only to find out where Rwanda was, but also to discover the name of the capital. It turned out, as doubtless every schoolboy knows, to be Kigali.

Rwanda forms the northern half of the former German colony of Ruanda-Urundi, administered by Belgium between 1920 and 1960 under a League of Nations mandate as a sort of appendage to the Belgian Congo (now Zaire). Lying just south of the Equator on the central spine of the African continent, Ruanda-Urundi had been ravaged by bitter tribal conflict between the tall, aristocratic Watutsi, Nilotic relatives of the Balozi people of Barotseland, and the shorter, more down-to-earth Bahutu, who for centuries had been peasant farmers and hewers of wood and drawers of water to the Watutsi. As elsewhere in Africa, the injection of European influence had upset the traditional tribal relationships; once the Watutsi spell was broken it turned out that the Bahutu were in many ways both more intelligent and more adaptable to western ways than their former masters. Unhappily, the years following their emancipation were marked by an appalling series of tribal massacres and counter-massacres. In the end, partition became the only solution. Rwanda and Burundi were born in 1962.

The British Government had originally been represented in the two territories by a single Ambassador resident in Bujumbura, the capital of Burundi. By the time we arrived, however, British relations with Burundi had effectively been suspended and it had been decided that the United Kingdom should be represented in Rwanda by a non-resident Ambassador based in Kampala. For Vera and myself the appointment involved some three or four visits a year, each lasting about a week and providing a short but enjoyable break from the more relentless tempo of life in Uganda. Almost every visit had its special feature.

The tone was set in September 1967, when I presented my letters to President Kayibanda. This was, I think, the only occasion on which Vera did not come with me. Instead, I was accompanied by Colonel Tommy Newton-Dunn, my Defence Attaché, and William Stober, a Second Secretary in the Kampala Chancery and the only member of my staff who had actually been to Rwanda before.

The permanent caretaker of our do-it-yourself-embassy in Kigali was André, a lean and silent maTutsi tribesman. André's presence was essential whenever we had to open the embassy, since in our absence he alone possessed the key. To make sure that he would be there to meet us after the long day's drive from Kampala always took some organizing; he lived some miles out of town and resolutely, and probably wisely, refused to entrust the key to his nocturnal *alter ego* Albert the night watchman.

On that first occasion, greatly to our relief, since we were much later than planned, André was on parade to greet us, though he made it very clear that once he had let us in and handed over the key his duties for the day were at an end. Unfortunately ours were not: we still had to unpack our stores and make the beds. After fourteen hours driving in the office Land-Rover, much of it over atrocious roads, I for one was too exhausted to bother about a meal and collapsed into bed.

The next day started early. I was woken up by mysterious sounds outside my window. When I dragged myself out of bed I found that Tommy Newton-Dunn and Will Stober were in the garden. I followed them out, only partly dressed, to discover them engaged in an apparently losing battle with the halliards on the embassy flag pole. It was only too clear that the Colonel's military training had not included instructions for raising an ambassadorial flag. By the time I arrived on the scene, the loose end of the halliard had escaped from his grasp and was firmly wedged about fifteen feet up in the rusty pulley at the top of the mast. A ladder was fetched and the Defence Attaché, in full uniform and bravely ignoring both the unhelpful suggestions from his Ambassador and the ironical (but fortunately incomprehensible) comments of the small crowd which was assembling in the road outside, climbed it and with difficulty retrieved the flapping end of the rope. There followed a battle with the toggle, which seemed to be at the wrong end of the flag. In due course, however, the flag was raised. A thin cheer went up from the crowd.

That, or so it seemed, was the precise moment at which André appeared. He was late, but doubtless considered himself entitled to some compensation for the overtime worked the previous evening. He might even have been mingling with the crowd outside. Without a word he walked over to the flag pole, where Tommy, not without satisfaction, was making fast the halliard. Still without a word, he gently but firmly pushed the Colonel on one side, loosened the rope and lowered the flag. Silently he reversed and reattached it, and raised it to the masthead. It had been flying upside down.

The next day I presented my letters to the President. Following normal diplomatic practice, a car was to be sent to take me and my staff the five hundred yards or so to the Presidential Palace. When the time of the appointment had passed by some ten minutes and no car had appeared I began to get anxious; Will Stober was instructed to ring the protocol department to find out what had happened. He got no very clear answer, though he was assured that the car was on its way; it duly turned up a few minutes later. I guessed afterwards that in fact it had probably been sent to collect the President from his home before it could come for us.

When the car did arrive, we were driven up to a tightly-closed entrance at the side of the palace. After a short delay the door was opened and I was ushered from the bright sunlight into a darkened room. The first thing I did was to collide violently at knee level with a low table just inside the door, narrowly avoiding falling flat on my face. President Kayibanda was already in position and waiting for me; we shook hands and it was indicated to me that I should take my place facing him across another low table. In my halting French I read my prepared speech, ending with a strictly orthodox, but admittedly rather pompous, expression of goodwill from Her Majesty The Queen and from the Government and people of the United Kingdom to His Excellency the President and the Government and people of Rwanda. While I was speaking, I was vaguely aware that a cork had popped and drinks were being poured out. When I stopped I thought there might be a formal reply. But instead of making a speech, President Kayibanda picked up from the table between us one of two tumblers each three-quarters full of champagne. 'Cheers,' he said, and sat down. I responded and we chatted for a few moments. But that was it. I was now a proper Ambassador.

After that first visit Vera always came with me, and often one or more of the children if they happened to be visiting us. Never has there been a less formal embassy. We did not have a major political role to play in Rwanda; my most important task was the co-ordination of a small aid programme, much of it concentrated on education, especially English language teaching. The fact that we were there at all was all that was demanded. I have a series of vignettes.

The Queen's Birthday, 1969: Robert, who had recently become administrator of the 69 Theatre Company (the forerunner of the Royal Exchange Theatre) in Manchester, had just joined us for a holiday. Taking our chance on the weather, which was far from settled, we spent the day preparing for the reception, which was due to take place in the garden at sunset. Robert, who was at the top of a rickety step-ladder fixing coloured lights in the trees, let out a howl of consciously operatic intensity. Beside him in the tree two monkeys, clearly under the impression that they were being provided with some new and delicious fruit, were trying to snatch the light bulbs as he fixed them. He was unsuccessfully trying to shoo them away. In due course we and the monkeys became firm friends, but that day we could have done without them.

Inspired by his theatrical experience, Robert wisely insisted on a full lighting rehearsal. Twice we blew the main fuse. Before the third attempt we came to the conclusion that we could use the lights, *or* the oven, *or* the amplifier, but that having more than one on at a time was too much for the system. So at least we knew that the food had to be heated before the guests arrived, and that when the Foreign Minister stood to propose the health of Her Majesty Queen Elizabeth the Second, the lights had to be dimmed so that the national anthem could be played. So that is what we did. None of our guests thought it strange because they also knew the problems. The party was a great success.

Our closest friends in Kigali were our American colleagues, Ambassador Leo Cyr and his delightful wife Kitty. In the course of a dinner party in their house a few days later, Robert found himself sitting next to the Papal Nuncio, a friendly and amusing cardinal, who was also dean of the diplomatic corps. It was clear that they were getting on well together, and in a short gap in the general conversation Robert was heard to observe, 'As I see it, Your Eminence, your problem is basically the same as mine: how to fill our houses.'

A later occasion: the fifth anniversary celebrations of the Université Nationale de Rwanda at Butare. The founder and first Rector of the university was a distinguished French Canadian academic, Père Georges-Henri Levesque, formerly holder of the Chair of Social Science at Laval University, Quebec. It was said that he had resigned from Laval following a disagreement with the authorities which involved a charge of heresy; whatever the truth of this story, he had clearly seized with both hands the opportunity to break new academic ground in Africa. To the outsider, he was a man of great, almost saintly, quality, with the added bonus of a wry sense of humour. The university at Butare was his creation, and he was rightly proud of it.

We attended the celebrations with Ambassador and Mrs Cyr, and for the journey from Kigali we pooled our transport. We and the Cyrs travelled in their jumbo-sized official Chrysler ('we are asking the manufacturers for a cash rebate on top gear, because we have never been able to use it in three years in Rwanda'), the baggage following with my driver in our Land-Rover. Unfortunately, our packing did not fully take account of the truly awful state of the road. When we arrived at Butare, Leo and I had to go straight to the university to meet the Hon. Paul Martin, former Canadian Foreign Minister and later High Commissioner in London, while Vera and Kitty went off to change and unpack. When I got back to the university rest-house where we were all staying, I was greeted with the grim news that a bottle of whisky, intended as a present for our hosts, had broken in my suitcase, and that all my clean underclothes were impregnated with good Scotch. Vera had wrung out what she could, but neither of us had time to do more before we were due on parade for the opening ceremony in the main university auditorium. I found myself seated next to Robert's friend, the Papal Nuncio, and while we were waiting for the academic procession to arrive I told him what had happened.

'I thought that was a very expensive smell,' he said. 'I have always myself regarded Scotch as being for internal rather than external application.'

CHAPTER 22

INAUGURATION OF THE
EAST AFRICAN COMMUNITY

IN SEPTEMBER 1967 the Commonwealth Parliamentary Association held their annual conference in Kampala. Mr George Thomson, who had recently taken over as Commonwealth Secretary, decided to combine his attendance at the conference with a first round of official talks with President Obote. This was particularly welcome to me, since it provided me with an early opportunity after my sticky start to take part in substantive and top-level discussions with Ugandan ministers. It was also useful from another point of view. Obote had perhaps inevitably opened the conference with a *pro forma* attack on British policy towards Rhodesia, and the foreign affairs debate had concentrated almost exclusively on this theme. He was supported by tough speeches from the Indian and Kenyan delegations, and it began to seem as if the conference would become a platform for a major assault on the United Kingdom. But in his talks with the Secretary of State behind the scenes Obote was moderate and constructive, and when Mr Thomson came to wind up the debate a much more accommodating atmosphere prevailed.

Towards the end of 1967, the existing East African Common Services Organization (EACSO), serving Kenya, Uganda and Tanzania, was replaced by a more ambitious form of association – the East African Community. It was decided to inaugurate the Community at a meeting at Arusha on 1 December, and at very short notice invitations were issued to all those states which were diplomatically represented in East Africa.

This invitation placed the British Government in something of a quandary; our relations with the host country, Tanzania, had been broken off because of Tanzania's disapproval of our handling of Rhodesia's unilateral declaration of independence. There was, therefore, a flurry of consultation between London, Nairobi and Kampala to decide whether, and if so how, HMG should be represented at Arusha. The obvious choice was Mr Malcolm MacDonald, who had recently retired as High Commissioner in Nairobi and had been designated as HMG's Special Representative in Africa with a roving commission. He was, moreover, a personal friend of President Nyerere. After he had been nominated, however, it turned out that he was already irrevocably committed elsewhere. The most convenient alternative choice lay between the High Commissioners in Kenya and Uganda. In the end, for a variety of reasons, the lot fell on me.

The final decision was taken only two days before the inauguration. Vera and I flew to Nairobi on the morning of 30 November, picked up an official car kindly lent to us for the occasion by Sir Edward Peck, the High Commissioner in Kenya, and after lunch set off southwards bearing a message of goodwill from the Secretary of State to President Nyerere in his capacity as first President of the Community. We crossed the border into Tanzania at Namanga, where we had our first sight of Masai tribesmen in their somewhat exiguous traditional finery. The drive also gave us magnificant views of the snow-capped crater of Mount Kilimanjaro, and later of the shattered cone of Mount Meru, the dormant volcano overlooking Arusha itself.

On our arrival at Arusha, we found a scene bordering on chaos. Our invitations had, understandably, been issued in the names of Mr and Mrs MacDonald. But when we reported at the New Safari Hotel to check in with the officer in charge of the accommodation arrangements we found that neither we nor the MacDonalds were on his list at all. We sought help from the only familiar face we could see: that of Mr Ian Buist, a former Colonial Service officer on loan from the Ministry of Overseas Development as Assistant Secretary-General of the East African Community. Ian had himself arrived from Nairobi only a few hours ahead of us and, though willing to be as helpful as he could, was also feeling somewhat disconsolate. He had just discovered not merely that he also was not on the list for accommodation, but that the filing cabinets housing his extensive documentation for the meeting had so far not arrived at Arusha at all.

Distrusting the protocol officer's assurance that accommodation would be available for us at Moshi, nearly fifty miles east of Arusha, I decided to put ourselves in the hands of the lady behind the desk at the New Safari Hotel. She was the first, and only, professional we had encountered so far, and after a single telephone call she found us a comfortable room at a hunting lodge only twelve miles out of Arusha.

The next morning we assembled, with several hundred others, in an open-sided marquee facing the dais on which the senior guests were to be seated. Comparing notes with our fellow diplomats we found that we had done exceptionally well in the accommodation stakes; it was, however, not altogether surprising that rooms were at a premium when we learned that the meeting was being attended not only by the three East African heads of state, but also by Emperor Haile Selassie of Ethiopia and President Shermake of Somalia, both of whom were accompanied by large staffs, as well as by President Kaunda of Zambia.

Having become accustomed to President Obote's penchant for punctuality, the one and three-quarter hours we had to wait for the arrival of the visiting heads of state became somewhat tedious, though my own boredom was relieved by being able to watch a small flock of trumpeter hornbills which, throughout the morning and entirely oblivious of the crowds, flapped and sailed in and out of the surrounding trees.

When the VIPs finally arrived, President Nyerere was brisk and business-like in his handling of the proceedings. The theme of his speech was summed up in his concluding words:

We in East Africa believe the institutions and machinery we have established will enable the Community to become quickly recognized as a great contribution to African unity and African development.

Brave words, with which all present must have sympathized. Alas, they failed to survive the test of time. To all intents and purposes the Community was dead within five years.

Although I did not secure the private interview with President Nyerere I had hoped for, and had to deliver the Secretary of State's message through Mr Dunstan Omari, the Community Secretary-General, I did manage to have a few words with him informally after the ceremony. Then, and throughout our visit Vera and I were received with great friendliness by all the Tanzanians we encountered, notwithstanding the fact that our two countries were not in diplomatic relations. We noticed in particular the attention paid to the flag flying on our car – a flag which had not been seen in Tanzania for the past eighteen months. As we drove slowly through the crowds away from the ceremony one young mother with a baby on her back drew her neighbour's attention to it with a delighted squeal of 'Ee-ee, Union Jacki'!

===

CHAPTER 23

ASIAN IMMIGRATION:
THE PRESSURE BUILDS UP

ONE POLITICAL FACTOR in East Africa, which was about to become a major political issue at Westminster also, was the question of the Asian community.

Just as the Indians in South Africa were mostly descended from the indentured labourers brought in to cut sugar cane in Natal, those in East Africa had originally arrived, mainly from Gujerat, to provide labour for the construction of the railway line from Mombasa to Nairobi. Their children and grandchildren had prospered greatly and had taken over an important role in the community as traders and businessmen. Initially there had been no complaints about this from the African population; the services the Indians provided – particularly those of the up-country traders, who were prepared to work long and unsociable hours for a reasonable profit – were not in competition with those offered by the indigenous population or by the established Europeans. But as time went by, the profits they made became the subject of envious criticism by Africans who were themselves beginning to take an interest in commerce.

A few of the Asians, by expanding and diversifying their companies, had become large employers and provided a large part of East Africa's export earnings as producers of sugar, coffee and cotton. Two of the leading Ugandan families, both of which had built up substantial commercial empires on the basis of their sugar estates, were the Mehtas and the Madhvanis. Even before we left India on our way to Uganda we had heard from Andrew in England that the father of one of his school friends, Nitin Madhvani, 'had a sweet factory' at Jinja, not far from Kampala. It turned out that the 'sweet factory' was a multi-million-pound complex of industrial and commercial undertakings, and that Jayant Madhvani, the boy's father, was one of the outstanding leaders of the Asian community in Uganda.

The legal position of the Asian community *vis-à-vis* the United Kingdom was a complicated one. It had been agreed as part of the independence settlements in each of the three East African territories that non-African residents, including Asians as well as whites, provided they were citizens of the United Kingdom and Colonies, should have the right to retain that citizenship if they opted to do so. Most of them had spent their entire lives in East Africa, and it was assumed – indeed they assumed it themselves – that they would in general wish to stay there. As holders of United Kingdom passports, however, they were entitled to believe that they would be admitted to Britain if they ever found it necessary to leave East Africa. During the disturbances after independence there had already been a trickle, which by now was increasing to a stream, of those who had decided to use their UK passports to seek entry to the British Isles. This flow, when added to the numbers of immigrants from elsewhere, was beginning to create social and political resistance in Britain; the law was accordingly amended so as to control and if necessary limit the numbers permitted to settle here.

Initially it was mainly in Kenya that the pressure built up to force the Asians to leave, but by the end of 1967 I was becoming aware, and starting to report to London, that, unless some sort of safety valve could be established under which a reasonable quota of immigrants could be admitted to the United Kingdom, there would sooner or later be an explosion in Uganda as well. Although President Obote had so far taken a pragmatic and tolerant line, he could not necessarily be expected to do so indefinitely in the face of action being taken elsewhere in East Africa.

This warning was confirmed even earlier than I expected. The first overt sign that Obote was taking a personal interest in the question came, characteristically, out of the blue. On 1 March 1968 I had been invited to attend the annual St David's Day dinner given by the Welsh Society of Uganda at the Kampala Club, of which the membership was still predominantly white. It had become known a few weeks earlier that the municipality of Kampala, doubtless with the knowledge of the Uganda Government, was considering the possibility of terminating the club's lease and using the site for its own purposes. The membership was in a somewhat jumpy state as a result.

At about ten o'clock, just as we were finishing dinner, but before the speeches, the club secretary came in looking somewhat flustered and gave me a note. This told me that a member of Obote's staff was waiting outside with instructions to ask me to accompany him to a meeting with the President immediately. There was no indication of what he wanted to see me about.

I was by then in a reasonable state of post-prandial euphoria, but I was uncomfortably aware that Obote would not have sent for me at that hour without good reason. A range of possibilities passed through my mind. In case something untoward was about to happen, I showed the note to the president of the society, who was sitting next to me, and told him, only half jokingly, that if I were not back within an hour he had better inform the Chief Justice – a rather dour Nigerian who lived only a few doors away from the club.

The President's emissary, who was waiting for me in the hall, offered me a lift. In the circumstances, however, I thought it wiser to use my official car and told my driver to follow our guide. Rather to my surprise we were led not to Obote's office in Parliament, where he often worked late, but to one of his private houses only a few hundred yards from my own.

When I arrived, I was taken straight in to a drawing room where the President was waiting. He seemed to be in a cheerful, but rather puckish, mood and started by commenting on the fact that I was in fancy dress, a reference to my dinner jacket. I explained that I had come from something that he would well understand, even if he did not necessarily approve of it – a tribal celebration – and that it was customary for Europeans as well as Africans to wear traditional finery on such occasions. He laughed and said that in that case I had better have a tribal drink, and pressed a large whisky into my hand.

Once we had settled down to talk, his mood changed. He said that he was extremely disturbed at the negative line being taken by HMG on the question of admitting Asians from Kenya to the United Kingdom. He professed to be all the more shocked that this line was being taken by a Labour government, which he expected to behave as a friend of Africa. He personally had no wish to drive large numbers of Asians out of Uganda; they were on the whole doing a useful job. But it was inevitable that over the years ahead more and more of their jobs would be required by Africans. The British Government acknowledged responsibility for them, otherwise why should they issue them with passports? But our policy seemed to be to admit them to Britain only if they were destitute. Surely it was better to take those who had to leave while they still had money to support themselves rather than to wait for months or years until their money ran out.

I replied that the question also presented serious problems for Britain. This was not strictly a party issue; we were willing to admit Asians as quickly as they could be absorbed, but we did not wish to encourage the establishment of ghettos, which could only lead to racial conflict. We appreciated the fact that up to now the Uganda Government had not been forcing the issue, and I hoped that he would continue to exercise restraint.

The discussion went on for some time. It was clear that I had not convinced him; equally, however, he seemed to indicate that the Uganda Government would not take drastic action until it became necessary. I felt, however, that we had managed to reach a certain measure of understanding and I decided on the spur of the moment to take the opportunity to raise an issue of my own. I therefore told him, in the context of the Welsh tribal celebration, of the anxiety among some British expatriates in Kampala that they might be in danger of losing their club. As he knew, the club was now open to African and Asian members, though my understanding was that not very many had applied for membership. In the meantime, however, on the assumption that he did not want the Europeans to leave so long as they had a useful part to play, I could assure him that the club offered a useful and harmless safety valve. If it were removed, the resulting discontent would not be to Uganda's advantage any more than it would be to that of the European community.

Rather to my surprise, Obote responded favourably to this argument, and gave me an assurance that no action would be taken against the club without further discussion. So long as he remained President he was as good as his word.

By the time I got back to the dinner it was nearly a quarter to twelve. The speeches were happily long since over, but it was clear that even if anyone had remembered my absence, they had certainly not reported it to the Chief Justice. I was able to pass on word of Obote's undertaking, and the news got around fairly quickly that the club had been given a reprieve.

The next day, HRH Princess Marina visited Uganda in the course of a tour of East Africa, and spent a few days as the guest of President Obote at State House, Entebbe. Princess Marina's beauty and serenity were as remarkable as ever, and her presence effectively reduced the political temperature. It came as a great shock to learn of her death only a few weeks later. During her stay she was joined for a few days by Prince Michael of Kent, who stayed on with us in Kampala for two nights after her departure. While he was with us he was taken out for the evening with a party of other young people by Barrie Gane, a First Secretary on my staff, and his wife Liza, to dance at one of the local night-clubs with which Kampala was well provided. We heard later that the party had got back to the house at about 4 a.m. after a swim in the Ganes' pool. Vera's mother, who was staying with us, heard nothing of Prince Michael's return and was touched when he told her the next morning that when he came to bed in the room next to hers he had taken off his shoes to avoid disturbing her.

In early March we were visited by an inspection team led by Peter Murray, a former Ambassador in Phnom Penh. While he was on the job we took Vera's mother for a short tour to show her something of the country. We spent two nights at a guest-house run by Mr Don Baggaley, a noted conservationist, on the edge of Uganda's largest remaining area of primary woodland, the Budongo Forest. On a later visit we were to see a family of wild chimpanzees in his garden. But this time our visit was rudely interrupted. During the afternoon, while I was out on Lake Albert fishing for Nile perch, Vera received a message reporting that there had been trouble earlier in the day at the High Commission offices in Kampala, and that I was to get in touch with the Deputy High Commissioner as soon as possible.

There was no telephone in the house and by the time I got back from the lake there was nothing we could usefully do that night, especially as the radio news reported that everything was now quiet in Kampala. The next morning we drove to Masindi, some twenty miles away, from where I telephoned Peter Foster, my deputy, in Kampala. Peter confirmed that all was quiet and that he did not expect any more trouble. I nevertheless felt that I should see things for myself, and asked him to arrange for an aircraft to pick me up from the airstrip at Chobe Lodge in the nearby Murchison National Park early the next morning.

We were at breakfast when a single-engined aircraft circled the camp; I had an overnight bag packed and Vera drove me the few hundred yards to the airstrip. The aircraft, which by then was standing in the clearing which did service for a terminal area, was almost surrounded by a large flock of Abdim's storks, which were then assembling for their migration north. As we taxied out the whole flock took off in front of us; the pilot had to give them two or three minutes to get clear before we could take off ourselves.

When I arrived in Kampala I heard the full story of the disturbance. It appeared that early on the Saturday morning the duty officer had been warned by contacts at the university, and later by the police, that a major student demonstration was to take place in support of the Asian UK passport-holders who were being compelled to wait their turn for admission to the United Kingdom. For most of its march from Makerere the procession was escorted by the police; when the crowd began to assemble outside our offices, however, the police faded into the background and made little or no attempt to control it. For some time the demonstrators shouted and chanted slogans, and then demanded to see me. Peter Foster told them that I was away; he was acting on my behalf. He added that he would be prepared to talk to a small deputation; quite rightly, however, he refused to allow more than a few individuals into the building. At some point the crowd began throwing stones, and since the front of the building was largely made of glass – a feature of post-war diplomatic buildings which the Department of the

Environment's architects for far too long persisted in providing – a good deal of damage was done in a short space of time.

It so happened that Peter Murray, the inspector, was working in a room on the first floor when half a brick came through his window and a fragment of flying glass made a tear in the sheet of paper on which he was writing his report. A young Ugandan university lecturer at the back of the crowd told me a week or two later that Murray had scarcely looked up from his writing when the window was broken; apparently his *sang froid* had a considerable effect on the demonstrators and helped to keep the temperature down. The question was going round the campus the next day. 'Who was the mad Englishman who went on writing when his windows were being smashed?'

I took the opportunity of my return to Kampala to inspect the damage and to deliver a strongly-worded protest to the Foreign Ministry, including a request for compensation. Although the Uganda Government strenuously denied that they had any part in organizing the demonstration, the noticeable failure of the police to disperse it or to take any action against the stone-throwers suggested that the authorities were not averse from indicating to me and to the British Government that they disapproved of our lack of action on the Asian question.

Over the following months the pressure on this issue built up steadily, though the Ugandans still left most of the running to Kenya. In June 1969 a meeting of heads of mission from African posts took place in London. The two main subjects were the future of Rhodesia, and Asian immigration. Sir Eric Norris, who had recently taken over as High Commissioner in Nairobi, and I were both convinced that some action to reduce the rapidly growing waiting lists was essential if we were to avoid a major explosion on the ground, and this view was shared by the Commonwealth Office. But parliamentary pressures were such that ministers in other departments were deeply reluctant to liberalize the quotas far, or quickly, enough to reduce the pressure in Kenya and Uganda significantly. Eric and I therefore suggested that we should be allowed to present our case directly to the department responsible for immigration policy, the Home Office, preferably at ministerial level. Somewhat to my surprise the idea was taken up, and it was arranged that we should meet the Home Secretary, then Mr James Callaghan.

I can't say that the meeting was a great success. Eric and I based our arguments mainly on what we believed to be enlightened British self-interest – that unless some limited action to speed up the process were taken quickly and voluntarily, we might find ourselves faced with an uncontrollable flow from all three East African countries simultaneously on a timetable not of our choosing. We also made use of the less hard-headed, but, we believed, valid, argument that the possession of a British passport, if it meant anything at all, must at the end of the day bear some relation to the possessor's right to enter, and even reside in, the United Kingdom if he should need to do so.

Neither of these arguments was effective. So far as the Home Office was concerned, considerations of domestic politics were, perhaps understandably, overriding. No concession was made to admit a substantially greater number of East African Asians until a year or so later when the pressure became so great, in Uganda as well as Kenya, that action became unavoidable. But by then, as we and others had forecast, the trickle had become a flood, and the problem of absorption had greatly increased.

CHAPTER 24

RHODESIA: NOISES OFF

ALTHOUGH PRESIDENT OBOTE was not always the easiest of men to do business with, his influence with the rest of black Africa was considerable and the British Government were understandably anxious to keep him broadly on their side in relation to the continuing negotiation on the future of Rhodesia.

In order to achieve this there was a fairly regular flow of top-level visitors to Uganda. Mr Malcolm MacDonald, HMG's Special Representative in Africa, was a particularly frequent and welcome visitor. He got on well with all the African Commonwealth leaders; his frank, friendly and unassuming approach enabled him to put across unpalatable facts in a positive and persuasive way. He and Obote had known each other for some years and had achieved a considerable *rapport*; I found it invaluable, especially during my settling-in period, to be able to use Mr MacDonald's ready access to the President to build up my own contacts with him. At a later stage Obote made the point that he would prefer to deal with one official representative of the British Government – the High Commissioner – rather than two, but he continued to welcome Malcolm to Kampala as a personal friend and counsellor.

Mr Ian Smith had displaced Mr Winston Field as Prime Minister of Southern Rhodesia in April 1964. In October of that year he had dismissed Major-General Jock Anderson, the loyal and courageous commander of the Rhodesian Army, and replaced him with the 'more pliable' Brigadier Putteril.[1] At the end of May 1965 Smith also removed the High Commissioner in London, Mr Evan Campbell, who had been outspoken against unconstitutional action, and on 11 November he took the ultimate and disastrous step of unilaterally and illegally declaring Rhodesia independent.

Viewed from London, the next few years were bedevilled by the problem of Rhodesia, which presented a real threat to the unity, and even, at times, the very existence of the Commonwealth.[2] At each successive Commonwealth Conference the issue was raised in one form or another with increasing vehemence. Why could Britain not terminate the rebellion by force of arms? Why did we continue to negotiate with the illegal regime? Why did we not impose effective sanctions to deprive Rhodesia of vital supplies? These were all highly logical questions, but the fact was that once the British Government had taken the decision in practical terms that armed intervention was not on – and the spectre of 1776 may not have been entirely absent from their minds – it had to be accepted that negotiation combined with some form of sanctions, the carrot and the stick, offered the only realistic way forward.

By the time I arrived in Uganda there had already been one major attempt to achieve a solution through negotiation – that by Mr Harold Wilson on HMS *Tiger* in December 1966. This had failed because Mr Smith, having apparently reached agreement in principle during the meeting, had been talked out of it by his Cabinet – or, some would say, their wives – on his return.

The next major attempt took place in October 1968. Vera and I were on home leave when I received a summons to attend a meeting with Sir Morrice James, the Permanent Under-Secretary of State at the Commonwealth Office. At this meeting I was told that the Prime Minister (Mr Wilson) had decided to have a second meeting with Mr Smith at Gibraltar, this time on HMS *Fearless*, and that this would start on 9 October. In order to prepare for this meeting it was proposed to send two emissaries, Mr Malcolm Mac-Donald and Mr Maurice Foley, the Parliamentary Under-Secretary of State, to visit between them most of the Commonwealth states in Africa. Because of Obote's expressed preference to deal with the High Commissioner rather than with special envoys, however, the Secretary of State proposed to send me to Kampala as a third member of the team with a personal message for him. I was to leave London on the following Monday, 7 October, so that I could see Obote the day before the *Fearless* meeting was due to take place.

This was not particularly welcome news, though I was assured that I could complete my leave after I had delivered my message. In another way, how-ever, it was professionally reassuring to be allowed to deal with Obote my-self. On 8 October 1968, therefore, I arrived back in Kampala. My return had been kept a complete secret, even from our house servants, because of the need to protect the security of the meeting on HMS *Fearless*, so that when I drove up to the house with Peter Foster, who had been Acting High Commissioner in my absence, my arrival came as a total surprise to the staff. It was a great credit to them that everything was in first class order and that Belinda, the dog, was obviously well and happy.

I called on President Obote the same afternoon and gave him my message, laying emphasis on the fact that I had been asked to interrupt my leave to do so. He pressed me in particular whether we were going to insist on the condition laid down at the 1966 Commonwealth Conference that NIBMAR ('no independence before majority rule') should be a prerequisite of any settlement. I made it clear that Mr Wilson would be entering the talks without preconditions, but that he had personally accepted NIBMAR and that I was in no doubt that majority rule was the ultimate aim. Obote responded well, and expressed appreciation at being kept informed of our intentions.

The ninth of October, as it happened, was the sixth anniversary of Uganda's independence, and I found myself swept up in a series of official engagements, including a military parade and an Independence Day ball. The same evening Mr Foley, who had completed his own round of talks in Zambia, Tanzania and Kenya, arrived in Kampala to attend a meeting of the East African Community. He called on President Obote the next day and sounded him out on a wider front, making particular reference to President Nyerere's recent decision to nationalize the (mainly British) banks in Tanzania. Obote restated his conviction that Smith should be removed by force, which he argued would not have the dire consequences forecast by successive British Governments. But for good measure he added that he regarded nationalization of the banks as irrelevant, making the point that the prompt and adequate compensation to which they would be entitled would be far too expensive for Uganda to contemplate, at least at that stage.

By the end of the week the talks on HMS *Fearless* ended, once again without result.[3] I had believed that I should be allowed to return to London as soon as my mission was completed, but day after day went by without any instructions from London, possibly because in the meantime the merger of the Commonwealth Office with the Foreign Office had taken place. The delay was all the more embarrassing because Foster had naturally undertaken a number of engagements as Acting High Commissioner; since he was no longer officially in charge there was often doubt whether he or I should attend them. Eventually, I decided that I had no alternative but to draw attention to the fact that I was still languishing in an official vacuum. I accordingly sent a personal telegram to Sir Paul Gore-Booth, the new head of the combined Foreign and Commonwealth Office, whose deputy I had been for a short time in Delhi, beseeching him to say something, if only goodbye. I received a sympathetic but firm telegram in reply, telling me that ministers were still considering their course of action following the breakdown of the talks and that in the meantime I was to remain at my post. It was a further week before I was finally let off the hook. I eventually returned to London on 27 October, having been away for almost three weeks to do one day's work.

For the rest of our time in Uganda Rhodesia remained a running sore, though Obote never made a major issue of it with me. It became increasingly apparent as the months went by that, although in theory sanctions had been tightened up following the failure of the *Fearless* talks, the only country that was enforcing them at all thoroughly was Great Britain. On several occasions I was instructed to draw the Uganda Government's attention to the fact that this or that aircraft calling at Entebbe was engaged in sanctions-busting. On at least one of these occasions an aircraft was stopped to enable possible contraband to be checked, but I cannot remember a single instance in which action followed in the courts of any African country.

In July 1969 one of the most memorable events of our tour of duty in Uganda took place. This was the visit of Pope Paul VI. Vera and I had met him briefly when, as Cardinal Montini, the Archbishop of Milan, he had visited Kariba while we were in the Federation. The specific occasion of the present visit was to celebrate the canonization of the twenty-two young Catholics who had suffered martyrdom under the perverted and unstable Kabaka Mwanga, who in 1884 succeeded Muthesa I. But the underlying purpose was the wider one of making the first visit to Africa by a reigning pontiff. In this context the Holy See made it clear that the visit was not to be regarded as one to Uganda alone. To underline this, one of the principal events of the visit was the Pope's consecration, before a huge congregation, of a number of new bishops drawn from all over Africa.

The visit was warmly welcomed by President Obote, who saw in it an opportunity to put Uganda – and himself – on the world map. It also fitted in well with his publicly announced policy of abolishing tribalism and sectarianism. (He tried, incidentally, to use the opportunity to bring together General Gowon and General Ojukwu for talks on the war in Biafra, but they declined the invitation.) The preparations were on a grand scale: the Kampala Municipality was asked to cater for a possible influx of two million people; vast quantities of flags and souvenirs were ordered, including several million yards of commemorative cloth bearing portraits of the Pope and Obote, and an enormous shrine and open-air auditorium was constructed at Namugongo, the scene of the martyrdom.

In reporting on the visit at the time I commented that it was perhaps not altogether fanciful to recall H. M. Stanley's famous letter to the *Daily*

Telegraph in 1875, in which he remarked on the high degree of organization he found in Buganda, and called for 'pious and practical men' to come and evangelize the local people. The Church Missionary Society responded by plunging holus-bolus into central Africa, instead of sticking to their announced plan to work gradually inland from the coast. The Catholic White Fathers shortly followed suit. In a spirit of enthusiastic competition the rival denominations built their cathedrals on the tops of opposing hills near Kampala, the Anglicans at Namirembe and the Roman Catholics at Rubaga. In the early years their followers from time to time engaged in shooting at one another across the intervening valley.

In this context the Pope's visit was of particular significance by laying emphasis on the ecumenical aspects, and went a long way to heal old wounds. For me, one special incident stands out. Since the original martyrs included Anglicans as well as Roman Catholics, there was a small Anglican shrine at Namugongo as well as the elaborate Catholic one. After the consecration of the Catholic shrine, which took place in a vast and colourful ceremony, the Pope also took part in a service in honour of the Protestant martyrs. This was conducted by the Anglican Archbishop, the Rt Rev. Erica Sabiti, whose sermon called for 'a greater realization of all that we share together in our one Saviour and Lord'; the Pope also made a short address and read several prayers. After the service, clergy and congregation moved in procession to the adjacent Anglican shrine. As representatives of the Protestant country most directly involved, Vera and I found ourselves close behind the Pope and Archbishop in the procession. When he reached the shrine the Pope prostrated himself. Knowing that Archbishop Sabiti was himself a low churchman from the London Missionary Society congregation, I watched with deep interest how he would react. There was a moment of agonized hesitation. Then he prostrated himself too.

A day or two later I met the Archbishop and ventured to congratulate him on his action, telling him that I realized that it had been a painful decision. He thanked me for what I said, adding that he believed that he had done the right thing. 'But I wish more of my flock felt as you do. I have had a lot of complaints from my clergy about what I did; I really think that some of them believe that I am going over to Rome.'

The Pope's visit was full to the point of exhaustion. Although the total number of pilgrims did not come up to expectation, heads of state from Zambia, Tanzania, Rwanda and Burundi attended, as well as ministers from the Congo (Kinshasa), Dahomey, Gabon, Kenya, Nigeria (and Biafra), Senegal, Sudan and Upper Volta. To all these the Pope gave audience. He addressed the Uganda Parliament; he attended a seminar organized by the Catholic hierarchy; he visited hospitals and clinics; he inducted bishops; he received a delegation of Muslims; he even received the diplomatic corps. All who met him were impressed; possibly more so in the informal and less organized atmosphere of a small African country than might have been the case in the more sophisticated atmosphere of the Vatican. It was undoubtedly a great occasion: what has happened subsequently in Uganda gives it at this distance an almost magical quality.

It is perhaps worth adding a footnote. Two Englishmen, Canon John Findlow, the representative at the Vatican of the Anglican Archbishoprics of Canterbury and York, and Mgr Basil Loftus, subsequently Pro-Nuncio in Rwanda, played an important part in advising on the preparations for, and organization of, the visit; one in the Vatican and the other in Kampala. I know enough of visits of this kind to be well aware that things do not go right by accident. This visit, especially as it applied to the delicate relationship between the Anglican and Roman communions, went conspicuously well. The fact that there were sensible and pragmatic people, both deeply aware of the problems, in key positions at both ends made a real contribution to this success.

CHAPTER 25

AMIN AND THE UGANDAN ARMY

IN VIEW OF what happened later, it would be difficult to write about Uganda without saying something about General Amin. I had only a limited personal acquaintance with him, though several members of my staff knew him better. But it was part of my job to form an assessment of the military and political significance both of Amin and of the forces under his command.[1]

The periods before and after the deposition of the Kabaka had been marked by serious unrest within the Ugandan armed forces. After the last British officers had left, the first Ugandan army commander, Brigadier Opolot, continued to maintain a mainly Baganda officer cadre. As Obote's conflict with the Kabaka built up, however, he moved Opolot sideways into the post of Inspector-General of the armed forces, promoting Amin, Opolot's exact contemporary in seniority, as Chief of Staff in his place. Shortly before Muthesa's overthrow, Opolot was arrested and imprisoned; by the time we arrived in Uganda Amin was firmly established in command. In the process, he had replaced most of the Baganda officers with cronies of his own, drawn mainly from the northern tribes of Acholi and West Nile, but had achieved some success in stabilizing the internal situation. Even in March 1968, however, I noted in a report to the CRO that the army had been curbed, not tamed.

What sort of a man, then, was Amin? Considering the disadvantages under which black members of the colonial defence forces operated until a short time before independence, he had a good and effective career in the King's African Rifles. Heavyweight boxing champion, service in Malaya, promotion to sergeant-major; all this without formal education other than the usual army courses. In British terms he could be regarded as a professional soldier with the qualities of a relatively uneducated warrant officer: powers of decision in a limited field; lack of imagination; respect for discipline; loyalty to his unit, to his officers and to the Queen. Not, I suspect, any great loyalty to Uganda as such: tribal loyalties almost certainly counted for a great deal more. (It is significant that in retrospect Amin seemed to resent the British intervention to quell the army mutiny in 1964 less than Obote, who had a

part in requesting it.) In 1961, a year before independence, Amin was commissioned as a lieutenant; ten years later he was President of Uganda, self-
promoted Field Marshal and 'Conqueror of the British Empire'.

There was a parallel between the recruitment of British colonial military
units in East Africa and those in the Indian sub-continent. It was always
assumed by British military pundits in India that the development of an
efficient army depended on drawing mainly on elements of the population
who had military traditions: it was, for example, firmly believed that, man for
man, the Muslims made better soldiers than the Hindus, and that northerners were militarily superior to southerners. Until India defeated Pakistan
in the 1965 war, almost every British Army officer who had any first-hand
knowledge of the pre-independence Indian Army confidently assumed that
the Pakistanis would wipe the floor with the Indians.

No doubt so long as it was possible to treat undivided India as a whole this
made good sense; it was easier to recruit and train adequate numbers of men
from tribes and areas with military traditions than to try to pick soldiers
from a representative cross-section of the population as a whole. Since,
moreover, the recruits were unlikely to have any influence on policy – the vast
majority of the officers continued to be drawn from the Imperial power – the
system merely confirmed the admirable military axiom that 'bullshit baffles
brains'.

It was much the same in East Africa. The traditionally military classes
in Uganda were the relatively uneducated northern tribes: Acholi, Madi,
Kakwa. By recruiting from the north, moreover, there was the added advantage of maintaining a geographical balance of power. In colonial days Britain
had chosen to exercise indirect (political) rule through the more sophisticated
Baganda; it was convenient – and only fair – to call on the apparently
apolitical but physically tough northern tribes to man the army. Before
independence, as in India, the officers were, and were expected to continue to
be, British; it did not seem to matter, therefore – indeed it was regarded as
helpful – that the troops on the whole lacked formal education.

This, then, was the background from which Amin emerged as commander
of the Ugandan forces, a background designed more for producing a platoon
commander than a general officer commanding, still less a president. He was,
moreover, virtually illiterate; his command even of Swahili, the language of
the army, let alone his command of English, was fairly basic. When decisions
were called for, he took them, as he had been trained to do. But he could not
easily weigh the pros and cons in discussion, nor could he argue effectively
with the better educated younger officers and civil servants. If the decision he

arrived at was too simple to meet a complicated situation, his answer, like that of Henry VIII, tended to be cut off someone's head, especially if that person had given him the advice on which he thought he had acted.

I have often been asked if I regard Amin as mad. My answer is no, not mad, but stupid and ruthless – a dangerous combination for a man in the position of absolute power in which he eventually found himself. Intellectually he was totally out of his depth. But he was a survivor and it was others who died.[2]

So much for Amin. What about his policies? So long as he was in a working symbiosis with President Obote, I have no doubt that the more difficult, politically-oriented decisions were taken by Obote. One of these the curious alliance with Israel. There was no doubt plenty in it from Israel's point of view. Uganda formed a vital link in the chain of allies and intelligence-gathering vantage-points around the Arab world which Israel desperately needed so long as the Arabs were united against her. Nevertheless, the close defence relationship between Israel and Uganda was never reflected in Ugandan support for Israel's policies in the Middle East. From Uganda's point of view, Israel's main value was to provide a Third World source of arms and technology which did not have the tag of alignment with Britain, the United States or the Soviet Union.

I have no doubt that this relationship was primarily established by Obote; apart from anything else, it would not have come naturally for Amin, a Muslim, to set up so close a working relationship with the Jewish state. As Amin gained in confidence and experience, however, it was almost certainly he who began to hedge Uganda's bets by encouraging a liaison with Czechoslovakia and the Soviet Union. Israel's French-designed Fouga trainers were all that the Ugandan Air Force really required – where after all was the threat? – but when Russia offered more powerful Mig 17s, why should he refuse?

The fact that Amin was beginning to switch to the Soviet bloc as a source of military supplies did not, however, mean that he entirely closed his options with the West. In January 1970, only a fortnight before we finally left Uganda, the British Aircraft Corporation arranged a demonstration flight of a BAC 1-11 for Amin's benefit. I accompanied the General on this flight and was fascinated at the somewhat naive interest he displayed in the aircraft not merely as a transport but also for dropping paratroops. Noticing that the aircraft was fitted with self-operating steps at the rear entrance, Amin cross-questioned the demonstration team closely on whether these could be lowered in flight. He made a good deal of the fact that he had made several parachute drops from a Dakota, and that it would be much more comfortable to jump from the rear of a sophisticated aircraft like the BAC 1-11. Perhaps fortunately, however, no purchase materialized.

All the new equipment Amin demanded cost money, and at quite an early stage Mr Wakhweya, the able Secretary for Finance, was advising his minister that defence expenditure was getting out of hand and must be reduced. But this may well be where Amin's personal hold over Obote came in; he may have made it clear that unless he got the money he would give away some of the secrets they shared. Once Obote had lost his financial control over Amin, the latter's power rapidly increased; so, in parallel, did the power of the Soviet bloc. It did not take long for the Israelis to be kicked out of their predominant position and replaced by an improbable consortium of the Libyans and the Soviet bloc. At this point the situation was ripe for Amin's own take-over bid.

In parallel with the deliberate strengthening of his position *vis-à-vis* Obote, Amin also took steps to build up his own protégés within the army itself. The murder of the garrison commander at Masindi in late 1969, and his replacement by an officer loyal to Amin, was a step in this process, which also included the removal from defence headquarters of several bright young officers loyal to Obote. Thus when the moment came for Amin's *coup* against Obote in January 1971, most of the potential resistance had been removed.

There is, however, still one unknown factor in the situation: why Obote, who must have been aware of the threat posed by Amin, should have allowed himself, by his absence at the Singapore conference, to be removed from power quite so easily. There is evidence quoted by both Judith Listowel[3] and David Martin[4] that before he left for the Commonwealth Conference he had instructed Colonel David Owito-Ojok, possibly together with Oryema, the Inspector-General of Police, to arrest Amin in his (Obote's) absence and to replace him with a commander of Obote's choosing. This would have been in line with the pattern of Obote's earlier action against the Kabaka, which was also conducted during his own absence from Kampala. If so, he fatally underestimated Amin.

CHAPTER 26

TRADE MISSION TO
THE EASTERN CONGO

ANDREW HAD ARRIVED for his 1969 summer holidays in late July, shortly before the Pope's visit. A week later, he was unexpectedly invited by the Madhvani family to spend a couple of nights with them at the Mount Kenya Safari Lodge. He naturally jumped at the invitation, not least because it involved being picked up in their private aircraft from the airstrip in Kampala. He had been reminded to take his passport but none of us remembered that his holiday visa for Uganda was only valid for a single journey. At Nairobi the party had to check through Kenyan immigration before flying on to the Safari Lodge. The Madhvanis' entry permits were all in order, but the immigration officer stopped Andrew, pointing out that he had no authority to make a second journey to Uganda: if he were admitted to Kenya, therefore, he would have to return direct from there to the United Kingdom. The argument became quite heated, much to the amusement of the Madhvani boys, who regarded it as a huge joke that the son of the British High Commissioner should have passport problems while they – the much criticized British Asians – had none. In the end the pilot generously offered to act as surety for Andrew's return to Uganda, and he was reluctantly allowed through.

Some weeks later we attended the celebration of the seventh anniversary of Ugandan independence. For this occasion General Amin had made elaborate arrangements for a grand parade and fly-past of virtually the whole of his forces, including Trooping the Colour. To plan this, he had asked my Information Officer, John MacQuiggan, if he could borrow a film of the Queen's Trooping ceremony; from my Defence Adviser, Lieutenant-Colonel Nigel Crawford, he obtained the exact measurements of the Royal Horseguards parade ground and gave the military bands the precise number of bars of music which were played on the film. In spite of the fact that his troops had to march on grass, the result was very creditable. The show of force represented by his newly-acquired Mig 17 fighters and Czech Delfin training aircraft and a small number of Sherman tanks acquired from the Israelis was impressive, though it was not clear at the time what he needed them for. But, with the benefit of hindsight, there is little doubt that he was primarily engaged in building up his image for the *coup* ahead.

In the second half of October we had a further visit from Mr Maurice Foley, the minister responsible for the aid programme to Uganda. One of the main forms which our aid took was the construction of roads, and a few days after he left we attended the opening of one of the new roads, from Kafu to Gulu, financed under the programme. This was designed to assist the tourist industry by providing a more direct route from Kampala to the Murchison National Park at Chobe, but it was also, I suspect, useful to Amin, who unknown to us was in the process of constructing, with Israeli assistance, a new air force base at Gulu.

Two days later we attended the opening by President Obote of a new railway bridge over the Nile at Pakwach. This had been built from East African Community funds and replaced a ferry on the main road from Amin's home province of West Nile. It also provided an improved route to the north-eastern districts of the Congo (Kinshasa). The new bridge was, I believe, only the second over the Nile between Khartoum and Lake Albert.

The opening ceremony, at which Amin was much in evidence, was also attended by a Kenyan minister, representing the East African Community, who made the tactical mistake of reading his long speech in Swahili, which few people in northern Uganda understood. Once the speeches were over, a train hauled by one of the first locomotives to operate in Uganda steamed slowly across the bridge, almost submerged in the huge crowd of singing and cheering local spectators who had gathered for the occasion. Later a group of Czech amphibious armoured cars, Amin's latest military acquisition, drove down to the old ferry ramp and began swimming across the river towards the spectators on the west bank. Excitement was added to the occasion when the engine of one of the cars stalled halfway across and the vehicle began drifting downstream with the strong current, apparently on a collision course with a pier of the new bridge. Fortunately for the prestige of the army it got going again just in time.

Our last major tour before we left Uganda took us to the extreme south-west of the country and to Rwanda and the Congo. As a result of the separation of responsibilities between the Foreign Office and the Commonwealth Office there had previously been little regular contact between the heads of our various missions in the francophone countries – the former French and Belgian colonies – and those, like myself, in the former British dependent territories. I had, therefore, been delighted when at the end of 1968 the incoming Ambassador to the Congo (Kinshasa), Paul Wright, suggested that he and his wife, Babs, might spend a few days in Uganda in order to get a feel of Africa before taking up his appointment at Kinshasa. This they duly did in January 1969, and we arranged for them to meet a number of leading Ugandans and to show them something of how life went on in a Commonwealth African country.

In the course of this visit we had also discussed the possibility of increasing British trade with the eastern Congo. Since Rwanda's imports had to come in overland, mainly through Uganda or Tanzania, we felt that we should try to find out whether British exports to the eastern provinces of the Congo could not similarly be channelled through Uganda. There were a number of possible routes, including the newly-opened Pakwach railway bridge, as well as two or three roads which either crossed direct into the Congo or entered through Rwanda.

We accordingly decided, with the approval of the Board of Trade, that we would jointly explore the possibilities and find out what, if any, new facilities might be needed. In this we were able to make use of the services of our existing trade correspondents in Rwanda and the Kivu Province; we were in the process helped by the goodwill created by the work of a small contingent of Royal Engineers who, as part of a highly imaginative training-*cum*-aid scheme, had been building bridges – in both senses of the phrase – in the Kisangani (formerly Stanleyville) area of the eastern Congo. The purpose of this exercise was to restore communications destroyed as a result of the Congo war and, for a relatively small outlay in cash and materials, it made an impact far beyond its actual results.

Paul and I agreed that it would be most convenient to start our expedition from Uganda, where I could provide transport. He and Babs accordingly flew from Kinshasa to Entebbe and spent a night with us in Kampala. The next day we set off by car for Kabale in the south-west corner of Uganda. From there the road to Kisoro and the Congo passes over the edge of the escarpment and drops almost three thousand feet. From the top there is one of the most spectacular views in the world. In front lies part of the great western rift valley which runs southwards from Lake Albert and the Nile valley through Lake Kivu to Lake Tanganyika; beyond it stands out the line of the three eastern volcanoes of the Virunga Mountains, which continue the line of the Ruwenzori and form the western edge of the rift. This is the central watershed of Africa: within a few miles of each other rise the head-waters of the Lualaba (Congo) River flowing westwards towards the Atlantic, and of the Kagera, the main river of Rwanda, which flows north and east into Lake Victoria and forms the ultimate source of the White Nile.

This is still some of the wildest and most remote country in Africa; the slopes of Mt Muhavura, one of the Virunga volcanoes, provide one of the last surviving homes of the mountain gorilla; in the Ituri Forest, a hundred miles to the north, pygmies of the Batwa tribe still flourish, as does the rare and elusive okapi.

Our first call after crossing into the Congo was on the local paramount chief at Rutshuru. From there we went north to spend two nights in the *Parc National Albert*. This visit was intended to give us some idea of the tourist facilities offered in the western Congo and to see how these would fit in with the neighbouring, but much better known, national parks in Uganda. The impression we took away with us was not very good; the main safari lodge was adequate, but it was badly run-down and game-watching facilities were almost non-existent. In the light of the conditions, it was hardly surprising to discover that we were almost the only visitors in the entire park.

After leaving the park, we drove south, past and between the volcanoes, to Goma on Lake Kivu. Here we were invited by the Prefect to attend a solemn mass at the cathedral to celebrate the second anniversary of the new Congolese constitution. At the end of the service we found a military band lined up in honour of the Prefect and, it appeared, ourselves. As we emerged onto the steps of the cathedral the band struck up the Congolese national anthem, with memorable *éclat*, though uncertain accuracy. Then, much to our surprise, it burst into an equally enthusiastic version of 'God Save The Queen'. Our view of the accuracy of the rendering was clearly shared by the bandmaster. After the playing of one particular 'bum note', he darted through the other players to beat an errant trombonist in the rear rank over the head with his baton. Within a couple of bars he was back in front and conducting again as if nothing had happened. The band, who were presumably familiar with his training methods, maintained their rhythm throughout.

We spent two night at Goma and had long and useful talks with the Congolese authorities and with our commercial correspondent, Mr Jetha Ismael. It was clear that opportunities existed for a number of British exports which had so far hardly been scratched. From Goma we crossed the border to Gisenyi in Rwanda, and sending our cars and drivers back to Uganda, we ourselves flew in two small chartered aircraft down Lake Kivu to Bukavu, the provincial capital. Bukavu must have been a delightful resort in Belgian times, but it had been fought over by the mercenaries and was clearly only a shadow of its former self. Nevertheless, it remained attractive; from our hotel window we were able to watch lake otters disporting themselves in the water just below us. While there, we called on the provincial President, a member of the central Congolese Cabinet, who expressed considerable interest in our mission and assured us that there was great scope for increased trade with Britain.

The next day the Wrights went on to Bujumbura in Burundi, while Vera and I flew back direct from Shyangugu to Entebbe, convinced that our mission had demonstrated real interest in new trading opportunities. Unfortunately our hopes were short-lived; the troubles which followed in Uganda quickly ruled it out as a trade route for places further west.

CHAPTER 27

DEPARTURE FROM UGANDA

ON 19 DECEMBER 1969 a big official reception was given at the Lugogo Stadium in Kampala attended by President Obote and most of his ministers, as well as by members of the army, the diplomatic corps and local notables. It so happened that we left early, before the President and most of the Ugandan guests. An hour or two later we heard two or three explosions, followed by bursts of machine-gun fire, apparently coming from the centre of Kampala. Andrew, who had just arrived for his Christmas holidays and had gone to bed early, joined us rather sleepily on the balcony outside our bedroom. Some desultory firing was still going on in the distance and I rang the High Commission duty officer to try to find out what was happening. He knew no more than I did, and after a time the firing stopped. Eventually we all went to bed.

Very early the next morning I was woken by the telephone. It turned out to be the *Daily Telegraph* correspondent in Nairobi. He said that an unconfirmed story was current in Nairobi that Obote had been assassinated. Did I know anything about it? I told him that we had heard shooting, but that we still had no idea exactly what had happened. Shortly afterwards a member of my staff rang to tell me that he now had firm information that there had been an attack on Obote as he was leaving the stadium the previous evening; that he had been wounded and that he was now undergoing treatment at Mulago Hospital. Roadblocks had been established round the town and the troops manning them were fairly trigger-happy, though there were no reports of any incidents involving the British community.

The facts of the attack took a long time to emerge, and even now some elements are obscure. What follows is put together from a number of sources, including an account given to me many years later by Hans-Joachim Eick, the German Ambassador, whose house was only a door or two from that of General Amin. My synthesis may not be correct in all details, but it seems to hang together.

It appears that President Obote left the reception at about 9.30 p.m. As he

173

was walking to his car, surrounded by a group of his ministers, two shots were fired at him from close range by an army officer sitting in the branches of a tree. One bullet missed. The other passed through Obote's face, knocking out two teeth from his upper jaw on one side and three from his lower jaw on the other. Fortunately for him, the pistol jammed after the second shot. In the ensuing confusion, Obote himself, though bleeding profusely and finding it very difficult to talk, characteristically took charge of the situation, instructing his driver to take him to Mulago Hospital and sending orders to Amin to report to him there.

From then on, all was confusion. Amin had apparently left the reception before the attack. Two vehicles, one an armoured personnel carrier full of troops, were sent to his house in Prince Charles Drive to collect him and take him to the hospital. Amin, who had already heard of the attack (whether he had been personally involved in advance is not clear), but presumably not knowing whether it had been successful, heard the vehicles arriving at his front gate. Possibly having a guilty conscience, and assuming that he was being held responsible for the attack, he guessed (wrongly) that the troops had been sent to arrest him. He had already taken off his boots, but he rushed out through a back door into his garden and, tearing his way through a dannert barbed wire fence which had been put there for his protection, scrambled up to the main road which ran along the back of his property. He arrived in the road with torn trousers and bleeding legs, but persuaded a passing van belonging to Radio Uganda to stop and take him to the barracks at Mubende some ninety miles out of Kampala, where a regiment loyal to him was stationed.

Whether or not this account is true in all its details, it ties up with the fact that for two crucial days Amin's whereabouts were not known to the public or to Obote.[1] When he did eventually report to the hospital, his meeting with Obote was far from cordial. But both men lived to fight another day.

Meanwhile, following the President's admission, the main hospital block at Mulago had been put under strict guard by Akena Adoko and his men. No one was allowed in or out without screening, and several doctors trying to visit their patients were manhandled in the process. Two senior consultants were summoned to deal with Obote's injuries: Sir Ian McAdam, then Professor of Surgery at Makerere University and the leading general surgeon on the staff of the hospital; and Dr Martin Aliker, the top Ugandan dentist and a personal friend of the President, to deal with the dental aspects.

The operation lasted into the small hours. Apart from the damage to the President's teeth, his tongue was also severely lacerated. It was an eloquent testimony to the skill of the two surgeons involved that within little more than six weeks after the incident Obote was able to make an important policy speech in Parliament.

During that night and the days which followed the shooting, Kampala was generally calm, though the streets were less than pleasant to move around in. A member of my staff, who had been at the local Christmas pantomime on the night of the incident, was stopped at an army roadblock shortly after leaving the theatre and had a bullet fired into one of his car tyres before being allowed to proceed. He said later that, even though he was forced to run on the rim, nothing would have induced him nor any of his party to get out and walk. Even three days later, when things were beginning to return to normal, Okongo, my driver, took Vera, Andrew and Belinda (the dog) into town for some last-minute Christmas shopping. On the way home they were stopped near Obote's private house by an armoured car. A soldier pushed his rifle into the car to persuade them (which he easily did) that they should take another route. Vera said afterwards that she was chiefly worried not that the soldier would deliberately shoot them, but that Belinda would take the law into her own hands and bite him. Anything could then have happened.

A year earlier, Mr Malcolm MacDonald had described Obote in a report to London as 'a skilful boxer who has had a clear lead on points in every round'. In my annual review for 1968 I recalled his analogy, adding, 'I would expect him to duck and weave his way through 1969 always ahead of his opponents. If by any chance he were unexpectedly knocked out, a highly unstable situation would ensue, in which the contending groups and personalities would almost certainly succeed in involving units of the army in their struggle for power; and violence, from which the local British population would not be immune, could hardly be avoided.'

At the beginning of 1970, a few days after the attack on Obote, I took up the analogy once again in my report for 1969, pointing out that any political leader, especially in Africa, needed both imagination and luck to survive. Obote was well aware that the pages of history were littered with the corpses of those who had been not quite lucky enough. 'He has just been knocked to the floor for a short count. He is up again, but his footwork will need to be still more adroit, and perhaps his punching heavier, if his supremacy is to be restored in 1970. In that process we may find him lashing out fairly wildly at times. To the extent that we may find ourselves getting in the way of some of his side-swipes I can only wish my successor what I have on the whole had myself – the best of British luck.' Because of his wound I was unable to pay a farewell call on Dr Obote; I did not see him again until, after his rest-oration to the Presidency, I paid a business visit to Uganda in January 1981.

Vera and I finally left Kampala on 28 January 1970. We also had to take leave of Rwanda, and since we were keen to travel home by sea we took the unusual opportunity to cross the continent and catch a ship from Zaire. At this point the army were still manning roadblocks between Kampala and Entebbe. We were therefore relieved to be given permission to depart in a chartered aircraft from the police airstrip in Kampala instead of having to use the international airport at Entebbe. As our aircraft climbed away over the centre of Kampala we congratulated each other in getting away in one piece. Years later, Hans Eick, our German colleague, told us that we nearly hadn't. Just as our aircraft was starting its take-off, a small van appeared and raced across the tarmac towards the runway. For seconds it looked as if there would be a collision, but at the last moment the aircraft lifted off the ground and the van passed underneath us.

After a round of farewell calls in Kigali, we flew down to Butare, where Père Levesque and several other members of the university staff laid on parties in our honour, including a delightful display of Rwandan dancing. Our onward route via Bujumbura involved flying over the range of moun-tains which form the eastern edge of the rift valley escarpment and rise to about 8,500 feet. When we arrived at the Butare airstrip we were not encour-aged to find that the twin-engined aeroplane that had brought us so far had been replaced by a single-engined Cessna Skywagon, just about the smallest passenger aircraft there is. Apart from a mass of ordinary luggage, we had Vera's sewing-machine, which she was going to need as soon as we got home and from which she was unwilling to be parted. The Belgian pilot looked at it a little doubtfully, but with proper pride in his aircraft said that it could take the lot. The weather was overcast and some of the mountain tops were shrouded in mist. However, he pointed to a thin sliver of clear sky over a pass high above us and said, 'We go there!' And go we did. As we scraped through the narrow gap between the clouds and the mountains, we abruptly found ourselves in cloudless blue sky, with a fantastic view of Lake Tanganyika some fifty miles ahead and nearly 7,000 feet below.

At Bujumbura, an attractive hilly town at the head of the lake, we had expected to make a direct connection with the Air Congo service from Nairobi to Kinshasa. After two hours' wait at a very hot and sticky airport, however, we were told that the scheduled Caravelle had been taken off at the last moment for the use of President Mobutu, and that it was being replaced by a much smaller Fokker Friendship. There would be no difficulty in taking all the passengers who were waiting, but there would have to be restrictions on the amount of baggage carried. Vera blanched visibly: if the sewing-machine had to be abandoned the chances of it catching up with us before we sailed seemed to be nil. The Friendship, which had been sitting out on the tarmac being loaded with freight for some other destination, now began to be unloaded again. Eventually the passengers were called forward, the Scotts loaded down with an impossible quantity of hand baggage, including the sewing-machine. At the steps of the aircraft the hostess looked at us doubtfully, but we carefully avoided catching her eye and squeezed past her.

Fortunately not every passenger had a sewing-machine under the seat, and after what seemed a very long run the aircraft managed to stagger into the air. The flight to Kinshasa, scheduled to take just over two hours in the Caravelle, took nearly four in the Friendship, but we made it in the end. Paul Wright, a welcoming figure at the airport, blinked slightly at the sewing-machine, but swept us through customs as if it was the most normal piece of hand baggage in the world.

We had a fascinating three days in Kinshasa, where we combined sightseeing with official calls. The British Embassy residence, where the Wrights put us up, looks across the Congo River to the city of Brazzaville on the north bank. Diplomatic relations between the two Congo republics had, however, been broken and the ferry service which normally crossed the river above the rapids was suspended. The two cities form the downstream terminus of a vast inland waterway system stretching from beyond Kisangani, 1,000 miles upstream. Below them the river falls in a series of cataracts and waterfalls and is unnavigable for a hundred miles.

Paul Wright took me to call on the minister responsible for overseas trade, to whom we expounded our ideas on the expansion of trade with the eastern provinces following our joint visit a month or two earlier. He also arranged for Vera and myself to be shown round Lovanium University, where we were astonished to find a research 'swimming-pool' nuclear reactor, a sophisticated piece of equipment which few British universities could boast at the time.

At the end of our short visit we were driven to Matadi, where we boarded a Belgian cargo-passenger liner, the 11,000-ton *Albertville*, bound for Antwerp. Matadi is at the foot of the final ladder of cataracts – from the quay the enormous Congo River looks as if it is coming down a long water-slide – and as the ship edged out into the stream we quickly found ourselves in an eight-knot current, sweeping us at an alarming speed towards a bend in the river. An hour or two later we reached Boma, our first port of call, where we had cargo to take on and where we spent the night. Another half-day's sailing took us to Banana, a real Somerset Maugham-style port consisting mainly of a few large warehouses surrounded by jungle. After two sweltering nights there we sailed again, but when we reached the open sea to our surprise we turned due south rather than west-north-west for Europe. Only then were we told that we were due to make a final call at Lobito Bay in Angola.

Lobito was then, and one hopes will one day be again, the main port for Zaire's Shaba Province, formerly Katanga, with which it is connected by the British-owned Benguela Railway. There we spent another couple of days, seeing something of how the Portuguese conducted one of their colonies. It was impossible to guess that only a few years later they would have withdrawn completely.

By the time loading was complete, the *Albertville*, which had seemed reasonably full when we left Banana, was a full two metres deeper in the water with the load of copper and cobalt we had taken on. We finally left West African waters ten days after we had sailed from Matadi; another ten days and we were sailing up a bitterly cold English Channel, past Dover and into the Schelde for Antwerp.

PART FOUR

REPUBLIC OF SOUTH AFRICA
1976–79

CHAPTER 28

BACK TO SOUTH AFRICA

I WAS IN THE Foreign and Commonwealth Office from 1970 to 1972 as Assistant Under-Secretary responsible for the administration of the remaining dependent territories – in effect the rump of the old Colonial Office. By 1970 their number had been greatly reduced. But they were still sufficiently far-flung to justify the boast that the sun never set on them; by travelling round the world more than once I managed to visit thirteen out of the total of seventeen territories in my bailiwick.

From 1973 to the end of 1975 we were in New Zealand – a delightful and relaxing posting – and during that period I was also Governor of Pitcairn Island, the smallest of all Her Majesty's overseas territories. We landed there from a Royal Fleet Auxiliary tanker, RFA *Plumleaf*, for a rewarding stay of four days in August 1973. Vera was, and I believe still is, the only Governor's wife ever to have set foot on the island.

In September 1975 we heard that our next, and final, post in the service was once again to be South Africa. By an odd coincidence I would be taking over as Ambassador from the same person, Sir James Bottomley, whom I had succeeded there as First Secretary in 1951. We were home for Christmas, and early in the New Year we had dinner with the Bottomleys to be briefed for our new appointment.

This was an eventful moment in South Africa's history: the South African Army was engaged in operations in Angola and was increasingly involved in the war in Rhodesia. I fully accepted Bottomley's comment that, although Britain still had close and valuable connections with the Republic in the economic and commercial fields, the Ambassador could no longer expect to be closely involved in the political scene. The facts that we were not now concerned with the administration of the High Commission Territories; that the Commonwealth link had been broken, and that in the defence field our traditional close relations had been replaced by an arms embargo, underlined the extent to which our common political interests had been eroded. Moreover, since South African internal policies continued to cause international embarrassment, both sides had in recent years tended to keep their distance.

Among the many calls I made to brief myself before leaving London to take up my new appointment was one on Mrs Margaret Thatcher, who in 1974 had been elected Leader of the Conservative Party. She herself had visited South Africa a year or two earlier as Secretary of State for Education and Science, primarily to attend the inauguration of an important new optical telescope commissioned and used jointly by the British and South African Departments of Scientific and Industrial Research. This telescope, which we later visited ourselves, occupies a spectacular site at Sutherland in the Karroo, about 250 miles north-east of Cape Town. I found her extremely well-informed on the political nuances in South Africa, and it became clear later that her visit had made a considerable impression on all who met her there, not least in the scientific community.

I also called on several trade union leaders, including Mr Len Murray and Mr Jack Jones, both of whom had been involved in the TUC's contacts with the trade union movement in South Africa, and on Mr Peter Plouviez, the General Secretary of Equity, the actors' union. Equity's decision to ban the sale to South Africa of television films in which its membership had taken part had, by closing to South Africans a window on the world, in my view, been counter-productive; the ban was secretly welcomed by the more bigoted members of the Afrikaner community and was most damaging to those who wanted to see change.

Vera and I arrived in Cape Town on Wednesday, 10 March 1976. Once again we had travelled by sea, though this time in a strictly functional refrigerated ship, the *Port Chalmers*. By a strange coincidence the new German Ambassador, who arrived in Johannesburg on the same day, was none other than our old friend Hans-Joachim Eick, who had earlier served with us in Salisbury and Kampala. We were to have a great deal more to do with one another in the years ahead.

It had been arranged that I should present my letters to the State President, Dr Diedrichs, on the following Tuesday, 16 March. As is normal, however, I made introductory calls on the Foreign Minister, Dr Hilgard Muller, and the Secretary of Foreign Affairs, Mr Brand Fourie, a few days in advance, on Friday, 12 March. These were formal calls in the sense that, since I had not yet presented my letters of accreditation, I was officially not qualified to carry out diplomatic business. To my surprise, however, as I was getting up to take my leave of Brand Fourie, whom I had known on and off since 1949, he asked whether I would mind if he raised a matter of substance with me. It was fairly urgent and could not really wait until the following week.

I naturally said that I would be delighted to do some real work, which, after all, was what I was paid for. Fourie then explained that, as I knew, South African troops were in the process of being withdrawn from Angola. He added something that I did not know – that the final contingents were expected to cross the bridge over the Cunene River back into South-West Africa in about six days' time. The South African Government were extremely anxious to avoid any incidents which might delay the withdrawal or involve casualties, but they had no channel of communication with the Angolan authorities. Was there any possibility that the British Government could arrange for a message to be conveyed to them?

I said that I had no idea whether we had any means of passing such a message, or indeed whether my Government would be willing to become involved, even indirectly, in an operation of which they thoroughly disapproved. We also had no diplomatic mission in Luanda. But I would certainly make enquiries and let him know the answer as soon as possible.

As soon as I got back to the office I sent a 'flash' (most immediate) telegram reporting what Fourie had said and commenting that, although I recognized that the request might involve political difficulties, it was clearly in all our interests, including presumably those of Angola, that the withdrawal should be completed rapidly and without incident. I therefore hoped that we would do anything we could to help.

That was on Friday afternoon. On Sunday I had the answer: through the embassy of a third country in London a message had been passed to the Angolan Government and a procedure agreed which could permit the troops to withdraw peacefully under mutually acceptable arrangements.

This was an extraordinarily lucky break for me. Not only did it give me a flying start in my relations with the South African Government; it also contradicted the idea that we were necessarily debarred from playing a political role, provided that it was in our interest to do so. Times had begun to change again with a vengeance.

One of my first official calls after presenting my letters was on the Prime Minister, the Hon. John Vorster. Mr Vorster had taken over the premiership in the traumatic aftermath of the murder of Dr Verwoerd in 1966, at which time he had been Minister of Justice and of the Police. It was not surprising, therefore, that he attached overriding importance to security; indeed, one of my most lasting impressions of Mr Vorster's government was of its rigid application of the 'need to know' principle at all levels. This situation has changed under Mr P.W. Botha, but was apparent in the relative absence of interdepartmental machinery for policy planning and for the exchange of information, and in the surprising lack of authority given to the Cabinet secretariat in the South African official hierarchy compared with the influ-. ence and prestige it carries in Whitehall.

Vera and I were often asked during our second posting to South Africa what changes, particularly in the area of race relations, we noticed from our earlier incarnation there in the 1950s. It was never an easy question to answer, not least because the questioner usually assumed that the answer would be unequivocal, and would confirm his or her own conviction that there had been tremendous changes for the better. In fact, such progress as had been made was often extremely difficult to define; to be honest one had to start by pointing out that in the early 1950s the Coloured community in the Cape had still been on the voters' roll. (It could have been added that at the time of Union in 1910 there had under British rule actually been 9,000 qualified blacks on the Cape roll as well as thousands of Coloureds.)

Between 1948 and Dr Verwoerd's assassination in 1966, indeed, the 'progress' was entirely negative. Even in the field of so-called 'petty *apartheid*' one had to make a conscious act of recall to remind oneself that the Cape Town buses were open to all races as recently as 1952: the unwelcome and expensive extension to the Cape of *apartheid* on municipal transport started by reserving the lower deck (or the front, on single-decker buses) for whites and, to the vocally expressed disgust of our own children, who always wanted to go on top, putting the non-whites upstairs. Only after 1953 were people of different races confined to separate buses. (Not until the late 1970s did the revolutionary concept begin to creep back that the word 'bus' is a contraction of *omnibus*, for all.)

When we left South Africa in 1953, I remember discussing with Vera how quickly we expected the political situation to develop. Our conclusion was that within a relatively short period - we guessed ten years - the numbers game would have begun to operate and signs of black revolution would become apparent. In March 1960, when at Mzimba in Nyasaland I heard the first reports of the Sharpeville massacre, I vividly remember thinking that we had after all underestimated the period required for the day of reckoning to arrive. That feeling seemed to be confirmed a few weeks later when I heard the news of the first attack on Dr Verwoerd. But I left out of account the weight of arms and authority in the hands of the white authorities and also, perhaps, the remarkable patience and docility of most of the black population. When we returned, therefore, the balance of surprise was not so much at the changes which had taken place, but that so much had remained the same.

In May and early June 1976 ominous rumblings began to make themselves heard from Soweto, the great complex of black townships to the south-west of Johannesburg. The immediate cause of complaint was the use of Afrikaans as the medium of instruction in the schools; it was the students who first began to form centres of unrest and civil disobedience. These warning noises were publicly discounted by the Government; in particular by the then Minister for Bantu Affairs, Mr. M.C. Botha, and by the Bantu Administration Boards operating under his department.

When Parliament rose at the end of the session in mid-June, Vera and I set off from Cape Town by car for an official visit to the Ciskei and the Transkei, the two 'homelands' of the Xhosa people. We had only reached Port Elizabeth on the second day of our journey when we heard the news of serious disturbances in Soweto, including attacks on schools and other public buildings, on the local offices of the West Rand Bantu Administration Board, and on one or two unfortunate whites who appeared to represent authority and who happened to get in the way. The police reacted violently and large numbers of casualties, almost all black, followed.

Realizing that there was little I could do in a highly confused situation, we decided to go on with our tour, not least because it was most unlikely that we should be able to visit the Transkei once it had achieved 'independence', which was expected to be granted before the end of the year in terms of the South African Government's homelands policy.

Although I had considerable personal sympathy with the black leaders involved in the homelands policy, our visit to Umtata, the capital of the Transkei, convinced me that the policy itself was basically a dead-end. I understood the view of the local politicians, who argued cogently that the limited measure of self-government available to them in the homelands was better than nothing and that it at least provided a training ground for the exercise of power. Chief Kaiser Matanzima pointed out forcibly to me that it was only an accident of history that the Transkei had not been included under Queen Victoria's protection in the same way that Basutoland had become a colony, the 'flea in the Queen's blanket', under King Moshoeshoe I; by being incorporated in the Cape Province, however, the Ciskei and the Transkei became part of the Union of South Africa in 1910. In theory that still gave the Xhosa people the benefit of the King's protection, but this lapsed unilaterally in 1961 when South Africa became a Republic. In short, Britain was basically responsible for their present defenceless position.

Unfortunately, however much one sympathizes with the difficulty of their choice, the 'independence' of the Transkei today is largely an illusion. Over 80 per cent of its total revenue comes from the Republic, either from the proceeds of the Customs Union (which Lesotho, Botswana and Swaziland also share) or in the form of direct grants. This dependence has led to more than a little corruption; there is evidence that prominent individuals have received substantial inducements in exchange for their willingness to go along with the homelands policy. In practical terms, it has also led to increasing over-population in the homelands themselves without the massive injection of capital which alone could make them self-supporting.

I came away with the conviction that the peoples of the homelands, whether nominally independent or not, were just as much the victims of *apartheid* as the urban blacks. It seemed wrong, therefore, that they should be further penalized by being regarded as ineligible for the development funds which their opposite numbers in the former High Commission Territories received from Britain and elsewhere. Later in the year I began to formulate proposals under which HMG might overcome this difficulty without at the same time appearing to support the homelands policy.

CHAPTER 29

ENTER DR KISSINGER

BY THE TIME we got to Pretoria in early July 1976, matters were beginning to warm up in another direction also. While we were still at sea on our way to South Africa, the Foreign Secretary, Mr Callaghan, had in March despatched Lord Greenhill to southern Africa to investigate the prospects for launching a new initiative on Rhodesia. This new approach had, however, been caught up in the Cabinet reshuffle following Mr Wilson's resignation as Prime Minister; a lengthy pause had then ensued while the new Foreign Secretary, Mr Anthony Crosland, prepared to get to grips with the situation. Eventually towards the end of August I heard that Sir Antony Duff, the Deputy Under-Secretary of State concerned, and a former High Commissioner to Kenya, was to visit a number of countries in southern Africa to discuss proposals for a new Anglo-American initiative in which Dr Henry Kissinger, the United States Secretary of State, was expected to play a leading part.

Duff's tour, which included a visit to Pretoria, went well, and the initiative assumed concrete form only two weeks later when Dr Kissinger made a comprehensive tour of southern Africa, calling on all the heads of state concerned. The only capital he did not visit was Salisbury, since this would have raised the awkward question of United States recognition of the regime, but it was arranged that Mr Smith would himself visit Pretoria while Dr Kissinger was there. There was, however, no prior commitment that they would meet.

Dr Kissinger's visit to Pretoria was a major event in which I became deeply involved. His impact was apparent at two distinct levels. At the public level it owed much to the extraordinary style in which he travelled. It has, of course, been common form ever since American Secretaries of State started to peregrinate by air that they and their immediate party should arrive in one of the presidential-style aircraft which seem to be collectively designated 'Air Force One'.

In Kissinger's case, however, the personal aircraft was preceded and followed by a sequence of other, sometimes even larger, aircraft. First the security team swept in - Vera called them the 'deaf-aid boys', because one ear was permanently linked through a radio intercom system to their mission controller - and went like a dose of salts through every aspect of the accommodation, conference and communications systems that the Secretary of State was to use. Next came an aircraft with the specially protected cars. On a round trip such as this one, which took in a number of capital cities, two of these aircraft, and two sets of cars, were required: one flew, say, to Pretoria to be ready for the Secretary's arrival there, while the other picked up cars from his last stop and leap-frogged them on to the next. A minimum of four four-engined jets were thus needed to get him around.

The second level of impact was the personal one. There is no doubt at all that the famous Kissinger charm is very compelling indeed. In his discussions with Mr Vorster, and later with Mr Ian Smith, Dr Kissinger was acting without a direct British presence, but he was speaking to a carefully prepared Anglo-American brief. It was therefore agreed that after each of his meetings with the South Africans and the Rhodesians he would hold a special debriefing session with me. At these meetings he was normally accompanied by four or five advisers, of whom Assistant Under-Secretary Bill Schauffely was the senior; I had Richard Samuel, a highly competent member of our delegation in New York, who travelled with the Kissinger party throughout the African tour. I was thus for three days subjected to the full force of Kissinger's personality, and greatly enjoyed the experience. I might not have enjoyed it quite so much, I suspect, if instead of being a relative outsider I had been, for example, the American Ambassador to South Africa, who was responsible for his minute-to-minute arrangements.

Our meetings were designed to enable me to report to the Foreign Secretary on the progress of the talks and to provide a channel through which United Kingdom comments and reactions could be fed back to Dr Kissinger. Since his meetings with Mr Vorster and Mr Smith went on until late at night, my sessions with him tended to take place in the early hours of the morning. I was deeply impressed with the thoroughness and conscientiousness with which he undertook this chore, even though he must have wanted nothing more than to go to sleep. In the middle of one of our sessions in his hotel suite, Mrs Kissinger came in from the bedroom next door in her stockinged feet to enquire if he was ever coming to bed. He politely introduced me to her, but continued, I fear, to keep her waiting for the better part of another hour. I felt guilty, not least because she reminded me vividly of my favourite film star, the late, and much lamented, Kay Kendall.

Apart from their reporting aspect, these briefing sessions also gave me an opportunity for lengthy tactical discussions with Dr Kissinger. It was widely alleged that Mr Smith's record as a negotiator had been one of consistent evasion and prevarication, even when he appeared to have reached an agreement. Unless, therefore, he could be publicly and irrevocably pinned down to any agreement arrived at, it might be found that he had once again gone back on what he appeared to have accepted. This could have left the whole negotiation even more intractably snarled up than when we started. Kissinger fully understood this point and made it clear that he had no intention of letting him wriggle off the hook once again.

It followed, however, that an important part of the discussion centred on the form of the announcement on the outcome of the talks, and who should make it. Various possibilities were considered. One was that there should be a joint Anglo-American statement setting out what had been agreed, which hopefully would be supported by the South Africans. Another was that Kissinger should make a unilateral announcement and yet a third that Smith should make a broadcast to the Rhodesian people in terms which had been cleared with us in advance. I argued very strongly for the last course on the ground that only after Smith had publicly committed himself to an agreed form of words would it be certain that he could not subsequently disavow what he had agreed in private. This is what was finally accepted.

With the benefit of hindsight, it may well be that I was wrong in advocating this course. On 27 September, in his historic television broadcast from Salisbury, Ian Smith, after a long preamble designed for internal consumption (which had not been discussed in advance with the Americans or ourselves), announced in the terms agreed that he accepted the principle of majority rule. Unfortunately, the fact that his statement, revolutionary as it was, appeared to have been made unilaterally and on his own initiative, created deep suspicion throughout the neighbouring African states. It seemed altogether too good to be true – even though it was true – and many convinced themselves that there must be some hidden catch. The result was that the Front Line States, under pressure from the Patriotic Front, failed to reach agreement to cash in on Smith's capitulation; the wriggling, which for a further two years seemed to have got Smith off his hook, was at that stage more the responsibility of his opponents than of himself. Once again he had secured room for manoeuvre – and tragically the war went on.

Undoubtedly the main reason for Kissinger's failure to reach finality on Rhodesia in 1976 was lack of time. The Ford administration had less than two months to run before the presidential elections, and in its last two months Rhodesia had to compete for the Secretary of State's attention with the Arab-Israeli problem, to which he had a prior commitment.

After he left Pretoria, but before Smith's announcement, Kissinger visited Lusaka and Dar es Salaam to explain orally to Presidents Kaunda and Nyerere the substance of what had been agreed. It seems likely that, since he was not authorized at that stage to give them anything in writing, he may have led them to expect more than in fact emerged. Given more time, his negotiating technique of 'constructive ambiguity' might well have worked; unfortunately, however, the ambiguities were never finally resolved. But the significance of his achievement should not be underestimated. What he secured from Smith *was* irreversible, and led eventually to Bishop Muzorewa's transitional government and thence to Lord Carrington's Constitutional Conference and Zimbabwe's independence under Mr Mugabe.

But all this was still in the future. At the time, my main concern was that, although the Kissinger visit had made considerable progress, follow-up action should be taken without delay. Mr Smith had made his statement, but how was it to be turned into action?

I had, of course, called on Mr Callaghan, the previous Foreign and Commonwealth Secretary, before leaving London to take up my appointment. But Mr Crosland had been appointed after I left and I had never met him. It seemed essential that sooner rather than later I should be briefed at first-hand on his thinking. Shortly after the Kissinger visit, therefore, I put in an informal request to visit London for consultation. I pointed out that I had spent some six or seven hours in *tête-à-tête* dialogue with Dr Kissinger and inevitably now knew his mind on the Rhodesian problem better than I knew that of my own ministers. This might indeed have become apparent in my reporting. In the weeks ahead, when much of the action could be expected to centre on our ability to influence South African, and through them Rhodesian, ministers, it was essential that I should be absolutely up-to-date and in tune with the Secretary of State's thinking.

There was no immediate response to this request, but the flow of high-level visitors from Whitehall, including a most useful one by Mr Ted Rowlands, then Parliamentary Under-Secretary of State, made it difficult to argue that I was not being kept in touch. Nevertheless, the Americans, having achieved their part of the deal by securing Mr Smith's acceptance of the principle of majority rule and now being themselves involved in an election campaign, understandably felt that the next step was up to the British.

As the weeks went by the South Africans also were getting restive. Not only had they stage-managed the Pretoria meetings, but they had taken some political risk in putting pressure on Smith to accept the Kissinger solution. Vorster said later, 'I did not twist Smith's arm – I merely pointed out the options to him.' But pointing out the options was widely believed to have included a practical demonstration of what might happen if he chose the wrong option: it was reliably reported that for a fortnight most of the freight trains on which Rhodesia depended for her essential imports were mysteriously 'lost' on their way north. Smith got the message.

At the end of November I was recalled to London for consultation. President Ford had been defeated at the polls and his administration, including Dr Kissinger, put into baulk. It was clear that no further American initiative could be expected for several months. On my arrival in London I had a number of useful meetings at official level, especially with Sir Michael Palliser, the Permanent Under-Secretary, and Sir John Hunt, the Secretary to the Cabinet, in which I stressed the urgency of following up the Kissinger initiative. The longer we failed to use the momentum created by Mr Smith's announcement of 27 September, the more difficult it was likely to be to persuade the South Africans to keep up the pressure on the Rhodesians, or – though this was not really for me to argue – to get the various guerrilla movements to attend talks, let alone to call off the war.

I finally saw Mr Crosland on my last day in London. At a personal level I found the meeting helpful. Instead of the half-hour I had been promised I had the better part of an hour; this gave me exactly the opportunity I needed to bring myself up to date on his thinking. He listened attentively to my arguments on the need for early action, and I returned to Pretoria feeling a good deal happier. Unfortunately, what eventually emerged did not go far enough to meet the rapidly deteriorating situation; although the idea of an all-party conference came to be accepted, the form it took was doomed from the start.

Early in the New Year Mr Ivor Richard, HM Ambassador to the United Nations, accompanied by a small team including Sir Antony Duff, visited South Africa and a number of the other African capitals involved, to canvass the prospects for a conference. The party arrived at Pretoria from Nairobi on 3 January, while Robert, his wife Su and their son David Scott II were with us. Since at that time South African ministers were mostly still away on their summer holidays, Mr Vorster invited Mr Richard, together with the rest of his team and myself, to meet him at his holiday house on the coast at Oubosrand, a small village some ninety miles west of Port Elizabeth. All the participants were lifted from Port Elizabeth by helicopter, landing on specially-constructed pads just outside the Prime Minister's house.

This occasion gave me an opportunity, unusual for an outsider, to see traditional Afrikaner hospitality in action. Oubosrand does not boast a single shop, let alone a restaurant, so Mrs Vorster had generously arranged, with the help of her daughter and daughter-in-law, to lay on an excellent lunch for the official parties, amounting to some sixteen people, in addition to her family. When the day arrived, however, she discovered that about sixty press reporters and photographers had also turned up, so without hesitation she organized lunch for them as well. As we were leaving I thanked her warmly for her hospitality and asked her how on earth she had managed to cope with the additional numbers. She said, 'Well, I had six springbok in the deep-freeze which the old man [Vorster] had shot before Christmas, so it wasn't difficult.' It turned out that she had been up since 5 a.m. making the preparations. I thought that in the circumstances her definition of 'not difficult' was remarkably generous, especially since she was supposed to be on holiday.

Mr Richard's reconnaissance confirmed that virtually all the parties concerned would be prepared to attend a conference, many of them on condition that HMG would foot the bill for transporting and accommodating enormous delegations. But it was at this point that things began to go wrong. It was agreed that the conference would assemble at Geneva in early February; instead of presiding over it himself, however, Mr Crosland announced that Mr Richard would take the chair.

For any ordinary conference Ivor Richard would have been an ideal chairman. He has all the necessary qualities of wisdom, enlightenment and patience. But, as the press did not fail to point out at the time, this was no ordinary conference. Its purpose was to achieve a lasting constitutional settlement for a technically dependent territory; such conferences were traditionally and invariably presided over by the responsible Secretary of State. One can well understand why Mr Crosland did not want to become too closely or personally involved: but without his authority the conference was a lost cause anyway.

Predictably, neither Mr Smith nor the Patriotic Front took kindly to the apparent downgrading of the status of the negotiations; the result was a series of undignified rows, often on trivia, in which the unfortunate chairman was inevitably and vulnerably in the middle. The ultimate weapon of breaking off the negotiations was denied him, and from all accounts he had a very uncomfortable time indeed. After ten inglorious weeks, the conference died in a welter of inconclusion.

CHAPTER 30

A NEW SECRETARY OF STATE

AT THIS MOMENT fate intervened with brutal decisiveness. On 19 February 1977 Mr Crosland died. Mr Callaghan, by an imaginative stroke, appointed Dr David Owen, Minister of State in the Foreign and Commonwealth Office, to succeed him. Within days of his appointment Dr Owen had taken a firm personal grip on the Rhodesian situation. In particular he secured the agreement of the new US administration to reopen a joint peace initiative in Rhodesia. He accepted that if a quick solution were to be found HMG could not afford to be too sensitive in holding the South Africans and the Rhodesians at arm's length, and he immediately began the process of establishing personal contact with the principal protagonists. In mid-April he visited Cape Town, where, by a convenient coincidence, Mr Ian Smith was on holiday.

Although Dr Owen had been promoted from a ministerial appointment within the FCO, he had been dealing mainly with European matters; few people in South Africa, either inside or outside the Embassy, had met him before. Apart from a very brief meeting between Mr Callaghan and Mr Vorster in Port Elizabeth in 1974, moreover, his was the first visit to South Africa by a Foreign Secretary for a number of years; it therefore caused great public interest and, for us, a certain amount of apprehension.

The visit began with a long session with Mr Vorster. Although the discussions centred on Rhodesia, the opportunity was taken to cover a number of other matters including South-West Africa (Namibia) and the international impact of South Africa's racial policies. Talks started in the morning and went on into the afternoon. Altogether, they covered the better part of six hours virtually non-stop, and were frank and surprisingly friendly. By the end of the afternoon a broad measure of agreement had been reached on the general lines of the approach to the Rhodesians.

During lunch, which Mr Vorster gave in Parliament, he embarked on a lengthy exposé of the philosophical background to the policy of separate development. At the end of it, Dr Owen commented that he had been extremely interested in what the Prime Minister had said, and could find no flaws in the logic with which he had expounded his views. 'You know, Prime Minister,' he ended 'we have someone in our House also whose arguments I find unassailable but whose basic assumptions, like yours, I find myself in total disagreement with. His name is Enoch Powell.' The Prime Minister took this in good part.

The following day Dr Owen's first meeting with Mr Ian Smith took place in the dining room of our official residence. The two delegations faced each other across the table, appropriately presided over by an imposing portrait of the Queen in her Coronation robes. On the whole this first meeting went well, not least, perhaps, because the Rhodesians appreciated the fact that the new Secretary of State had no intention of distancing himself from the negotiations. There was, nevertheless, a fairly major disagreement on whether or not the approval of the Rhodesian Parliament was necessary to ratify any solution approved by Parliament at Westminster. In effect this argument hinged on whether a 'return to legality' was a prerequisite of an agreed solution. Ian Smith maintained strongly that he could not give away in advance the right of his parliament to vote on, and hence by implication to reject, any legislation affecting its own powers. Against this, the Secretary of State argued equally forcibly that since the Crown could not accept the legal existence of the post-UDI Rhodesian Parliament, there could be no question of delegating to that body the right of veto on matters affecting its own future. If, however, it were prepared to vote itself out of existence, clearly no one would wish to prevent it from doing so.

This argument, which had a certain air of unreality, was eventually put on one side for further consideration by the legal advisers, but it went some way to sour the proceedings. Nevertheless, the meetings in Cape Town took matters appreciably further forward, not least by once again involving the South African Government. They also opened the way for a meeting between Dr Owen and Mr Cyrus Vance, the new American Secretary of State, in London on 6 May. This resulted in full American involvement in the negotiations and included agreement to set up a joint Anglo-American consultative group with instructions to establish a dialogue with all the parties concerned with the Rhodesian problem, including the Rhodesians themselves, South Africa and the so-called Front Line States (Tanzania, Zambia, Botswana, Mozambique and Angola). The consultative group consisted of John Graham (later Sir John Graham, KCMG, HM Ambassador to Iran), the Deputy Under-Secretary of State concerned in the FCO, and Stephen Low, the US Ambassador to Zambia, who together spent most of the next year in consultations in Africa, Washington and London.

Rhodesia was, of course, not the only subject with which we were currently concerned. Shortly after Dr Owen's appointment as Secretary of State, but before his visit to Cape Town, I had made a speech to the Cape Town Press Club which attracted a certain amount of publicity both in South Africa and overseas. In it I reminded my audience that the only four recent occasions on which a British Labour Government had exercised the veto in the Security Council had been to avoid a head-on collision between that body and South Africa. I ended by saying:

We [Britain] now find ourselves with very little ammunition left to defend ourselves against intense international criticism that we are leaning over backwards to defend South African internal policies. Unless you can give us more ammunition, we may not be able to go on doing so. What form this ammunition can take is not for me to say: but I have to warn you that the stocks are already perilously low ...

I have spoken frankly, but I hope you will accept that I have spoken as a friend. The need for friends in a troubled world has perhaps never been greater for all of us than it is today. But friendship is a two-way affair and sometimes it has to be worked for. I hope we are all working for it today.

This speech received a generally approving response from the South African press, both English- and Afrikaans-language; I even received sympathetic personal comments on it from more than one South African minister. But it was symptomatic of the knife-edge on which a British Ambassador in South Africa has to operate that two questions were put down for answer in the House of Commons asking whether it was acceptable for the British Ambassador to claim to speak as a friend of South Africa. Happily for me, the new Secretary of State replied on the lines that, if the honourable members had read the full text of the speech as he had, they would recognize that it was intended to persuade the South African Government to change their ways rather than to support their policies.

Shortly before the meeting between Dr Owen and Mr Vorster, Dr Muller had resigned as South African Foreign Minister and had been replaced by Mr R.F. (Pik) Botha, the South African Ambassador to the United Nations. Mr Botha had started his career as a member of the South African Diplomatic Service, and his period in New York had made him familiar with the realities of the international scene and the pressures on South Africa to change her internal as well as her external policies. One particular international problem of which he had extensive first-hand knowledge was that of Namibia (South-West Africa).

South-West Africa had been placed under a League of Nations mandate following Germany's defeat in the First World War, and for some sixty years had been administered on behalf of the League of Nations, and subsequently of the United Nations, by South Africa, for much of that time as an integral part of the Republic. Latterly, there had been increasing pressure in the United Nations to remove the territory from South Africa's 'illegal occupation', but this had been strongly resisted by the South African Government until 1975, when Mr Vorster announced that he accepted the principle of independence for South-West Africa, provided that it was allowed to evolve gradually and peacefully. This major reversal of policy unfortunately came too late to take the heat off South Africa in the United Nations, especially since Mr Vorster made it clear that he was not prepared to negotiate with SWAPO, whose claim to be the sole legitimate representatives of the people of Namibia had by then been recognized by the United Nations.

Following this change of policy a South African-sponsored constitutional conference was established to decide the future of South-West Africa (Namibia); its meetings were held in the old German drill hall, the Turnhalle, in Windhoek and it became universally known as the Turnhalle Conference.

Although the parties to this conference were drawn from all the main ethnic groups in South-West Africa, they had not all been democratically elected and in any case did not include representatives of several of the main political parties, including SWAPO, many of whose top leaders were either in prison or in exile.

Dr Kissinger, while he was still Secretary of State, had begun to interest himself in the question of Namibia, but here also he ran out of time, and once again it was Dr Owen who initiated action for a new approach. After consultation with the new American administration and with our EEC colleagues it was agreed that it was essential to tackle the problem at the main point of international pressure – i.e. at the United Nations. To achieve this, the five Western members of the Security Council, three of them permanent members (United States, United Kingdom and France) and two elected (Canada and West Germany), agreed to get together to work out proposals for a new Constitution. In order to be acceptable to the Security Council, these proposals would have to be saleable both to SWAPO and to the South Africans. On past form this looked like being an almost impossible task; to try to achieve it a contact group of the five powers was set up in New York, consisting of their Permanent Representatives or their deputies. A parallel group was set up in South Africa consisting of the five ambassadors in Cape Town/Pretoria. In local parlance we became known as 'the Gang of Five', and on matters affecting Namibia we rarely acted separately thereafter.

Looking back, I am amazed how quickly the new machinery was set up. Dr Owen's visit had taken place between 12 and 14 April 1977; on 24 April the New York contact group arrived in Cape Town to hold preliminary talks with the South African Government. The British representative on the group was James Murray, Ivor Richard's deputy; the United States was represented initially by Mr Andrew Young but subsequently mainly by his deputy, Mr Don MacHenry. The group's first task was, in a sense, a negative one – to persuade the South Africans to abandon the recommendations now nearing completion by the Turnhalle Conference and to agree to consider a new set of proposals, not yet formulated, which would stand some chance of acceptance by the Security Council and the international community as a whole.

Once the South African Government had hoisted in that the aim of the five powers was to secure an internationally acceptable solution they acted quickly, though always in a sense designed to keep as much as possible of the initiative in their own hands. In spite of the fact that on 17 May the white voters of Namibia voted overwhelmingly in favour of the Turnhalle proposals for an interim government followed by independence, the South African

197

Government announced only three weeks later that these proposals would, temporarily at least, be set aside and that an Administrator-General, responsible to the State President, would be appointed to administer the territory until a Constituent Assembly was elected. On 6 July Mr Justice M.T. Steyn was appointed Administrator-General.

This reversal of policy, wise as it was, naturally caused much concern among the members of the Turnhalle Conference both black and white, many of whom were by now coming to see themselves as the future rulers of an independent Namibia. It also made some of them physically as well as politically vulnerable, since the decision to go for an internationally acceptable solution gave a clear signal to their opponents, particularly SWAPO, that they would, after all, have some chance of assuming power.

Perhaps the person who had most reason to be upset at the change of plan was Mr Dirk Mudge, one of the leaders of the white delegation and chairman of the constitutional committee, who had taken his colleagues in the National Party a long way along the path towards a multi-racial, even if ethnically structured, constitution. Before I was permitted to visit South-West Africa myself, I established close personal contact with him through my minister, David Summerhayes, who was a frequent visitor to Windhoek, reinforced by personal meetings when Mr Mudge visited Cape Town or Pretoria. I always found him intellectually honest in his arguments; even when we did not see eye to eye on what would be politically saleable in Windhoek or in New York, we were able to discuss the problems calmly and objectively. I wish him well, whatever solution eventually emerges in the country he loves. He has an uphill row to hoe.

CHAPTER 31

SILVER JUBILEE YEAR

ALTHOUGH FOR ME the first half of 1977 was dominated by Dr Owen's initiatives on Rhodesia and Namibia, the South African domestic scene was also in a state of some turmoil.

The stage had been set by an unusually gloomy New Year message to white South Africans in which Mr Vorster spelt out the extent of the country's international isolation. He warned that if South Africa's head should be demanded on a platter, the United Nations 'with the odd vote against and a few abstentions' would happily oblige. After Angola, he said, the Communists knew that they could attack any part of Africa, including South Africa, without evoking any reaction in the rest of the world other than protests, or at best threats. The West had lost the will to take a firm stand against Communism: South Africa would have to stand alone if a Communist assault were made on her. He admitted that South Africa had been harmed 'in no uncertain manner' by the previous year's rioting in the black townships, but he gave no hint that any changes in his Government's racial policies were contemplated. Neither did he explain how South Africa, after nearly thirty years of uninterrupted National Party rule, had managed to become simultaneously isolated from all three of the world groupings he identified; namely the West, the Soviet bloc and the Third World. Nor, curiously enough, did many of his audience even ask the question.

In party political terms the traumatic results of the Portuguese withdrawal from Mozambique and Angola following the 1974 revolution had polarized white opinion in South Africa to the advantage of the National Party (NP) on the right and of the Progressive Reform Party (PRP) on the left. The middle of the road United Party (UP) had been steadily declining in strength since General Smuts's defeat in 1948; now, under the pressure of events, the centre ground it had formerly straddled was itself being eroded. Many of the party's faithful supporters had begun to desert it for either the NP or the PRP. Already the latter had increased its parliamentary representation from one (the indomitable Mrs Helen Suzman) in 1974 to twelve members, and it looked set to gain more from the imminent disintegration of the UP.

Nevertheless, in spite of their dramatic gains, the PRP were doing little more than securing a bigger share of a diminishing opposition vote. The disarray in which the opposition parties found themselves was somewhat maliciously underlined by Mr Vorster at the end of his meeting with Ivor Richard in January. Mr Richard had referred to the difficulties experienced by Mr Callaghan's government in operating without an overall majority in the House of Commons. 'You will understand, Mr Richard,' Mr Vorster replied, 'that we also have a problem with our Opposition.' Ivor Richard, conscious of the size of the Government's parliamentary majority, expressed polite incredulity. 'You see, Mr Richard,' Mr Vorster went on, 'our problem is to keep it in existence.'

However, the National Party was also having serious problems. Evidence was accumulating that important groups within the Afrikaner establishment were becoming dissatisfied with particular aspects of the Government's philosophy and were increasingly prepared to express that dissatisfaction publicly. One was the Afrikaans-language press, which was beginning openly to criticize key areas of Government policy, especially towards the urban blacks. Another consisted of academics at the Afrikaans-medium universities, including members of the *Broederbond* inner circle, who were starting to question some of the basic implications of *apartheid*. Underlying this intellectual ferment, the Afrikaner business community, who were specially well placed to appreciate the economic interdependence of South Africa's racial groups within its highly developed industrial society, began to advocate changes in the laws regulating labour and employment practices, especially as these affected the urban black communities. But possibly most important of all, because the army affected the lives of almost every young South African, the new and dynamic Chief of the Defence Force, General Magnus Malan, was beginning to argue not only that non-whites should be brought in larger numbers into the armed forces, but that their potential should be more fully developed in civil life as well. Evidence was emerging that these theories were actually being put into practice in the army; stories circulated about the abolition of racial segregation in army messes on the Angolan border, and even of white and non-white soldiers sharing the same tents.

Added to these constructive pressures, the first indications of possible malpractice and corruption in the government information field were beginning to leak out; it was alleged - and immediately denied - that unfair influence, possibly even involving the use of official funds, had been used in the setting up of the new pro-National Party daily newspaper, the *Citizen*. A fuse had been lit which was to have profound effects on South African politics in the year ahead.

In this troubled atmosphere it was a relief to be conscious that 1977 was also the year of the Queen's Silver Jubilee. An Ambassador needs occasionally to be able to stand back and recall that, even though most of his work is concerned with prosecuting the policies and interests of Her Majesty's Government – of whichever political party may at the time be in power – he is also, in a real as well as a formal sense, the representative of the Crown itself. In South Africa this was brought home in a number of ways.

For climatic and other reasons the British National Day – the Queen's Birthday – is celebrated in South Africa on 21 April, the Queen's natural birthday, rather than on her official birthday in June. There is a natural tendency in most foreign countries for the local British community to regard the official Queen's Birthday party as primarily an occasion for themselves, though this is not necessarily the official view. In South Africa the numbers who (when it suits them) claim to regard themselves as British, even though many no longer hold British passports, run into hundreds of thousands; in Cape Town alone we had reason to believe that there were still upwards of 10,000 British passport holders. It was, therefore, physically impossible to invite to an official reception more than a small fraction of those who might regard themselves as entitled to attend. This led to endless ill-feeling. Successive British Ambassadors had accordingly organized their Queen's Birthday reception as a deliberately multi-racial occasion, designed to demonstrate that they regarded Britain's (and the Crown's) relations as being with *all* the racial elements in South Africa and not solely with the white minority, still less exclusively with the English-speaking element.

There is one special aspect of the Queen's Birthday which is unique to Cape Town. This is the fact that, as Princess Elizabeth, the Queen celebrated her twenty-first birthday there in 1947. Silver Jubilee year in Cape Town, therefore, was marked by a particular warmth and family feeling which made me determined to celebrate the occasion in appropriate style with a garden party and a band. Fortunately we had glorious weather, and when we drank the Queen's health there was scarcely a dry eye in the place.

The Silver Jubilee itself was celebrated in a special service of thanksgiving in Cape Town Anglican Cathedral, at which I was asked to read the lesson. I found it moving to remember that exactly twenty-five years earlier, in the same cathedral, we had attended the memorial service for the Queen's father, the late King George VI, at which my predecessor, Sir John Le Rougetel, had also read the lesson. Continuity of this kind is strangely reassuring.

The Ambassador also represents the Queen in a more informal way at the annual meeting of the South African Turf Club at which the Queen's Plate is run. The trophy had originally been presented by Queen Victoria in 1861; each year since then the Sovereign had continued to present prize money for the race. By tradition it is the Ambassador's pleasant duty to attend the meeting at Kenilworth race-course and present the plate to the winning owner. In 1977, knowing nothing of local form, Vera and I decided to back every horse whose name had a royal connection. By a remarkable coincidence this brought us winners in four of the first six races; the Queen's Plate itself was appropriately won by Bold Monarch. Our only failure came in the seventh race when we backed a filly called Wild Anne, which finished last – we could only assume that she had been named after the wrong Anne.

Yet another Cape Town connection with the Royal Family was the fact that up to 1978 HRH Princess Alice, Countess of Athlone, remained a regular visitor to the city in which she had lived during the 1930s when her husband was Governor-General. By the time we arrived in South Africa she was already well over ninety, but she remained lively and attractive and had a fund of anecdotes going well back into the last century. In Silver Jubilee year she recalled at lunch in our house how on the occasion of Queen Victoria's Golden Jubilee in 1887 she and her brother had been driven from their parents' home at Claremont Park, Esher, to Buckingham Palace, changing horses at Richmond. After lunch her grandmother had sent for her and placed her on her lap. Queen Victoria had very short legs, and her black silk dress was extremely slippery – 'Grandmama's lap was like a landslide' – but she was well aware that it would never do for her to fall off until she was given permission to leave. In order to stay in place she had to keep pushing herself up with her feet – 'it was like treading water' – and she was greatly relieved when she was finally allowed to get down.

CHAPTER 32

═══

DEVELOPMENTS ON
RHODESIA AND NAMIBIA

WHEN THE 1977 parliamentary session ended in mid-June, we spent our usual ten days touring on our way back to Pretoria. This time we set off due north from Cape Town, skirting the western edge of the Cedarberg range. From the rich fruit-growing areas of Citrusdal and Clanwilliam, we crossed the Pakhuis Pass through landscapes resembling huge cemeteries of shattered rock and made a brief diversion to visit the small and isolated Coloured community at Wuppertal. From there, after a night at Calvinia, we drove north through increasingly barren karroo country.

Although the flat, almost desert, landscape is scarcely touched by agriculture, brackish water is often close to the surface. On one stretch of flooded land – one could hardly dignify it by calling it a lake – a mass of pink and white birds struck a magnificently discordant note. Who could possibly have expected to find a flock of flamingos and spoonbills in the middle of the karroo? Further north the surface water vanished but trees reappeared, some of them bowed down by the weight of huge nests of sociable weavers. These multiple nests can weigh up to two or three tons, and contain thousands of pairs of birds.

Eventually, coming over a slight rise, the parched brown land gave way to a strip of vivid green: the irrigated area of the Orange River. For perhaps two hundred miles, from far above the market town of Upington downstream to the spectacular Augrabies Falls, the valley is cultivated as a vast market garden: citrus, grapes, apricots and peaches, ground-nuts and vegetables, grow in controlled profusion. Irrigation canals, some of them fifty kilometres long, are taken off the river further and further upstream, so constantly widening the area under cultivation. The whole project is a remarkable tribute to the work over the past sixty years of the Water Department, whose development budget in the area runs into millions of rands.

From Upington our route took us eastwards to the manganese and iron mining areas of Postmasburg and Sishen. The latter is the site of a vast opencast iron mine from which an eight-hundred-mile railway line has been built solely to lift ore to a new loading terminal at Saldanha Bay. At Sishen we were entertained by the local management of the South African Iron and Steel Corporation (ISCOR) and taken round the mine in company with representatives of the British consultants responsible for designing the plant to upgrade the iron content of the ore before shipment.

At Kuruman, a few miles further on, we visited the historic mission station first opened by Robert Moffat in 1829, from which his daughter Mary had married David Livingstone. The tree under which he is said to have proposed still exists though much mutilated by souvenir-hunters.

Our tour ended with a visit to Mafeking and the homeland of Bophuthatswana, where we were the guests of the South African Commissioner-General. Here we visited medical and agricultural establishments, and I had a long meeting with Chief Mangope, the Chief Minister, and his Cabinet. Once again I encountered the dilemma faced by the homeland leaders; Mangope made an impassioned plea, to which I was far from unsympathetic, for British help, particularly in the fields of medicine and the teaching of English. He argued convincingly that only by securing help of this kind from third parties could Bophuthatswana shake off the restrictive influence of the South African Department of Bantu Administration, and so achieve a measure of true independence. This argument formed an important element in my subsequent recommendation that we should embark on a modest programme of aid and technical assistance for black South Africans, both urban and rural. provided this could be done without appearing to endorse the homelands policy or recognizing their so-called independence.

Back in Pretoria we were visited by my mother, who, having seen something of Cape Town the year before, had expressed a wish to visit the Transvaal. Unfortunately her stay was dogged with misfortune. Two days after her arrival I was struck by a violent attack of asthma, which involved my being taken off to hospital in the middle of the night; no sooner was I back in circulation than my mother had a serious fall on the highly dangerous marble spiral staircase in our official residence, with the result that she spent the remaining three weeks of her holiday in hospital.

Vera and I had been due to start a period of home leave in September 1977, but in early August I was asked to convey an invitation to Mr Pik Botha to attend a further round of talks on Rhodesia with Dr Owen and Mr Vance in London. I was asked to attend these talks myself and we decided that, although I should have to return to Pretoria for a few weeks after the London meeting, it would be best for Vera to accompany my mother back to London as soon as she was fit to travel and to remain in England until our leave proper began.

The London meetings were highly concentrated. In addition to the two Secretaries of State and the South African Foreign Minister, they were attended by Johnnie Graham and Steve Low, the consultative group on Rhodesia; by the American Ambassadors in London and Pretoria, and by myself. In the course of them it was agreed that HMG, in collaboration with the United States Government, should put forward firm proposals to allow Rhodesia to make an orderly transition to recognized independence during 1978. This would involve the holding of free and impartial elections, the establishment of a transitional British administration supported by a United Nations presence, the drawing up of an independence constitution, and the underwriting of a Zimbabwe Development Fund of between $1,000 million and $1,500 million by a number of countries led by the United States and Great Britain. The interim administration would be headed by a British Resident Commissioner, not yet named.

Ten days after my return to Pretoria the Secretary of State, this time accompanied by Mr Andrew Young representing Mr Vance, and by the consultative group, made another lightning tour of southern Africa to tie up the loose ends of the Rhodesian proposals.

While in Pretoria Dr Owen's time was mainly taken up by meetings with Mr Vorster and Mr Pik Botha, but he also asked to meet some of the leading protagonists in the South African internal scene. At very short notice, therefore, I got together two groups to meet him. The first was a mixed party of trade unionists, both black and white, and leading businessmen, with whom he had a useful discussion on labour relations, including the so-called 'code of conduct' drawn up to guide British companies operating in South Africa. The second was a group including the veteran South African financier, Mr Harry Oppenheimer, consisting of members of the South African political and economic establishments. I even managed to persuade Chief Gatsha Buthelezi, the leader of Kwazulu, to fly up from Durban to join us for dinner. Dr Owen contrived to have useful conversations with most of the guests. After the party Chief Buthelezi took me warmly by both hands and said, 'Thank you, David. That was a great evening for the Anglo-Zulu love-hate relationship.'

Early in September the Rhodesia settlement proposals were promulgated as a White Paper[1] and published simultaneously in London and Salisbury. Initially they made a considerable impact. They were, however, seriously prejudiced a few weeks later by a reported gloss put on them in a private letter from President Carter to President Nyerere of Tanzania. This letter was understood to affirm that the new Zimbabwe National Army would be 'based on the liberation armies', a reference to the guerrilla forces under the command of Mr Mugabe and Mr Nkomo. The White Paper itself had used a carefully chosen and neutral form of words on this point – that the Zimbabwe Army would 'in due course replace all existing armed forces in Rhodesia', which left open the precise way in which the army of the future independent Zimbabwe should be formed. When reports of this gloss leaked out, it was castigated by the South African Government, whose good offices with the Rhodesians had been specifically enlisted at the London meeting in August, as a deliberate breach of faith which would inevitably damage both the atmosphere in Salisbury and their own future willingness to co-operate.

While the Rhodesian proposals were still being digested, the New York contact group on Namibia once again assembled in Pretoria. This time they met the South African Government in the shadow, not only of the inherent negotiating differences, but also of a deeply repugnant extraneous event. On 12 September 1977 Mr Steve Biko, the leader of the Black Consciousness movement in South Africa, died in detention following interrogation in brutal and degrading circumstances in the course of which he received fatal brain damage. It subsequently emerged that when the seriousness of his injuries had become apparent he was transported a distance of seven hundred miles, naked in the back of a Land-Rover, from Port Elizabeth to a prison hospital at Pretoria where he died.

In a statement made shortly after Biko's death, the then Minister of Justice, Mr James Kruger, implied that he had died as the result of a hunger strike. By the time the five-power group met, however, it was clear that this was not the correct explanation, and their feelings of genuine outrage came close to wrecking the talks altogether.

In the event, both sides stopped short of the brink. In an unexpected gesture, the South African Government went out of their way to inform the National Party in South-West Africa that they accepted the need for far-reaching changes on the lines proposed by the contact group; this led to a split in the National Party, Mr Mudge breaking away from his extreme right-wing colleagues to form the Republican Party. At the same time the constitutional links between the South African Parliament and the South-West African Legislative Assembly were broken with the termination of South-West African representation in Parliament at Cape Town. Two weeks later, the Administrator-General announced that a number of discriminatory South African laws would cease to be applicable in South-West Africa (Namibia).

These included the controversial Immorality and Mixed Marriages Acts, which still make sexual relations between the races, whether inside or outside marriage, a criminal offence in South Africa itself. The revoking of these laws, which are regarded by the more strait-laced members of the Afrikaner community as fundamental to the policy of *apartheid*, did not cause the skies to fall in Namibia. On the contrary, taken in conjunction with the simultaneous relaxation of the laws on mixing in hotels and restaurants, they led, at least in the eyes of an outsider, to a marked improvement in the racial atmosphere in the territory.

CHAPTER 33

1978: SOUTH AFRICA'S YEAR OF CRISIS

I STARTED MY DEFERRED leave in early October 1977. A few hours before I left Pretoria I learned that Field Marshal Lord Carver, the former Chief of Defence Staff, with whom I had briefly served on the Joint Planning Staff in 1954, was about to be appointed Resident Commissioner in Rhodesia in terms of the Anglo-American plan, and I was asked to pass this information to Air Vice-Marshal Hawkins, the Rhodesian diplomatic representative in Pretoria, for transmission to his Government. Although Harold Hawkins was not officially recognized by the rest of the diplomatic corps in South Africa as one of their number, he and his wife had been personal friends of ours from our earlier service in Salisbury and I and my predecessor had been specifically authorized to use him as a channel of communication with the Salisbury regime. He was, of course, well aware of Lord Carver's outstanding reputation as a soldier, and of his highly relevant experience of bush warfare, particularly during the Mau Mau emergency in Kenya. I was confident, therefore, that he would commend the appointment to his Government.

On my arrival in London, I contacted Lord Carver in order to bring him up to date on my talks with Hawkins and the South Africans. He responded by inviting me to lunch with him at the House of Lords two days later. When we met he asked me bluntly whether I thought he was mad to have accepted the appointment of Resident Commissioner. I said, truthfully, that I believed there was now a better chance of reaching a solution to the problem than at any time in the immediate past, but that few reputations had so far been enhanced by becoming involved in it. In the light of my meeting with Air Vice-Marshal Hawkins, however, I felt sure that if anyone had a hope of succeeding, he had. Nevertheless, I would not put his chances too high.

The rest of my leave was fairly fully occupied. Because of the rapidly developing situation, particularly in relation to Rhodesia and Namibia, I was invited to a succession of City and business lunches and dinners and had a

208

number of meetings with ministers and officials in Whitehall. Among these was a particularly useful meeting with Dr Owen, at which we were able to take further the question of aid for the black communities in South Africa, particularly in the field of English language teaching. I felt that at last we were beginning to get somewhere, though I well realized what a sensitive subject it was in strictly political terms. I also had a valuable meeting over lunch with Lord Carrington and the then shadow Foreign Secretary, the late Mr John Davies.

Vera and I decided to spend the last week of our leave in January 1978 where we could not easily be got hold of. We settled for Malta, which Vera had never visited. One special advantage of this was that we were able to look up the Monsarrats, who lived in Gozo, Malta's sister island. Nicholas met us at the ferry terminal and took us to their delightful house at San Lawrenz, where we spent a happy day gossiping and making plans for Ann and him to visit us in Cape Town the following year. Alas, before our plans could mature Nicholas was taken ill and we never saw him again.

From Malta we had an unexpectedly roundabout journey back to Johannesburg, via Rome and Madrid. The last part of the flight took us over Namibia near the mouth of the Cunene River on the Angolan border and thence across Botswana before touching down at Jan Smuts airport. It was an appropriate route to follow back into action.

During our absence, the National Party had been returned with an increased majority at the South African general election in October 1977. It had been widely assumed that the election had been called by Mr Vorster with the aim of securing a vote of confidence which would enable him, *inter alia*, to make certain changes in his Cabinet, particularly in relation to the irregularities in the Information Department and to the Biko affair. When it came to the point it seemed that the ministers concerned refused to go quietly, and Mr Vorster at the last moment jibbed at the possible consequences of dismissing them. When Parliament reassembled, therefore, the mixture was very much as before except that Dr Mulder was transferred to the Department of Bantu Administration, now renamed the Department of Plural Relations.

Our first public engagement after our return to Cape Town was the State President's banquet on 26 January 1978, on the eve of the opening of Parliament. After the banquet, I had an opportunity for a short talk with Mr Vorster. I was very shocked at his appearance: he had a bad colour and was obviously far from well, and he told me that he was under doctor's orders to take things very quietly.

While we had been away, a number of developments had taken place in Namibia. The Administrator-General had in October revoked the Pass Laws requiring Africans to carry special documentation, and in December he had taken over a number of governmental functions from South African departments in Pretoria in order to administer them directly from Windhoek. At the same time he issued a proclamation allowing blacks for the first time to own freehold property – something that had always been prohibited in South Africa. Following the breakup of the National Party in the territory, moreover, Mr Dirk Mudge had helped to form a new multi-racial alliance of political parties, the Democratic Turnhalle Alliance (DTA), of which the first President was the Herero leader, Chief Clemens Kapuuo.

On 2 February the five powers presented a new set of proposals on Namibia, the most detailed so far, to the South African Government and to SWAPO. Although the substance of these proposals had been extensively discussed with both sides in advance, they inevitably contained phraseology which it had not been possible specifically to clear with either; the whole purpose of the negotiations was, after all, to bridge a gap between the two sides which had previously been regarded as unbridgeable. The best we could hope for, therefore, was the 'parity of disesteem' to which Lord Alport had referred in Rhodesia. One aspect to which the South Africans objected in particular was the proposal for the phased withdrawal of all but 1,500 of their troops stationed in the territory, and the demobilization of the white 'kommandos' and other ethnic forces.

In an attempt to resolve the outstanding differences, therefore, the five powers invited both sides to take part in 'proximity talks' between themselves and the UN Secretary-General in New York. This invitation was designed to get round Mr Vorster's publicly declared refusal to sit down at the same table as SWAPO. On the second day of the talks, however, to everyone's disappointment, Mr Pik Botha withdrew from them on the ground that he needed to consult his Government, and returned to Pretoria.

At this point a curious reversal of roles became apparent in the negotiations. Up to then it had been the five powers, responding to pressures in the Security Council, who had been urging the South Africans to speed up the talks. After Mr Botha had reported back to his colleagues on 14 February it was Mr Vorster who began to say that he was committed to giving South-West Africa independence by the end of the year and that, in order to avoid further political uncertainty in the territory, he had every intention of sticking to that date, whether or not by then SWAPO and the Security Council had reached agreement on the terms of the settlement. This argument was given added significance when on 27 March Chief Kapuuo, President of the DTA, was assassinated outside his shop in Katutura, the black township near Windhoek.

On 30 March 1978, following further intensive discussions, the New York contact group came up with some important clarifications. These took into account anxieties expressed by both sides at the proximity talks in February. It was made clear, however, that if the latest package were not accepted there would be very little room for further manœuvre without prejudicing legitimate concerns of either SWAPO or the South Africans. Ten days later the new proposal[1] was transmitted to the Security Council.

At this precise moment I had, for the first time, been given permission to visit Namibia. Following a ruling by the International Court of Justice in 1971 that the South African presence in South-West Africa was illegal, a convention had grown up among most of the countries represented in South Africa that their Ambassadors should not visit the territory so long as it continued to be administered from Pretoria. With the increasing Western interest in solving the problem, however, this convention had begun to be called in question, not least by myself, and the Secretary of State accepted the argument that, if we were to take an active part in reaching an agreed solution in the territory, we could not afford to tie one hand behind our back by refusing to go there.

Vera and I spent our first night at Swakopmund, from where the next morning we visited the Rössing uranium mine, run by an international consortium headed by the British mining group, Rio Tinto-Zinc. We had only just arrived at the mine when I was told that there was a telephone call for me in the manager's office. This turned out to be my deputy, David Summerhayes, telling me in guarded terms that 'two very important visitors' were expected in Pretoria at the week-end and that it had been suggested that I should meet them there rather than return to Cape Town on Sunday as planned. I guessed from the context that one of the visitors must be Dr Owen; who the other might be I had no idea. It was only three days later, as we were coming to the end of our stay in Windhoek, that I heard that the second visitor was the American Secretary of State Cyrus Vance.

In Windhoek I met a number of local personalities and political parties, including representatives of SWAPO, DTA, the Namibian National Front (NNF) and AKTUR, the extreme right-wing element of the former National Party. I also called on Mr Justice M.T. Steyn, the Administrator-General. We subsequently had the chance of a more informal talk with him at a dinner kindly given for us by the doyens of Windhoek society, Jack and Olga Levinson. I was highly impressed with the grasp he had acquired of the local political scene in a short time.

Vera and I arrived in Pretoria an hour or two before the two Secretaries of State were due. Since our official residence was closed for the Parliamentary session, we had booked ourselves into the Burgerspark Hotel, where Dr Owen and Mr Vance were also staying. By the time we arrived, the 'deaf-aid boys' were in full possession: three complete floors of the hotel had been taken over and a number of somewhat disgruntled guests had been moved out to make way for the official delegations.

For security reasons the lifts had been programmed not to stop at the eighth floor where the ministers were accommodated, with the result that it became extremely difficult to get any form of room service. Vera and I had a suite next to Dr Owen's, and it seemed to happen that we became the refreshment centre for the floor. At one particular gap in the proceedings, Vera had managed with great difficulty to get a pot of tea for herself and me and Joanna Lowis, my secretary, who had joined us from Cape Town, when Dr Owen wandered in and said, 'Hurrah, a cup of tea. Can I join you?' Joanna dutifully gave him her cup and went off to get another; before she got back, however, Andy Young and Mr Vance had also detected the tea and had gone off to collect cups from their rooms. Vera said that it reminded her of our university days at Birmingham, when as impecunious students we went to the Union tea-room and ordered 'tea for three and seven cups, please'. By the time Cy Vance had had his cup, Vera was reduced to refilling the teapot from the hot tap in our bathroom. But I don't think anyone noticed.

The meeting had been arranged primarily to discuss Rhodesia, and the consultative group and Lord Carver were also of the party. Already by then, however, the Rhodesian white ants had been eating away at Lord Carver's appointment as Resident Commissioner: the word was going around in Salisbury that he was a 'political general' and that, far from being neutral, he was committed to the policy attributed to President Carter of ensuring that the future armed forces of Zimbabwe should be 'based on the liberation armies'. Once again the familiar syndrome was at work – the politicians in Salisbury seemed determined to denigrate and antagonize the very people who were in the best position to help them.

Namibia was also on the agenda, however, and the fact that I had just been there proved extremely useful. The new proposal was the subject of particular examination. South African ministers had earlier made it clear that they would have to discuss it with the parties in Windhoek before they could give a final answer, but the same night, after a lot of coming and going, Dirk Mudge let it be known that the security aspects of the proposal, always one of the more sensitive points, were broadly acceptable to the DTA. On 25 April, just after the special session of the General Assembly had begun in New York, the South African Government announced their acceptance of the proposal as a whole.

This was a great step forward. It was, however, followed by a prolonged silence from SWAPO, who had clearly been relying on the special session to secure them better terms. Indeed, the resolution which the Assembly passed on 3 May blandly ignored the fact that the dispute was *sub judice* in the Security Council and called, wholly unrealistically, for Namibia to be handed over to SWAPO immediately. As if in reply, the South African Defence Force carried out a major raid on the SWAPO base at Kassinga in Angola on 4 May, inflicting heavy loss of life.

From the point of view of the five powers' negotiations this raid could scarcely have been more disastrously timed; there was for a time an inclination on the part of the contact group to throw in their hands, arguing that the reaction to the raid in New York would make further progress in the Security Council impossible. The other side of the coin was, of course, that the South Africans had made it clear beyond doubt where the military balance of power lay, and this message was not entirely lost on SWAPO. Although the Security Council unanimously condemned the raid, they stopped short of a determination under Chapter 7 of the UN Charter, which would have invoked mandatory action against South Africa as creating a threat to peace.

During the three months which followed South Africa's acceptance of the five powers' proposal, the Front Line States began to put pressure on SWAPO to follow suit. The Tanzanians in particular took the decisive step of releasing Mr Andreas Shipanga, a former member of the SWAPO Executive Committee, and eighteen other SWAPO members who had been held in detention, first in Zambia and later in Tanzania, following a split between them and Mr Sam Nujoma some two years earlier. (On his return to Namibia Shipanga formed a new party, SWAPO (Democratic), which later formed a working alliance with the NNF.) A meeting of the Front Line Presidents was held in Luanda on 11 June, at the end of which SWAPO announced that they would be prepared to resume talks to resolve the outstanding issues.

Meanwhile the South Africans, ignoring the fact that the delay was at least partly a result of the Kassinga raid, continued to press for the electoral process to be started; on 20 June the Administrator-General announced that the registration of voters throughout Namibia would begin on 26 June and continue until 22 September. The South Africans represented this registration as a precautionary process to enable an election to take place without delay once the procedures for a UN-supervised election had been agreed. From the point of view of the five-power group and of the Security Council, however, it was clearly inconsistent with the electoral process envisaged in our proposal, not least because the registration would not be internationally supervised.

On 11 July, Don MacHenry, acting on behalf of the New York contact group, met SWAPO representatives in Luanda. The next day a statement was issued as follows:

During two days of frank and cordial discussion certain points in the proposal of the Five Powers were clarified and the two delegations accordingly agreed to proceed to the Security Council, thus opening the way to an early internationally acceptable settlement of the question of Namibia.

It looked almost as if we had arrived. But there were still plenty of reefs ahead.

CHAPTER 34

NAMIBIA BACK IN
THE MELTING-POT

THE 1978 PARLIAMENTARY SESSION ended in June with a flurry of activity on the Information Department scandal. The Government managed to play out time, but the press and opposition were howling for blood. One of the last acts of the session was the establishment of a judicial inquiry under Mr Justice Anton Mostert to investigate the possible misappropriation of funds in the department. As Parliament adjourned, Mr Vorster was taken ill, and went into hospital in Cape Town for treatment and a complete rest.

A few days later the State President, Dr Diedrichs, also fell ill; in the middle of August he died. A State funeral was held in his home city of Bloemfontein on 26 August. Two special aircraft were laid on from the military airfield at Waterkloof, just outside Pretoria, to enable ministers and members of the diplomatic corps to attend. It was a cold and wet day, and it was widely remarked that Mr Vorster, who had interrupted his convalescence to be present, was looking far from well. Within a matter of days he was back in hospital.

It was generally expected that Mr Laurens Muller, the Minister of Transport, would succeed Dr Diedrichs as State President, but before the election for the presidency was due to take place Mr Vorster let it be known that, bearing in mind his state of health, he would himself be available for the post. On the correct assumption that he would be elected this created a vacancy for the prime ministership. A period of intense political activity opened.

Meanwhile in early August, the South African Government having approved the presence of a UN mission, Mr Martti Ahtisaari, the (Finnish) former UN Commissioner for Namibia who had been designated the Secretary-General's Special Representative in terms of the five powers' proposal, paid a short visit to Namibia to carry out a preliminary survey in connection with its implementation. He was accompanied by a .eam of about fifty, including General Philipp, the Austrian army officer who had been named as Commander-designate of the UN Transitional Assistance Group (UNTAG). Although the five ambassadors had virtually no contact with the UN party, the visit subsequently led to the first of a series of misunderstandings between us and the South Africans, and for that reason must be referred to briefly here.

So far as we could tell at the time, it was a highly successful visit. By all accounts Ahtisaari got on well with Judge Steyn, with whom under the plan he would have to work in double harness. In parallel, General Philipp had frank and detailed discussions with General Geldenhuys, the South African GOC in South-West Africa, and quickly established a close working *rapport* with him. As professional soldiers they had no difficulty in first identifying and then agreeing on the tasks to be carried out by UNTAG. It was clear that this definition of the tasks pointed inexorably to the need for a larger force than the South Africans had previously had in mind; it was not, however, apparently fully understood by the soldiers that the results of their discussion could not be regarded as the basis of a final agreement, but would have to be cleared with the South African Government at ministerial level.

Mr Ahtisaari, who by then had also consulted the SWAPO leaders in Luanda, returned to New York on 22 August and reported to the Secretary-General. On 30 August, Dr Waldheim submitted his own formal report to the Security Council for approval and implementation. In it he proposed that UNTAG should consist of 7,500 troops plus a further 1,500 officials and police, and laid down a programme under which UN-supervised elections would take place seven months after acceptance of the proposal by the Security Council. The numbers suggested were considerably bigger than had been anticipated, particularly in relation to the size of the residual South African force, though they could be fully justified on military grounds. It could, moreover, be argued that the larger UNTAG was, the less the chance of intimidation on either side and hence the less need for substantial numbers of South African troops. This view was not accepted by the South African Government, however, who described the Secretary-General's report as totally inconsistent with the five powers' proposal. In addition, they accused the Five of duplicity in allowing the report to emerge in such a form, arguing that their original proposal had placed the Secretary-General under a special obligation to consult them on the number and composition of UNTAG.

At this point the Namibian problem became even more closely involved with South Africa's internal politics. On 20 September, in a televised press conference, with Mr Pik Botha at his side, Mr Vorster formally announced his resignation from the premiership; in the same conference he said that the Administrator-General would call an election in South-West Africa to elect a Constituent Assembly. All options would be open to this assembly: it could accept the Secretary-General's report; it could proceed with the implementation of the five powers' proposal, or it could itself go ahead and draw up a new Constitution.

This announcement was once again clearly inconsistent with the Five's proposal. Worse, it confirmed the fears of those who suspected that the South African Government had never genuinely intended to allow internationally-supervised elections to take place in Namibia. It also, predictably, stimulated SWAPO to declare that they would intensify the armed struggle. There was even a danger that the Security Council would decide to reject the Five's proposal on the grounds that it failed to satisfy either of the main protagonists and was unenforceable.

On 25 September Dr Owen, who had spent the previous two days attending a meeting between Mr Callaghan and Dr Kenneth Kaunda at Kano, arrived in New York to attend the General Assembly. It was clear that matters were coming to a head. The only source of encouragement on Namibia was an announcement from Mr Justice Steyn in Windhoek that the elections planned for October would be postponed until 4 December on the ground that no section of the community should feel that its views were being disregarded for want of time.

What happened next affected me closely and can perhaps best be recorded by quoting from a diary which, exceptionally, I kept at the time.

26 September 1978 (on BA *Flight to London)*
Had the somewhat eerie experience of hearing on this morning's 8 o'clock SABC News that the five Pretoria ambassadors had been summoned to New York for consultation with our Ministers prior to the Security Council meeting on Thursday. When I told Vera, she said, 'They have to be joking. They *must* have got it wrong.' I said that I wasn't so sure. On arrival at the office at 8.45 the news was confirmed by a telegram which had just come in from the Secretary of State in New York, asking me to be in New York by Wednesday (tomorrow) afternoon: I am grateful that he did not have me woken in the middle of the night to tell me. After a good deal of telephoning by Joanna I was booked on this evening's 747 flight to London, and Concorde on to New York tomorrow morning. Bernard Dorin [my French colleague] was only wait-listed for the BA flight J'burg-London, but very properly insisted on Concorde for the London-NY sector and eventually got himself on.

I saw Brand Fourie this morning. He was highly pessimistic about what we could do on the Namibia *débâcle*, but urged the Five to delay a decision until the SWA elections take place in November. I was v. doubtful whether this cd. be achieved. He got v. hot under the collar at my suggestion that [General] Magnus Malan had never seen Gen. Philipp's justification of the figure of 7,500 for UNTAG. He threatened to ring up the General on the spot to check, but did not carry this out. The fact is that

Generals Philipp and Geldenhuys *did* discuss the detailed tasks for UNTAG but did *not* discuss total numbers. . . .

My date with Fourie this morning was partly to tell him . . . of D. Owen's latest views on Rhodesia. We would *not* be prepared to accept a return to legality on the basis of taking over responsibility for a racial war in Rhodesia. Any such proposal must accept the principle of an all-party conference and the AAP [Anglo-American Plan]. Fourie accepted this – and indicated that the S. African Govt. 'did not know what these people [Smith & Co.] were up to'.

Had to leave Vera to host dinner party for tonight as well as cancelling visits to Potchefstroom, Bloemfontein and Fort Hare Universities for this week and next, as well as a speech at St Andrew's, Grahamstown.

28 September (New York, U.N. Plaza Hotel)
I distinguished myself by getting on to Concorde (my first flight) yesterday morning with a violent *migraine* and being violently sick into a brown paper bag even before we had taken off. I sat next to a nice & sympathetic man from Hill Samuel – poor chap! Earlier I had had a talk with Martin Reid [H.M.S. Reid, CMG, head of Central & Southern African Department, FCO, and later my deputy as Minister, Cape Town/ Pretoria] at the Excelsior Hotel during my stop-over at LAP. This was v. useful in bringing me up to date, but contributed to the *migraine*.

On arrival at JFK (10 am NY time) I found that the S. of S. was speaking in the General Assembly at 12.45. This gave me an opportunity to make my number with him before he got up to speak, as well as to listen to the speech myself. I also met two old friends in the Assembly – Leslie Harriman, the outspoken Nigerian chairman of the Committee on Apartheid, who had been on the same course as me at the IDC [Imperial Defence College, now Royal College of Defence Studies]; and Shirley Amerasinghe, a former President of the Assembly, who had served with us in Delhi as High Cr. for Ceylon. Leslie embraced me warmly, with the comment that he didn't think the British Ambassador to S.A. should be seen talking to him.

We had delegation talks at lunch and throughout the afternoon, but I managed to steal an hour's excellent sleep between 6 & 7. At 7.45 we had a meeting of the Pretoria Ambassadors with the Contact Group; after which Mervyn Brown took me off to a quick dinner at his Park Avenue apartment, cooked by James Murray's renowned Chinese cook, Ah Ngee. After ¾-hour we had to be back at the US Delegation Office for a further meeting of the contact groups with Martti Ahtisaari.

I was able to get together with Ahtisaari before the meeting started, and explained our difficulties over the assurances of consultation given to the S. Africans by the Five as long ago as 30 March. He made quite a lot of the fact that he had consulted Judge Steyn, though not specifically on numbers, and that Gen. Philipp had had very full discussions with Gen. Geldenhuys. I pointed out that the latter was not regarded as equivalent to Governmental consultation – on the strictly military net there was no real argument about numbers – and that the S.A. argument was entirely a political one.

The meeting then started in earnest. Debate on the draft for the Sec-Gen's speech to the Security Council the next day went on until 1.30 a.m. (New York time), by which time I calculated that I had been on the go for almost exactly 50 hours with only cat-naps in the aeroplanes and one hour's sleep in New York. By then I had got my second wind and I continued to press Ahtisaari for the inclusion in the speech of some acknowledgement that South Africa was still owed a genuine measure of consultation on the size of UNTAG. He gave no ground during our discussion, but I was delighted to discover the next morning that a new paragraph accepting the need for further consultation had been added to the draft by the Secretariat. For once I felt that I had made a genuine contribution.

The next day the Security Council debate took place. Thanks to Mervyn Brown offering me his seat I sat with Ivor Richard immediately behind David Owen at the table. No fewer than 9 Foreign Ministers attended the debate. It was characteristic of New York double standards that Adriaan Eksteen [the South African Chargé d'Affaires] was not allowed to take any part in the debate, even though it was about a territory for which South Africa was *de facto* responsible, while Sam Nujoma had a place at the table from which he made a lengthy and mainly unhelpful speech. (I heard that a distinguished Commonwealth statesman commented privately some weeks ago that Nujoma enjoyed the fruits of the struggle so much that he feared he would be reluctant to take on the responsibilities of victory.)

CHAPTER 35

MR P.W. BOTHA TAKES
UP THE REINS

IN THE MIDST of the excitement in New York, a new Prime Minister was elected in Pretoria on 29 September 1978. Initially there had been four contenders, of whom three, oddly enough, were called Botha. These were Mr S.P. (Fanie) Botha, Minister of Mines; Mr R.F. (Pik) Botha, Minister of Foreign Affairs; Dr Connie Mulder, Minister of Plural Relations, and Mr P.W. Botha, Minister of Defence. At a fairly early stage Mr Fanie Botha withdrew. Of the other three, Pik Botha was not generally regarded as a strong contender at such an early stage in his ministerial career; the main significance of his standing was that he could be expected to split the Transvaal vote with Dr Mulder. And that was how it turned out. On the first vote Mulder received the greatest support, with Mr P.W. Botha a close second; Pik then dropped out and P.W. was elected by a comfortable majority.

Naturally the outcome was of the greatest interest to the Secretary of State, and indeed to all the ministers of the five powers in New York. The UK delegation therefore arranged with Summerhayes in Pretoria that as soon as the announcement was made from the Parliament building in Cape Town it would be telephoned direct to Dr Owen's party in the UN Plaza Hotel in New York. In fact, the system worked so well that Summerhayes managed to beat the news agencies by almost half an hour – a rare achievement.

Particular interest centred on the policies which the new Prime Minister might be expected to adopt. Although Mr Botha had a reputation as a hardliner in National Party terms, I did not assume that he would necessarily adopt a hard line in the field of external relations. There were two reasons for caution. One was that, since he had been Minister of Defence for a number of years during which Britain had operated an arms embargo against South Africa, there had been far less opportunity than with most other ministers for successive British Ambassadors to get to know him personally. We had therefore relatively little first-hand experience on which to form a judgment. The second was that, as Minister of Defence, he would naturally pay great attention to the advice of his principal official adviser General Malan, who com-

'Sorry, I can't sell you a Dinky, m'boy ...
they fall under the British arms embargo!'

bined the post of Chief of the Defence Force with that of Secretary for Defence. General Malan had consistently made it clear that he was aware of the danger of over-extending the military task by including South-West Africa and Rhodesia in South Africa's defence perimeter, and for this reason seemed likely to favour the side of caution.

The Security Council met the same afternoon and adopted Resolution 435, thereby approving the Secretary-General's report on the implementation of the five powers' proposal on Namibia. In the process it condemned the holding of unsupervised elections by the South Africans. This was in line with the attitude of the five governments, and I left New York feeling reasonably content with the outcome of the meeting.

After two days of consultation in London, I returned to Pretoria on 4 October to find myself immediately involved in a meeting of the five ambassadors at the German Embassy as a preliminary to our calling on Mr Pik Botha later the same afternoon. At this meeting Mr Botha raised a number of difficulties on the implementation of Resolution 435, particularly in relation to the number and composition of the UN force, and indicated that there could be no question of delaying the elections beyond the date of 4 December already announced by the Administrator-General. Since there was no possibility of the Security Council being able either to arrange for these elections to be supervised in the time available or to accept the result of elections unsupervised by, the United Nations, this looked like putting the whole negotiation back to square one.

However, the five governments were not prepared to accept that we had reached the end of the road after getting so near to a solution. In a final attempt to put the talks back on the rails, I was instructed to deliver a personal message to Mr P.W. Botha from Mr Callaghan. Its main purpose was to congratulate the new Prime Minister on his appointment, but at the same time I was authorized to suggest to him that the five foreign ministers might be prepared collectively to visit Pretoria for talks on Namibia. After some initial hesitation this proposal was accepted, though again Mr Botha made the fair point that in the last resort it would be up to the people of Namibia to decide whether or not there was room for manœuvre in reaching a solution. Dr Owen responded to this by suggesting to his colleagues that they might start their visit by spending a day at Windhoek to meet the political parties there. In the event, Herr Hans-Dietrich Genscher, the German Foreign Minister, and Mr Don Jamieson, the Canadian Minister of External Affairs, as well as Dr Owen himself, agreed to go to Windhoek.

Between my delivery of Mr Callaghan's message and the arrival of the foreign ministers, Mr Vorster was sworn in as State President at a solemn service in the Groote Kerk in Pretoria. This was followed by a vast ceremonial gathering in Church Square at which he made his inaugural address. During those few days I also made a series of calls on some of the leading newspaper editors in Pretoria and Johannesburg. I drew attention to the efforts which the five powers had made to secure an internationally acceptable solution to the Namibian problem, and in particular to the additional paragraph which had been included in the Secretary-General's speech acknowledging the need for further consultation on the strength and composition of UNTAG.

Altogether, it was an extremely busy week. As well as the work on Namibia, I had my annual Embassy commercial and consular conferences taking place successively in Johannesburg and Pretoria and involving our Consuls-General in Johannesburg, Cape Town and Durban, as well as representatives from departments in Whitehall. On Friday, 13 October, even before the Pretoria conference was over, I took off for Windhoek with George Grande and Hans-Joachim Eick, my Canadian and German colleagues, to meet our ministers.

The ministers' programme in Windhoek followed a pattern previously

222

established by the contact group, under which each of the political parties and various groups of church and business leaders were received in succession. As always happened, each group tended to overrun their time, so that the later interviews fell progressively further behind schedule. This understandably irritated those whose appointments came last. But by dint of working almost without a break the ministers managed to meet all concerned by about midnight. On Sunday morning, before taking off for Pretoria, they also fitted in a meeting at the airport with Mr Andreas Shipanga and his SWAPO (D) colleagues who had flown in that morning from Europe.

In Pretoria the ministers joined up with Secretary of State Vance and M. Olivier Stirn, the French Minister of State (the French alone were not represented at foreign minister level), over a splendid luncheon laid on by Anne Eick at the German Embassy. The afternoon was occupied in delegation talks and the first meeting with the South Africans was fixed for the following morning.

Throughout the trip Dr Owen was accompanied by a BBC *Panorama* team headed by Mr Richard Lindley. This had the object of making a programme on an overseas tour by the Secretary of State, while at the same time providing some news coverage of the meeting. I am personally not at my best before 9 a.m., and when the team announced that they wanted to photograph the party at breakfast at 8 o'clock on Monday morning, my heart sank. Fortunately the show was largely stolen by Portia, the boxer we had brought with us from New Zealand, who was highly suspicious of the activities of the photographer and kept interposing herself between the camera and the breakfast table. For the next few weeks our letters from England seemed to contain little but comments, rude or otherwise, on our public breakfast with Minister and dog.

Much of the ministerial discussions with the South Africans took place on this occasion in restricted session without advisers present. One result was that the five Pretoria ambassadors were often ignorant of what was going on from hour to hour. This made planning difficult. During the course of Tuesday afternoon the contact group were waiting in my office for an expected summons to join our ministers in the Union Building where the talks were taking place. At about half-past four we received a message from the 'deaf-aid boys' outside the conference room to the effect that the ministers were about to leave and were on their way to the British Embassy. Fine, we thought; we shall now hear what is going on.

Two minutes later we heard the approaching sirens of the motorcycle outriders accompanying the ministers. To our amazement, however, the cavalcade swept by without turning in at the Embassy drive. After a moment's frantic speculation as to where they might be going, it occurred to me that 'the British Embassy' might have been intended to mean my house rather than the Chancery offices. I therefore rang Vera to warn her that she might find five ministers turning up at any moment. She, too, however, had just had a warning call from the American operations centre and confirmed that tea and drinks were being whistled up. While we were still talking she heard the motorcade turning in at the gate, and rang off. At least this was firm news, and on the assumption that a party was about to begin in my own house, I invited my colleagues to join it. Eventually there were about twenty-five people having a well-earned drink on our lawn, plus perhaps double that number of hangers-on. Fortunately I have an adaptable and unflappable wife.

By the end of the second day, it looked as if the ministers' visit might end in deadlock. The South Africans were still taking a tough line on the terms of the Security Council resolution, and insisted that they must go ahead with their own elections in December come what may. It was only at the eleventh hour that an entirely new formula emerged, under which the two opposing points of view were spelt out in successive paragraphs of a joint statement. The South African Government, while continuing to insist that the elections planned for December should go ahead, accepted that they should be regarded merely as an internal process to elect leaders; the five powers reiterated their view that such elections would be null and void. Both sides, however, agreed that the UN Special Representative should resume discussions with the Administrator-General to work out the modalities of later elections to be held in accordance with Resolution 435 and to fix a date for them.

The day after the ministers left Mr P.W. Botha held a press conference at which he was closely cross-questioned on the real measure of agreement reached. In spite of the fact that he had been Prime Minister for only a matter of days, he answered the difficult questions levelled at him with great skill, laying particular emphasis on the point which he had made all along – that it was for the people of South-West Africa to decide what sort of government they wanted, and that their decision should receive international recognition.

In New York the ambiguity of the agreement was viewed with less than complete satisfaction. At SWAPO's request, the Security Council met again on 13 November 1978 and passed – the five powers abstaining – SCR 439 calling for the cancellation of the December elections. At this point Dr Waldheim invited Mr Pik Botha to visit New York for further talks to clarify the position. For a week or more Mr Botha delayed his answer, but after an exploratory visit to New York by Mr Brand Fourie he finally met the Secretary-General on 27 November; three days later he had talks with President Carter and Mr Vance in Washington. On his way back to South Africa he also met Dr Owen. The best that could be said was that we were still in business; the talks had not finally broken down. But it was difficult to be particularly optimistic.

CHAPTER 36

THE INFORMATION SCANDAL

MEANWHILE, MATTERS HAD not stood still on the internal front. One of the first problems the new Prime Minister had had to face was the publication on 2 November 1978 of an interim report by the Mostert Commission. Judge Mostert found, *inter alia*, that there had been an improper application of taxpayers' money running into millions of rands, and that there were indications of corruption in the disposal of public funds. The report created a considerable furore, not least because it was argued by some of those concerned that the Judge had gone appreciably beyond his terms of reference. On 7 November, however, Dr Mulder resigned from the Cabinet and from the leadership of the National Party in the Transvaal, though not at that stage from Parliament. On the same day the Prime Minister announced that the Mostert Commission had been terminated. Shortly afterwards, in response to public accusations that the Government intended to sweep the whole matter under the carpet, he appointed a new judicial commission headed by Mr Justice Erasmus, and instructed it to report in time for a special session of Parliament on 7 December.

In retrospect, it seems likely that the original revelations on the Information affair by the press and the Opposition had not been taken as seriously as they deserved by the then National Party establishment. The Erasmus Commission revealed, however, that in 1972, under Mr Vorster's premiership, a ministerial decision had been taken to launch a major campaign to support and improve the Government's image overseas. Under the Prime Minister and the Minister of Information (Dr Mulder) the two officials mainly concerned in the organization of this campaign were Dr Eschel Rhoodie, the Secretary of Information, and General H.J. van den Bergh, the head of BOSS. The campaign itself was carried out through a wide range of projects, some of which, including the funding of the *Citizen* newspaper and the establishment of the so-called Committee of Ten in London, were ultimately 'blown', but others still remained secret. The Commission commented on the fact that many of these projects had been carried on secret votes and had thus been excluded from public or Parliamentary scrutiny, and found that in executing them there had been a notable lack of financial control and a substantial misappropriation of funds.

In view of the importance of the issues involved, and the public interest evinced in them, I went down to Cape Town to attend the debate. At the start of the proceedings the Speaker made an unusual, but obviously carefully worded, statement to the effect that although under the rules of procedure members were debarred from making any form of attack on the office of the State President, they were free to draw on factual information relating to the actions of the former Prime Minister (Mr Vorster). This statement was fairly broadly interpreted, and as the debate proceeded there was little doubt that Mr Vorster's position was under only slightly less direct attack than that of Dr Mulder. Although the Erasmus Commission had formally cleared Mr Vorster of direct responsibility for what had gone wrong, it was clear that a substantial area of doubt remained. Largely because of the unwonted frankness with which a matter of this nature, involving as it did the actions of government ministers, was treated, however, the debate ended without the display of political bitterness which had been widely forecast.

In the meantime, on 3 December 1978, Mr Cledwyn Hughes, MP, who had been appointed by Mr Callaghan to report on the feasibility of a further conference on Zimbabwe/Rhodesia, arrived in Pretoria for consultations with the South African Government *en route* to Salisbury. Lord Carver had resigned from his frustrated appointment as Resident-Commissioner in Salisbury a few days earlier, and it could not be said that the immediate prospects were bright.

Mr Hughes was accompanied by Tony Duff from the FCO and US Ambassador Steve Low, both of whom had been immersed in the Rhodesian problem for many months past. He had a long talk in my house with Air Vice-Marshal Hawkins, the Rhodesian representative, and the following morning called on the Minister of Foreign Affairs. Mr Botha was understandably doubtful whether at such an early stage in its existence the new Executive Council headed by Bishop Muzorewa would be likely to display any marked enthusiasm for a fresh approach, but emphasized the South African Government's desire for a peaceful settlement and wished Mr Hughes well.

The evening Mr Hughes left for Salisbury we gave a small dinner party in honour of another notable South African personality, Dr Kobus Loubscher, the General Manager of South African Railways and Harbours. Dr Loubscher, himself a pillar of the Afrikaner establishment, had for long appreciated the key part the railways (and airways) could play, not only in the development of South Africa itself, but also in assisting her neighbours. It was no secret that a small team from the Railways Administration had for some months past played an important practical role in helping the Mozambique authorities in the running of the docks at Maputo. And at a crucial moment a few months earlier, when other routes were closed, it was Dr Loubscher who flew to Lusaka to finalize arrangements to keep Zambia's copper exports flowing through Rhodesia to East London for despatch to world markets. The returning trains carried fertilizer, desperately needed in Zambia. It is not too much to say that, over the years,, Dr Loubscher became South Africa's most effective ambassador to the rest of Africa.

By the time I got back from Cape Town after the special session of Parliament, Christmas was nearly on us. Although we usually remained in Pretoria until early in the New Year, we had been unable through pressure of work to take more than a few days' leave in 1978 and I decided that for once we would have Christmas in the Cape. Since it was also our last summer in South Africa, we had invited Diana and Brian and their three boys, together with Andrew and a friend, Tessa Mayhew, to spend their Christmas holidays with us. Unfortunately Brian, who had recently taken over as head of the central division in the Treasury, found it difficult to get away for long enough to make the journey worthwhile. The rest of the party arrived between 12 and 14 December, and on 16 December we set out in convoy on a four-day journey which took us to Cape Town via Mafeking, Kimberley and Beaufort West.

One of my most treasured relaxations in Cape Town was membership of the St George's singers, a small choir which once a month in the cathedral gave a liturgical performance of a Mass by one of the classical composers. I had been introduced to Barry Smith, the organist and choir master, some two years earlier by Mary Rayner, Vera's social secretary, who was herself a member of the choir. I happened soon afterwards to suggest to Barry that he might like to add the splendid little Mozart *Missa Brevis*, K275, to the choir's repertoire; he agreed, and invited me to take part as a supernumerary bass. Having got in I stayed, and sang in performances of three or four of the great Haydn Masses as well as a number of others.

On Christmas Day we were due to sing Schubert's Mass in G, and since several of the regular members of the choir were away on their summer holidays Barry invited Andrew and Tessa, both of whom were members of the London Bach Choir, to take part. It was a most enjoyable occasion, and I don't think we disgraced ourselves. We did a lot of singing that Christmas; we formed a family party to sing carols at an orphanage and an old people's home for members of the Coloured community and we took part in the cathedral choir for the service of nine lessons and carols on Christmas Eve. Even for an agnostic like myself it was a nostalgic reminder of schooldays at Charterhouse, where forty years earlier I had been head of the choir.

Although I could not cut myself off entirely from the office during the holiday, and was indeed summoned just before Christmas by Mr Heunis, the Minister of Economic Affairs, to discuss certain implications of Rhodesian oil sanctions, we had an excellent break. We climbed Table Mountain, we saw the New Year in on the beach at Hermanus, we watched at close quarters the colony of jackass penguins at Saldanha Bay and we visited the rondavels at Ysterfontein where Andrew had been conceived twenty-seven years before. But for our grandson, Michael Unwin, the young ornithologist of the family and an illustrator of this book, the highlight was the visit to the Cape Town sewage farm near Retreat, one of the finest areas for watching waders, terns, flamingos and grebes anywhere in the world. When, on his return to England at the end of the holiday he was asked by his father what he had enjoyed most, he answered without hesitation, 'the sewage works'!

Shortly before the new session of Parliament opened, I heard that Sir Roy Welensky was spending a holiday in Cape Town with his second wife Valerie and their two small daughters. I had not seen him since 1963, and it seemed a wonderful opportunity to talk over old times. We accordingly asked him and his family to lunch; during the afternoon, while Val and their elder daughter Aletta had a swim with Vera in the pool, Sir Roy and I minded the baby and had a long and nostalgic talk.

Sir Roy did not conceal that he had little confidence in, or love for, the Smith regime, which he felt had missed too many opportunities to reach an honourable settlement, and had always ended by facing worse conditions on the next round. He told me an amusing story, which he said was going the rounds in Salisbury. Smith was represented in it as a young man with a series of girl-friends he wanted to get rid of. He took each of them in turn through an old-fashioned tunnel of love. First there was Miss Harold Wilson. The two got into the car with their arms round each other's waists and were launched off into the tunnel with spooks and monsters appearing at every turn. Eventually the car came out into daylight at the other end. There was Ian Smith with a grin on his face, but where was Miss Wilson? Nowhere to be seen. She had disappeared somewhere along the route. A year or two later the same thing happened with Miss Douglas-Home. They got into the car together ('all lovey-dovey,' said Sir Roy with relish), but when they reached the end of the track, 'Where's Alec?' Somewhere in the ditch with Harold. The third party was the sedate Miss Vorster. This time it was a new tunnel, which went over a dizzying replica of the Victoria Falls Bridge. When the car emerged, no sign of Vorster. Smith had pushed him into the Zambezi. 'What an amazing track record that fellow has,' Welensky ended. 'He has taken the whole country for a ride.' I was sorry that I hadn't heard that story when I was talking to Dr Kissinger two years earlier.

Later in the afternoon the baby woke up and began to complain. Sir Roy, with a confidence based on up-to-date experience, set about changing her nappy. I held her while he put the new one on. When we had finished, he chuckled wickedly. 'I hope you remember that, my girl. It's not everybody who can say that they have had their nappy changed by a former Prime Minister and one of Her Majesty's Ambassadors!'

Before he left Cape Town Sir Roy, hearing that I was planning to write a book, offered me the use of his papers, which he had sent for safekeeping to the Bodleian Library at Oxford. It was typical of his generosity that, without imposing any condition on the use I might make of them, he should put his vast collection of private and state papers at the disposal of someone who had spent much of his professional career on the other side of the hill from himself. Although the Federation he had loved – not, perhaps, altogether wisely, but too well – had failed to survive, and the rump was still in the throes of a vicious civil war, he was altogether without personal bitterness.

CHAPTER 37

FURTHER PROBLEMS
ON NAMIBIA

AFTER CONSIDERABLE HESITATION on the part of the United Nations, based on doubts whether the South Africans were genuinely committed to a solution compatible with the five powers' original proposal, Mr Martti Ahtisaari paid a second visit to Namibia and South Africa in January 1979. Once again he was accompanied by a strong team, including General Philipp, and once again the military experts on both sides got on well together. After forty-eight hours of hard work they produced a draft paper setting out in some detail proposals for the tasks and deployment of UNTAG and its relations with the South African armed forces.

Once again, however, things went wrong. Section 8A of the proposal had referred to 'a cessation of all hostile acts by all parties and the restriction of South African and SWAPO armed forces to base', but it did not attempt to define the areas in which 'restriction to base' should take place, or indeed exactly what the phrase implied. So far as the South African forces were concerned, it would not have been impossible to reach agreement on a mutually acceptable interpretation, but SWAPO claimed vigorously that they also had bases within Namibia, and refused to accept that their forces should be confined to bases outside Namibia as the UN now proposed. They and the Government of Angola also rejected the suggestion that SWAPO bases in Angola should be subject to UN supervision, or that Namibian refugees returning to Namibia should be confined to specified reception centres.

The South Africans in reply categorically rejected SWAPO's claim to have any permanent presence in Namibia which could be described as a base, though they did not contest that there might be areas or villages in which SWAPO forces could lie up temporarily while conducting operations. In an attempt to resolve the difficulty, Dr Waldheim on 26 February submitted a further report to the Security Council on the implementation of Resolution 435. This provided for SWAPO forces to be confined to 'locations' (not 'bases') inside Namibia where they would be monitored by UNTAG but not, as the South Africans demanded, for the monitoring of SWAPO forces outside Namibia.

This further interpretation of our proposal by the Secretary-General led to yet another crisis in relations between the South African Government and the five powers. Although Dr Waldheim's report as published was couched in neutral terms, the South African mission in New York had managed to get hold of a copy of an earlier draft – what I like to call the 'kitchen sink' version, since it incorporated some of the more extravagant claims by both sides – and published it as evidence that the Secretary-General, and by implication the five powers, approved what was contained in it. In fact, this suspicion was unfounded; the draft had been one of a number circulated for comments and the contact group had immediately themselves made clear that parts of it were incompatible with their proposal and were likely to make it unacceptable to SWAPO as well as to the South Africans. The South African decision to give credence to an unapproved draft in this way was in fact a classic demonstration of the danger of acting on the basis of undigested intelligence: an hour's serious research should have revealed that the draft they had got hold of had never been regarded as the final version.

In order to try to restore the position, three of the Cape Town Ambassadors of the five powers – Edmonson, Eick and myself – flew to Windhoek on 3 March. We did our best to persuade the politicians there that this was a storm in an imaginary teacup. But grave damage had been done, and in a major speech in Parliament on 6 March, the Prime Minister, Mr P. W. Botha, accused the Five of bad faith in the negotiations, claiming that Dr Waldheim's report, although supported by the five powers, could not be regarded as a fair or reasonable interpretation of the original proposal.

The Cape Town Ambassadors were deeply disturbed by this apparent attack on their negotiating integrity and immediately recommended to their capitals and to the New York contact group that a joint statement should be issued repudiating the charges of bad faith and putting the matter in perspective. For a variety of reasons this advice could not be acted on at once, and in the absence of a public disavowal the belief rapidly grew within South Africa – and even more damagingly among the moderate parties in Namibia itself – that the five powers were in collusion with SWAPO and the United Nations to mislead them and the South African Government. On 9 March, in an attempt to limit the damage, I therefore put out an interim statement of my own, rejecting the accusations of duplicity and bad faith levelled against the Five and suggesting that repeated accusations of this kind were potentially very damaging to relations between our two countries.

This statement was followed within twenty-four hours by a communiqué in almost identical terms by the five powers; but understandably it was I who drew the Government's main fire. In a pained background article, the senior editor of the Johannesburg newspaper *Beeld*, writing under the pen-name of 'Dawie', said that the British Ambassador seemed to think that the best form of defence was attack:

This is the only explanation imaginable for his breathtaking statement that the Prime Minister's rebuke to the Western Powers on the subject of their role in the SWA question is unhelpful and very damaging to future relations between our two countries. This is the height of temerity, and the word 'temerity' is deliberately used in English to lighten the task of the translators ... It was often said in the past that South Africa must behave in one way or another in order to make it possible for its Western friends to help it. What friends? What help? ...

Attacks in the press were followed on Monday afternoon by a private rebuke to me by the South African Prime Minister himself. For several weeks thereafter I adopted a low posture, though my relationships at official level remained unimpaired and the conduct of business in other directions was not affected. Before very long, moreover, evidence began to accumulate that the South African Government were themselves coming to realize that perhaps the earlier draft of the Secretary-General's report did not, as they had believed, reflect the five powers' view. The fact that in its published form it did not contain any of SWAPO's more far-fetched demands provided strong collateral for our claim that the Five had been taking a genuinely impartial role.

On 19 March Mr Pik Botha again travelled to New York to attend a second round of proximity talks arranged by the foreign ministers of the five powers with SWAPO, the Front Line States and the UN Secretariat. These talks resulted in certain understandings being reached, and on 27 March the five ambassadors in Cape Town were instructed to pass a further message of clarification on the implementation of our proposals to the South African Government. The same evening the new South African Ambassador-designate to London, Dr Dawie de Villiers, and his delightful wife Suzaan came to an informal dinner party at our house, so I had some reason to feel that I was no longer entirely in the dog-house.

233

CHAPTER 38

FINAL LAP

FOLLOWING NORMAL CIVIL service retirement procedures, I had been warned that I should plan to take my accumulated leave by the date of my sixtieth birthday in early August 1979; that meant that we should aim at leaving South Africa by the middle of May. In late February, therefore, we began the first of a series of farewell tours by visiting Port Elizabeth and East London.

At Port Elizabeth I made a speech to the local Chamber of Commerce in

We note with interest that presentations of musical concerts at a city hotel, attended by ambassadors, professors and doctors, have been disallowed by the Divisional Council because of the noise of buzzbikes and motorcycles.

which I emphasized the continuing importance of the trade links between our two countries, at the same time pointing out that Britain was exposed to economic as well as political risks in South Africa as a result of our historically-established ownership of over 50 per cent of all foreign investment in the country. This led to a further question being asked in Parliament at Westminster, this time by Lord Hatch in the House of Lords, who, on the basis of an abbreviated report in the London papers, asked whether what I had said represented HMG's policy towards South Africa. The short answer, given by Lord Goronwy-Roberts, the Minister of State, was 'Yes', but the question led to a mini-debate in which I received generous support from an eminent predecessor as Ambassador in South Africa, Lord Redcliffe-Maud.

That was on 22 March; a week or two later another and altogether more significant event took place at Westminster. The Government was defeated on a motion of no confidence; Mr Callaghan submitted his resignation and called an election. This had some effect on our own plans, since to depart in mid-May, only a week after a new Government might be taking up the reins, hardly made sense. It was therefore agreed that I should provide some local continuity by staying on for a further six weeks until the end of the South African parliamentary session when the tempo of Government business normally slowed down. A change-over then had the further advantage that neither I nor my successor would have to undertake the move from Cape Town to Pretoria: Vera and I would leave from the Cape, preferably by sea, and our successors could fly direct to Pretoria.

One development which pleased me greatly was announced in London just before the change of Government; my recommendation that a modest amount of aid should be allocated to help black South Africans was finally approved. This news reached me only a day or two before Vera and I paid our farewell visit to the University of Zululand. I was thus able to discuss with the Rector, Professor Nkabinde, a former post-graduate student at Edinburgh University, possible ways in which his university might benefit from such funds. He said that he had been alarmed to find on taking up his appointment that the standard of English among new entrants to the university was so low that 80 per cent of those who passed the entrance exams nevertheless failed a Standard 8 (lower school certificate) test in English language comprehension. He was therefore faced with the problem whether to start all his degree students with a crash course in English, or to try to organize special sixth-form courses in English at the secondary schools.

I was able to tell him that the British Council had recently sponsored the appointment of an expatriate English language teacher at Fort Hare

University to meet precisely this need, and that with increased funds I saw no reason why we could not do the same for the University of Zululand. He was delighted, and I felt that our visit had been justified. A few weeks later, during our farewell visit to Soweto, I made the first presentations under the new scheme and at the same time opened a branch of the British Inform-ation Library in Soweto. I hope and believe that contacts of this kind can only be helpful in the years ahead.

We were in Natal on British election day. When the results began coming through there was predictable rejoicing at a prospective Conservative victory from the high Tory white settler community. More than once I found my-self pointing out that, although there would undoubtedly be changes in style, British foreign policy tended to be broadly bipartisan and the scope for a fundamental change of policy towards South Africa was strictly limited.

We were staying with a cousin, Tim Scott, and his wife Rosemary at Howick when the news reached us that Lord Carrington had been appointed as our new Secretary of State. This was pleasing for us personally, since we knew him better than anyone else in the new administration; he was, more-over, well known in southern Africa and had kept closely in touch with developments there during his period in opposition.

On our return to Cape Town news was waiting for me of a proposed visit by Mr Richard Luce, the Parliamentary Under-Secretary of State concerned with African affairs; the first visit to South Africa by a member of the new Government. By this time we were committed to an embarrassingly full programme of farewell functions, but on one of the nights he was with us we had arranged a large buffet supper party for our friends in the Cape Town musical community. Unusually, therefore, a visiting minister was entertained at a party at which he met not the political or business leaders of the country, but some of the leading conductors, singers and instrumentalists. Needless to say, his official engagements included more orthodox meetings with Mr Pik Botha and the Prime Minister's principal adviser, General Magnus Malan, as well as with opposition leaders.

Since the beginning of the parliamentary session there had continued to be rumblings about the Information Department scandal. Eschel Rhoodie had fled overseas, and by an ironic twist of fate General van den Bergh, the former head of BOSS, was woken by the police in the middle of the night - a tactic he had often used against his own former clients - to have his passport removed. Criticism of Mr Vorster's role in the affair continued to be heard, notwithstanding the fact that he was now State President. I was not altogether surprised, therefore, that when I called on Mr Vorster to say good-bye I found him friendly but very depressed.

Vera's farewell call on Mrs Vorster took place a few days later, on Monday 4 June, and turned out to be a poignant occasion. An hour or two afterwards it became clear that this was Mrs Vorster's last official engagement; Mr Vorster had resigned. A fortnight later, with none of the *panache* which had accompanied Mr Vorster's own inauguration, the President of the Senate, Senator Viljoen, was quietly sworn in as the new State President. In many ways it was the end of an era.

A few days later I took my leave of Mr Vorster's successor as Prime Minister, Mr P.W. Botha. I was reassured to find that our differences of February had been buried; we parted on friendly and constructive terms.

In the three-and-a-half years since our arrival, the difficulty of finding a ship for our return to the United Kingdom had increased dramatically. The mailships had finally vanished and the only passenger ship which offered a regular sailing was a small vessel, the *St Helena*, which had been put on the route mainly to maintain a passenger and supply service to St Helena and Ascension Islands. This ran a two-monthly round trip service with terminals at Cape Town and Avonmouth. We had heard that there was a northbound sailing on about 20 June and we made a provisional booking on this. There was, however, still uncertainty about when Parliament would rise, as well as about the exact sailing date. We therefore arranged to complete the majority of our farewell calls by 9 June, keeping the last ten days free. During this period we would have to pay a final visit to Namibia, but its duration had not finally been settled.

As soon as it was announced that the inauguration of the new President would take place on 19 June, we went on firm visits to two places we had long set our hearts on seeing, the Namib Desert, and the diamond-mining operations in the coastal area between the mouth of the Orange River and the old German port of Luderitz. So it was that on 11 June, Vera and I, accompanied by Sophia Lambert, my Economic First Secretary, found ourselves flying up the west coast in a small aircraft of Namib Airlines bound for Alexander Bay, the small town at the extreme north-western tip of the Cape Province. There we were met by an official of Consolidated Diamond Mines (CDM) and taken across the Orange River to the company town of Oranjemund, the Namibian headquarters of the present mining operation.

For the next two days we were given a comprehensive and highly illuminating view, including a tour by helicopter, of the mining and extraction activities of the CDM. Broadly, this involves turning over immense tonnages of sand and rock to separate out a relatively few ounces of diamonds which over millions of years have been carried down the Orange River and deposited on the beaches at its mouth. From there some of them have been progressively washed up the coast, often being cövered by many feet of sand in the process. Fortunately the sea itself does some of the sorting, but there is plenty left for man to do. (We were told that about a hundred tons of sand have to be processed for every carat of diamond discovered.)

Although the coastal strip is a hive of sophisticated activity, employing enormous mechanical shovels and earth-movers, a mile or two back from the sea the barren scrub is still the undisturbed home of the gemsbok oryx and a wide variety of other desert wild life. Indeed, the very fact that the diamond areas are carefully guarded provides them with an unusual degree of protection. The rich fishing grounds off the coast support vast flocks of sea birds – cormorants and pelicans, gulls and terns predominate, with rafts of black-necked grebes covering some of the inshore lagoons. The never-ceasing onslaught of cold Atlantic rollers provides unlimited food for the birds, but offers a constant hazard for opencast mining, which is often taking place twenty or thirty feet below sea-level and only separated from the breakers by a shifting line of largely man-made sand dunes.

We left Oranjemund for Windhoek in CDM's own aircraft, and spent the next two nights as guests of Olga and Jack Levinson at Heynitz Castle, their attractive and historic house perched on one of the highest points of the ridge overlooking the city. During our visit I had final meetings with representatives of the political parties, including a long session with Mr Daniel Tjöngarero, the Information Secretary of SWAPO (Internal).

On our second night in Windhoek we gave a farewell party for a wide cross-section of our political friends, including Mr and Mrs Dirk Mudge (DTA), Mr and Mrs Andreas Shipanga and Dr Kenneth and Mrs Ottilie Abrahams (SWAPO [D]), Mr and Mrs John Kirkpatrick (NNF), Bishop and Mrs Lukas de Vries of the Evangelical Lutheran Church and Mr and Mrs John Viall of the Administrator-General's office. The party went well, and in a graceful speech wishing us well for our retirement, Dirk Mudge said that, although in Windhoek the DTA were accustomed to being in the political majority, on that occasion he was delighted, even though he was in a minority, to find himself still among friends.

At noon the next day we flew to Walvis Bay, the chief port of South-West Africa and still a potential bone of contention in the Namibia settlement. There we were met by a member of the staff of the Namib Desert Research

Station, who drove us the sixty-odd miles to Gobabeb. The research station lies on the Kuiseb River, which forms the dividing line between the scrub plain running back from Walvis Bay and the sea of sand which constitutes the Namib Desert proper.

A number of remarkable films have been produced about the Namib, recording its beauty and the extraordinary range of life it supports in spite of the virtually total absence of rain. Moisture is obtained from the sea fogs which at certain times of the year cover the dunes; highly specialized insects, reptiles and even mammals survive by trapping and drinking the water which condenses from this fog – even going so far as to lick the moisture from their own eyeballs – and spend the heat of the day lying up a few inches below the surface of the sand. This desert is also the home of one of the most primitive plants in the world, the *Welwitschia bainesii*, whose single pair of leaves may grow to a length of dozens of feet and live to be some two thousand years old, 'in stubborn defiance of its environment' as Olga Levinson says in her authoritative *Story of Namibia*.[1]

The superintendent of the Gobabeb station, a remarkable American scientist, Dr Mary Seely, whose knowledge of the life of the Namib is unrivalled, was away when we arrived, but she returned the same evening bringing with her Professor Louw from the University of Cape Town, who two years earlier had been responsible for interesting us in the visit. Until her return we were looked after by the resident warden and his wife, and spent the late afternoon driving through the dunes in a specially adapted truck fitted with low-pressure desert tyres. The dunes themselves are surprisingly stable and, although they demand a certain driving expertise, they are easier to penetrate by vehicle than I had expected. In places they rise to 1,200 feet or more; every now and again among them one comes across the tracks of the ubiquitous gemsbok.

The next morning we drove for miles up the sandy track of the Kuiseb River itself to the start of the gorge through which it emerges from the Gamsberg Mountains. For most of the year the water is, except in rare pools, below the level of the sand, though occasional flash floods occur. Fresh water is, however, always available a few feet below the surface, and this is made use of by the handful of Topnaar (Hottentot) tribesmen who live in the valley with their goats.

Back in Cape Town, our last few days passed very quickly. The night before we sailed Rex and Mardee Wilson asked us to a family dinner with them; it was more than twenty-eight years since we had first met, and our children and grandchildren were still friends. The next day we embarked before lunch and, through the courtesy of the captain, had a large and cheerful party for a host of friends, official as well as personal, in the main lounge of the *St Helena*. This went on, with periodic interruptions for press and television interviews, until just before the ship sailed.

It was a perfect evening – more than we could possibly have hoped for on a midwinter day. Our ship was only just over three thousand tons, and a roaring south-easter on our first day at sea would inevitably have sent us scurrying for shelter. As we moved out of Table Bay we saw penguins, seals and dolphins enjoying the sunshine and the glassy sea as much as we were. Behind us the cliff of Table Mountain tailing off into the serrated ridge of the Twelve Apostles looked as beautiful as we had ever seen it.

On our starboard beam, in stark contrast, the low and unbeautiful outline of Robben Island, so near and yet a world apart, reminded us that not all South Africans enjoyed the freedom to come and go at will. Mr Nelson Mandela, the freedom fighter, or convicted terrorist, depending on which view one took, and Mr Toivo ja Toivo, the imprisoned leader of SWAPO, could at that very moment have been watching us as, in a sense, we were watching them. Could one look for a peaceful and constructive future for South Africa so long as some of the most influential black leaders were still confined in apparently permanent detention? Whatever the answer to that question, we should not now be there to see it.

CHAPTER 39

PROSPECT

IF MY PERSONAL account of Africa in transition seems to end in mid-air, it is because that is precisely and inevitably what it does. Diplomacy, like life itself, is a continuing business; it is rare indeed that an Ambassador can claim to have reached a final solution. The best he can usually hope for is to have contributed to a better understanding of the problems, and perhaps in the process to have secured some lessening of the tensions to which they gave rise. His successor will take on from where he left off.

Dominating all long-term international relationships is the time-scale in which the human individual has to operate. Historians are able to observe and record the secular movements in which nations and philosophies rise and fall; with the benefit of hindsight they may even be able to rationalize how and why these movements took place. Occasionally such movements are the result of action taken by individuals; far more often they are a response to conditions which have taken generations to mature. I have little doubt that, viewed from the end of the twenty-first century, many of the tensions which exist in Africa today, and which result from the dramatic social and political changes in the continent over the past century-and-a-half, will have been resolved, though at what cost in human lives and resources it is impossible to guess. Those of us who work on the shop-floor of history, as it were, may be well aware of the nature of the problems but quite unable to find a solution to them in the time available to us.

The diplomat's strongest weapon is probably detachment, and it is a weapon he must hang on to for all he is worth. Only by standing a little outside the struggle in which the politicians are engaged can he hope to reconcile the aims of the government he represents with those of the governments to which he is accredited. But this very detachment can also be his Achilles' heel. By definition, an Ambassador cannot afford to be a voice crying in the wilderness, or to be inaudible, or unintelligible, to his political masters. He has to make himself heard: his art, like theirs, is the art of the possible.

In writing of southern Africa today one is writing of a conflict between cultures; perhaps unfortunately this is made starkly visible as a conflict between black and white. But race is not the sole element in the conflict; it is almost as hard for the average Englishman as I assume it is for the average black to appreciate that the Afrikaner, like the black, sees his struggle over the past 150 years largely as a struggle against colonialism.

Professor René de Villiers, himself an Afrikaner, begins his illuminating section on Afrikaner Nationalism in the *Oxford History of South Africa* with this sentence:

From their earliest days the Afrikaner people have felt themselves threatened, from inside their borders and from without, to a degree few other nations or groups have experienced or believed ...

This, I am sure, is a key concept in any attempt to understand South Africa and the South Africans. It does not make the Afrikaners a comfortable people for an outsider to live among, especially since their sense of being threatened is often combined with a remarkable certainty of the God-given rightness of their beliefs. But it cannot be ignored.

Afrikanerdom has felt itself threatened on two fronts in particular. First, politically, by the British, from whom they fled in the Great Trek and by whom they were temporarily defeated in the war of 1899-1902. Second, racially, by the blacks, who have always out-numbered them and with whose women their ancestors (they hate to admit) did not shrink from begetting children. In order to retain their identity they felt themselves compelled to continue the war against the British by other means, and at the same time to build an impregnable psychological barrier between themselves and the blacks. In the process they rejected the Coloured community, for whom they had some responsibility and who could have been their allies. Thus their sense of insecurity on two fronts led to the development of a siege mentality probably matched by only one other country in the world today – South Africa's ally and strange bedfellow, Israel.

This is not the place to analyse the anomalous, but entirely understandable, *rapport* between South Africa and Israel, though I much hope that before long someone will do so. Nor is it for me to make a value judgment on the unenviable position in which the Afrikaners – appropriately called the 'white tribe of Africa' in David Dimbleby's perceptive television series – have found themselves through much of the nineteenth and twentieth centuries. But a significant manifestation of their insecurity has been the adoption first by the Afrikaner community itself, and more recently by the whites throughout southern Africa, of racial attitudes which are repugnant to world opinion and therefore probably in the long run self-defeating.

South Africans are prone to attribute the hostility of world opinion entirely to the success of Communist propaganda. Objectively, few would dispute that blacks in the Republic are materially better off than their opposite numbers in most, if not all, the African countries to the north. The statistics, indeed, suggest that in 1980, for the first time, black spending power in South Africa exceeded white. This still leaves a *per capita* income differential of the order of 4:1; nevertheless it is a significant milestone. It is doubtless unfair, therefore, that the world seems to condemn the unacceptable face of *apartheid* more strongly than it has condemned the absence of personal freedom in many other countries, including the Soviet Union. South African politicians sometimes say that they are 'too honest' in discussing their domestic racial policies: possibly they are. Certainly the relative freedom of their press is difficult to reconcile with the existence of a police state as it is known, for example, in many countries of eastern Europe. But perhaps we in Britain expect more of South Africa than we do of the Russians.

To acknowledge that blacks in South Africa have a high standard of living relative to blacks in the rest of the continent is, however, to ignore that they compare themselves not with other blacks whom they have never seen, but with the whites they see every day. It is true that limited steps have been taken already, particularly in the labour field, to remove some of the more glaring disabilities under which they work. The Wiehahn and Rieckert Commissions have pointed the way to a better utilization of South Africa's limited human resources; the work of the Urban Foundation has also begun to ameliorate the quality of life for those living in the black townships.

But such action remains within the framework of *apartheid*; even improved economic conditions do not alter the facts that in political terms South African legislation remains almost totally discriminatory and that blacks have few personal or political rights within the Republic. The cry of 'no taxation without representation' still has real significance in South Africa today: there is not a single South African member of Parliament whose seat is threatened as a result of his failure to protect black interests – quite the reverse. Communists did not invent the discrimination, they merely capitalized on it.

The anomalies inherent in the pure doctrine of *apartheid* are, of course, becoming increasingly apparent to a growing body of thinking Afrikaners, including many members of the present Government. When as long ago as 1978 I paid my first call on Dr Mulder after he had taken over the

Department of Plural Relations, he surprised me by saying that he recognized that no politician, black or white, could today be satisfied with anything less than one man, one vote. But he went on to say that one man, one vote in a unitary state would mean that the whites would have to give up the way of life they had created for themselves – *ergo* they could only accept universal franchise in a plural state.

My personal reaction was that the world would probably not seriously object to South Africa being broken down into a racially separated federal or confederal state, so long as the resources of the country were fairly divided. But a federal system of the sort he had in mind did not seem to give anything approaching a fair deal to the homelands, or to offer any satisfactory representation to the urban blacks who could be expected to play an increasing, not a diminishing, part in the white economy. Could they accept that their vote should only be exercised in a homeland in which they did not live, nor in many cases even have roots? Dr Mulder replied that he would not rule out the creation of a 'city-state' in Soweto. It is, however, not altogether easy to see how a dormitory city-state, entirely dependent for its revenue on incomes earned outside its boundaries, could be made to work.

Where, then, does the future lie? First, it is absolutely clear, as Mr P.W. Botha's Government have themselves indicated, that the present situation cannot be expected to continue indefinitely without change. Even if the numbers game, in which the whites are already outnumbered by five to one, were maintainable *sine die* within South Africa's borders, the rest of Africa is hardly likely to allow matters to rest there for ever. My guess is that the military advice being given to Mr P.W. Botha is that, as in pre-Zimbabwe Rhodesia, a civil war between black and white could only lead to a 'no-win' situation. That is to say, the whites could not be defeated, at least in the short term; but since the blacks could be reinforced and resupplied from an inexhaustible reservoir in the rest of Africa, the whites could never hope to bring the war to a final conclusion favourable to themselves.

If that is correct, the options are limited. Few, other than her most implacable enemies, would wish on South Africa a solution of the Amin type. By displaying to the world the image of black tribalism in its most extreme form, Amin did the cause of genuine African nationalism a profound disservice and played into the hands of white extremists elsewhere. (It should be added – though it does him no credit – that Amin still fell short of the most extreme form of black nationalism: almost all his atrocities were directed against Ugandan blacks of tribes other than his own, and relatively few against whites as such.)

On the other hand, the precedents for peaceful evolution, including eventual coexistence between black and white, are by no means totally discouraging. For one thing, the Soviet Union's track record in Africa is very far from being the monolithic success that many white South Africans believe – or seem to wish to believe. In country after country – in Egypt, Zaire, the Sudan, Somalia, even perhaps in Mozambique – the Russians seem to have set things up for themselves, only to discover that Africans are Africans first and Communists only so long as it is made worth their while. Indeed, I believe that the whole concept of African tribal democracy – the system of the *kgotla* or the *ndaba*, under which the young men speak first and the elders later, the chief summing up with a consensus-based ruling – is totally antipathetic to a Communist system under which policy is handed down from on high.

Ultimately there are two extremes between which an evolutionary policy has to steer if effective change is to take place peacefully. The first is that of immobilism – demonstrated in Algeria – in which the dam-wall of repression has to be built ever higher if the growing volume of discontent is to be contained. Eventually the dam breaks, or is blown up; everyone except the revolutionaries suffers.

The second is the slippery slope. The sluice gates are opened voluntarily, but too wide or too suddenly; restraining influences are swept away, and the pace of evolution may quickly become indistinguishable from that of revolution.[1]

Thus the speed of the advance has somehow to be controlled. But this can clearly only be done with goodwill on both sides. Paradoxically, the most urgent need now may be for greater self-confidence among the whites. As I have already noted, some of the more obviously discriminatory South African legislation has already been repealed in Namibia without the skies falling. The extension of this process to the Republic itself would be an invaluable demonstration of goodwill. The release, for example, of Mr Toivo ja Toivo – and indeed of Mr Nelson Mandela – could be seen, like the release in their time of Dr Banda, of Mzee Jomo Kenyatta and of Bishop Makarios, as a gesture of confidence rather than of capitulation. Such gestures might well lead to more moderate opposition attitudes rather than to harder ones. If the lessons of Zimbabwe demonstrate anything it is that, as the years went by, the options for the Rhodesian whites became progressively less attractive. Timing is of the essence; in the last resort, however, only Africans, hopefully white as well as black, can decide it.

I regard myself as deeply fortunate in being able to claim many close

friends in southern Africa, both black and white. Like others of my countrymen, I do not want to have to choose between them. I am well aware that
many whites in Africa feel that wé in Britain have let them down. But I
believe passionately that they are wrong. We have been detached, but not
perfidious. The most bitter accusation the whites make against us is that we
have consistently refused to align ourselves with them, our kith and kin,
against the blacks. Instead, we have acted on the assumption that men *can*
learn to live together; that evolution is the desirable, indeed the only, alternative to revolution. In the process we have earned disesteem from both sides.
But in voluntarily handing over our former colonies to independence we have
avoided both the ignominy of an Algeria and the horror of a Vietnam. We
desperately hope that our friends in southern Africa, both black and white,
will be able to avoid them too.

SOURCE NOTES

CHAPTER 2

1 Frank Clements, *Rhodesia: The Course to Collision*, Pall Mall Press, 1969.

CHAPTER 3

1 Nicholas Monsarrat, *The Tribe that Lost its Head*, Cassell, 1956.

CHAPTER 10

1 Sir Roy Welensky, *Welensky's 4000 Days*, Collins, 1964, pp. 117-18.
2 Sir Roy Welensky, *op. cit.*, p. 139.
3 Welensky papers.
4 Cmnd 1149 and 1150, HMSO, 1960.
5 Julian Greenfield, *Testimony of a Rhodesian Federal*, Books of Rhodesia, Salisbury, 1978.
6 Welensky papers.

CHAPTER 11

1 *cf.* the account on pp. 131-2 of *The Way the Wind Blows* by Lord Home, Collins, 1976.
2 Doris Lessing, *Martha Quest*, MacGibbon & Kee, 1965.
3 Lord Birkenhead, *Walter Monckton*, Weidenfeld & Nicolson, 1969, Chapters 34 and 35.
4 Elspeth Huxley, *The Merry Hippo*, Chatto & Windus, 1963.
5 Welensky papers.
6 Sir Nigel Fisher, *Iain Macleod*, André Deutsch, 1973, p. 157.

CHAPTER 12

1 Welensky papers.
2 Welensky papers.
3 Lord Home, *The Way the Wind Blows*, Collins, 1976, p. 142.
4 Cmnd 1148, HMSO, 1960.
5 Welensky papers.
6 Welensky papers.
7 Julian Greenfield, *op. cit.*
8 Harold Macmillan, *At the End of the Day*, Macmillan, 1973, pp. 299-301.
9 Welensky papers.
10 *cf.* Lord Alport, *The Sudden Assignment*, Hodder & Stoughton, 1965, p. 152.
11 Harold Macmillan, *op. cit.*, p. 313.
12 Harold Macmillan, *op. cit.*, p. 300.
13 House of Lords, *Official Report*, 16 November 1960.
14 Harold Macmillan, *op. cit.*, pp. 301-5.

SOURCE NOTES

CHAPTER 13

1 Lord Alport, *op. cit.*, Chapter 1.
2 Sir Roy Welensky, *op. cit.*, pp. 291–307.
3 Lord Alport, *op. cit.*, p. 51.
4 Welensky papers.

CHAPTER 14

1 Conor Cruise O'Brien, *To Katanga and Back*, Hutchinson, 1962.
2 Welensky papers.
3 Conor Cruise O'Brien, *op. cit.*, p. 236.
4 Conor Cruise O'Brien, *op. cit.*, pp. 284–5.
5 Lord Alport, *op. cit.*, pp. 104–22.
6 Lord Alport, *op. cit.*, p. 89.
7 Lord Alport, *op. cit.*, pp. 112–13.
8. Lord Alport, *op. cit.*, pp. 123–37.

CHAPTER 15

1 Sir Roy Welensky, *op. cit.*, p. 315.
2 Sir Roy Welensky, *op. cit.*, p. 316.
3 Lord Alport, *op. cit.*, p. 161.

CHAPTER 16

1 Julian Greenfield, *op. cit.*, p. 206.
2 Sir Roy Welensky, *op. cit.*, p. 318.
3 Lord Alport, *op. cit.*, pp. 169–71.
4 Lord Butler, *The Art of the Possible*, Hamish Hamilton, 1971, pp. 212–13.
5 Sir Roy Welensky, *op. cit.*, p. 339.
6 Lord Alport, *op. cit.*, p. 183.
7 Stevens papers.
8 Lord Butler, *op. cit.*, p. 217.
9 Stevens papers.
10 Stevens papers.
11 Lord Butler, *op. cit.*, Penguin Edition, Preface.

CHAPTER 17

1 Lord Alport, *op. cit.*, pp. 179 *et seq.*
2 Robert Blake, *A History of Rhodesia*, Eyre Methuen, 1977, p. 344.
3 Sir Roy Welensky, *op. cit.*, p. 352.
4 Robert Blake, *op. cit.*, p. 342.
5 Harold Macmillan, *op. cit.*, p. 328.

CHAPTER 18

1 Lord Alport, *op. cit.*, p. 221.
2 Lord Alport, *op. cit.*, p. 224.
3 Welensky papers.
4 Conor Cruise O'Brien, *op. cit.*, pp. 319–26.

SOURCE NOTES

CHAPTER 19

1 Lord Butler, *op. cit.*, p. 229.

CHAPTER 20

1 Alan Moorehead, *The White Nile*, Hamish Hamilton, 1960, p. 48.

CHAPTER 24

1 Robert Blake, *op. cit.*, p. 367.

2 *cf.* the account by Lord Garner in *The Commonwealth Office 1925-68*, Heinemann, 1978, pp. 383-97.

3 Robert Blake (*op. cit.* p. 400) reports that a certain amount of headway was made in the *Fearless* talks, but that final agreement failed to be reached largely as a result of the intransigent attitude adopted by H. Nicolle, the Rhodesian Secretary for African Affairs.

CHAPTER 25

1 Possibly the most accurate and unemotional account of Amin's life and background is contained in Major Iain Grahame's *Amin & Uganda*, Granada, 1980.

2 *cf.* the horrifying report in *Transition*, issue no. 49 (Accra, Ghana, 1975), which includes an open letter to Amin by his brother-in-law and former Foreign Minister, Wanume Kibedi. Also George Ivan Smith's *Ghosts of Kampala*, Weidenfeld & Nicolson, 1980.

3 Judith Listowel, *Amin*, I.U.P., 1973.

4 David Martin, *General Amin* (revised edition), Sphere Books, 1978.

CHAPTER 27

1 This is confirmed by M.A. Obote's own account reported by George Ivan Smith (*op. cit.*, p. 79).

CHAPTER 32

1 Cmnd 6919, HMSO, 1977.

CHAPTER 33

1 Security Council document *S/12636* of 10 April 1978.

CHAPTER 38

1 Olga Levinson, *Story of Namibia*, Tafelberg Publishers, Cape Town, 1978, p. 3.

CHAPTER 39

1 The case for a revolutionary, rather than an evolutionary, solution is argued strongly in Joe Slovo's paper *South Africa - No Middle Road*, contained in *Southern Africa: The New Politics of Revolution* (ed. Ronald Segal), Pelican Books, 1976.

BIBLIOGRAPHY

Allighan, Garry, *The Welensky Story*, Purnell & Sons (SA), 1962.

Alport, Lord, *The Sudden Assignment*, Hodder & Stoughton, 1965.

Birkenhead, Lord, *Walter Monckton*, Weidenfeld & Nicolson, 1969.

Blake, Robert (Lord), *A History of Rhodesia*, Eyre Methuen, 1977.

Bledisloe, Lord, 'Rhodesia & Nyasaland Royal Commission', Cmnd 5929, HMSO, 1939.

Blundell, Sir Michael, *So Rough a Wind*, Weidenfeld & Nicolson, 1964.

Butler, Lord, *The Art of the Possible*, Hamish Hamilton, 1971.

Churchill, Sir Winston, *History of the English Speaking Peoples*, Vol. I, Cassell, 1956.

Clements, Frank, *Rhodesia: The Course to Collision*, Pall Mall Press, 1969.

Davidson, Slovo & Wilkinson, *Southern Africa: The New Politics of Revolution*, Pelican Books, 1976.

Fisher, Sir Nigel, *Iain Macleod*, André Deutsch, 1973.

Garner, Joe (Lord), *The Commonwealth Office 1925–68*, Heinemann, 1978.

Gore-Booth, Paul (Lord), *With Great Truth and Respect*, Constable, 1974.

Grahame, Iain, *Amin & Uganda*, Granada, 1980.

Greenfield, J.M., *Testimony of a Rhodesian Federal*, Books of Rhodesia, 1978.

Home, Charles Douglas-, *Everyn Baring: The Last Pro-Consul*, Collins, 1978.

Home, Lord, *The Way the Wind Blows*, Collins, 1976.

Huxley, Elspeth, *The Merry Hippo*, Chatto & Windus, 1963.

Johnson, R. W., *How Long Will South Africa Survive?*, Macmillan, 1977.

Lessing, Doris, *Martha Quest*, MacGibbon & Kee, 1965.

Levinson, Olga, *Story of Namibia*, Tafelberg, Cape Town, 1978.

Listowel, Judith, *Amin*, I.U.P., 1973.

Macmillan, Harold, *At the End of the Day*, Macmillan, 1973.

Martin, David, *General Amin* (revised edition), Sphere Books, 1978.

Mason, Philip, *The Birth of a Dilemma*, O.U.P., 1958.

Mason, Philip, *The Year of Decision*, O.U.P., 1960.

Monckton, Lord, 'Report of the Advisory Committee on Review of the Federal Constitution', Cmnd 1148–51, HMSO, 1960.

Monsarrat, Nicholas, *Life Is a Four-Letter Word*, Cassell, 1966.

Moorehead, Alan, *The White Nile*, Hamish Hamilton, 1960.

O'Brien, Conor Cruise, *To Katanga and Back*, Hutchinson, 1962.

Pakenham, Thomas, *The Boer War*, Weidenfeld & Nicolson, 1979.

Smith, George Ivan, *Ghosts of Kampala*, Weidenfeld & Nicholson, 1980.

Stevens, Sir Roger, Private papers, unpublished.

BIBLIOGRAPHY

Todd, Judith, *The Right to Say No*, Sidgwick & Jackson, 1972.

Transition No. 49, 'The Anti-Man Cometh, etc.', Transition Ltd, Accra, Ghana, 1975.

Tredgold, Sir Robert, *The Rhodesia That Was My Life*, Allen & Unwin, 1968.

Welensky, Sir Roy, *Welensky's 4000 Days*, Collins, 1964.

Welensky, Sir Roy, Private papers, unpublished.

Wilson, Sir Harold, *The Labour Government 1964-70*, Weidenfeld & Nicolson, 1971.

Wilson, Monica, and Thompson, Leonard (ed.), *The Oxford History of South Africa*, Vol. 2, O.U.P., 1971.

Woods, Donald, *Biko*, Paddington Press, 1978.

Young, Kenneth, *Rhodesia and Independence* (2nd edition), Dent, 1969.

INDEX

INDEX

INDEX